FAMILY ROMANCES

FAMILY ROMANCES

George Sand's Early Novels

Kathryn J. Crecelius

Indiana
University
Press

Bloomington and Indianapolis

For E.A.C.

This book was brought to publication
with the assistance of a grant from the
Andrew W. Mellon Foundation.

Library of Congress Cataloging-in-Publication Data
Crecelius, Kathryn J.
Family romances.

Bibliography: p.
Includes index
1. Sand, George, 1804–1876—Criticism and interpretation.   2. Psychoanalysis and literature.   3. Domestic
fiction, French—History and criticism.   4. Family in
literature.   I. Title.
PQ2417.C74   1987   843'.7   86–43051
ISBN 0–253–32175–1

1 2 3 4 5 91 90 89 88 87

CONTENTS

Acknowledgments

Many people and organizations have helped me see this book to completion.

I am grateful to the Camargo Foundation in Cassis, France, for providing an apartment and access to a library in an idyllic setting conducive to reading and reflection. The American Council of Learned Societies, whose research fellowship allowed me free time to write, deserves particular thanks.

A travel grant from the Massachusetts Institute of Technology permitted me to use the incomparable Collection Spoelberch de Lovenjoul in Chantilly, the Bibliothèque Nationale, and the Bibliothèque Historique de la Ville de Paris; all three libraries generously made their resources available to me. Georges Lubin, without whose edition of Sand's correspondence and autobiography this book would most likely have been impossible, kindly invited me into his home and discussed many points with me.

The M.I.T. humanities library and interlibrary borrowing service staff, especially librarian Marlene Manoff and Tom Kiely, were most helpful. I would also like to thank my colleagues in Foreign Languages and Literatures who read the manuscript and made useful suggestions. Special thanks are due to Julia Alissandratos for her friendship and moral support throughout the project.

I would like to express my appreciation to all those at the Indiana University Press who capably saw the manuscript through the various stages of production.

Parts of this book have already appeared in print. I gratefully acknowledge permission to reprint the following three articles: "*Rose et Blanche,* la dernière oeuvre d'apprentissage de George Sand" (French version), *Présence de George Sand* (Association pour l'étude et la diffusion de l'oeuvre de George Sand, Echirolles, France), 22 (1985): 54–57; "Tristan and Iseut in the *Berry*," *Tristania* IX, 1 2 (Autumn 1983–Spring 1984): 82–90; "Writing a Self: From Aurore Dudevant to George Sand," *Tulsa Studies in Women's Literature* 4, i (Spring 1985): 47–59.

The jacket photo of George Sand's 1831 self-portrait was provided through the courtesy of Christiane Sand and the Musée George Sand et de la Vallée Noire, La Châtre, France, and was taken by Studio Gesell, Argenton-sur-Creuse, France.

My debt to Andy, for his unstinting encouragement and devotion, can only partially be repaid by my dedicating this book to him.

INTRODUCTION

George Sand's literary debut was most impressive. She made her mark on the Paris literary world at the age of twenty-eight with her first novel, *Indiana* (1832), after serving a brief apprenticeship at Nohant and in Paris and composing a relatively small number of preliminary works. This initial success was followed in the next five years by a wealth of novels and short stories, including *Valentine, Lélia, André, Jacques, Mauprat,* and *La Dernière Aldini,* works that show a narrative vitality and variety of invention rare in so young an author.

My initial interest in Sand's early works was provoked by her ability to change registers with each new project, by her talent for writing a romance, an epistolary novel, and a *Bildungsroman* in quick succession. This book is about Sand's rewriting of traditional plots and her use of familiar forms for new and unfamiliar ends. As this study progressed, however, it became apparent that beyond the seeming distinctions between these novels lay an uncanny similarity, a subplot that Sand reworked in some form or another in every text. One of my goals is to elucidate this substructure, of which Sand was most certainly unaware, while relating it to the themes and plots more readily discernible in her fiction, in order to produce a detailed study of Sand's achievements in the early years of her career.

I deliberately limited my corpus to the years 1827–37 for three reasons. First, Sand's *oeuvre* is so vast that no one book could encompass all her works, or even all her novels. Second, this period saw the publication of her most famous and enduring novels, novels that are among the best she produced. Finally, these novels were written before Sand was exposed to the social theories of Lamennais and Pierre Leroux, before she began consciously to incorporate political and social considerations into her work. For all these reasons, the novels discussed form a coherent body of writing that readily lends itself to exploration within the scope of a book.

Examined closely, George Sand's first novels obsessively repeat the same pattern. *Rose et Blanche, Indiana, Valentine,* and *Jacques* present what can be termed Sand's personal scenario in its entirety. *Mauprat* collapses the structure into its central matrix, while *Lélia,* the most formally innovative of Sand's novels, reproduces only a fragment of the whole. *André* and *Leone Leoni* describe one side of the story and are the least personal of Sand's novels. Read together, these novels tell the same story, however different the characters, the plots, or even the narrative form, a story that is personally meaningful for George Sand while holding importance for women in general as well as for students of literature.

This story is an old and familiar one, newly told and with far-reaching consequences. It is that of the child's oedipal struggle. But in Sand's case, a girl's development is described and a woman is writing the novels.[1] Up until now, the oedipal triangle in literature has been fruitfully studied by such writers as Marthe Robert, John T. Irwin, and Otto Rank in male characters and male authors. The conclusions to be drawn from Sand's elaboration of a female oedipal structure are unexpected and disconcerting, with respect both to Sand's own life and to literary theory.

My thesis is that George Sand's novels depict the heroine's journey away from a stern, virile father figure to union with a gentler, more caring man, who is not an overt father figure, as in the beginning of the novel, but who may nonetheless be identified with the father for two reasons. First, the heroine is introduced to this second man only after he has initially, and usually briefly, been the lover of her sister, half sister, or *soeur de lait* (foster sister). Raymon (the wrong man who is replaced by Ralph, Indiana's right object choice), is first Noun's lover. Louise is in love with Bénédict before he meets Valentine; Octave is Sylvia's lover before realizing that Fernande is more suited to him; Pulchérie tricks Sténio into believing he is at last making love to Lélia. These female doubles have often been noted in Sand's work and seen as Sand's splitting of the female character into a chaste and a carnal side—the sexual Noun, who is impregnated by Raymon, as opposed to the still-virgin, although married, Indiana; Louise, the adolescent mother of an illegitimate child, and her sister Valentine, whose marriage also remains unconsummated; the courtesan Pulchérie and the frigid Lélia. Such doubling has been criticized as Sand's inability to imagine a whole, sexual woman.[2]

This explanation has never seemed sufficient, though, and I propose to look at these female couples not as two sides of one woman, but as two women, mother and daughter. As noted, these women are all half or full sisters or else *soeurs de lait*, an expression that itself incorporates the word "sister." In fact, Sand's novels are all built on incestuous, or at the very least overdetermined, relationships, where cousins intermarry, husbands are viewed more as fathers, and characters use *brother, sister, mother, son* as terms of endearment. Following Rank's and others' reasoning as regards incestuous scenarios, it is possible to argue that these sisters really represent mother and daughter, and that the man for whom they are rivals is none other than the father.[3] Thus, although the first man in Sand's scenario— Capitaine Delmare, Jacques, Hubert de Mauprat—is explicitly designated in the text as a father figure, the second never is but is only apparent as such through his relationship to the women.

The sexual woman (Noun, Pulchérie) disappears from the novel immediately after her encounter with the "father" or else turns her attention to another man (Sylvia). Louise is an exception, and this accounts for the further complications the structure takes in *Valentine*. The heroine-daughter therefore has the father to herself; this is precisely the girl's desire in the oedipal fantasy. Her union with this man is fruitful, not only spiritually but also physically: Fernande becomes pregnant with Octave's child, Bernard and Edmée de Mauprat have six children, Athénaïs and Valentin have a daughter, Indiana and Ralph "adopt" the narrator who hears their story and perpetuates their experience. The bearing of a child to the father is part of the girl's oedipal fantasy and is realized in Sand's novels. These marriages are furthermore accompanied by social and economic changes that lead to a more just and egalitarian society: Indiana and Ralph free as many slaves as they can; Athénaïs the peasant marries a count and purchases a château with her parents' money; the Mauprats are models of civic and charitable duty.

This happy, productive incest is contrary to all received ideas about literary incest, which are based on male paradigms. Marthe Robert, in her discussions of Balzac and Flaubert, especially "La Fille aux yeux d'or" and *L'Education sentimentale*, points out how incest is scrupulously avoided, in de Marsey's case so that Henri can achieve the brilliant political future Balzac has in mind for him, and in Frédéric's because of his realization that possessing Mme Arnoux would be tantamount to incest.[4] In his latest book, Peter Brooks argues: "Narrative is in a state of temptation to over-sameness, and where we have no literal threat of incest (as in Chateaubriand, or Faulkner) lovers choose to turn the beloved into a soul sister so that possession will be either impossible or mortal. . . ."[5] Chateaubriand illustrates both the "literal threat of incest" and the "soul sister" models. René's sister Amélie becomes a nun to escape her passion for René and soon dies, while Atala and Chactas, "brother" and "sister" through their relationship to Lopez, Atala's real father and Chactas's adoptive father, are parted by Atala's suicide. Rousseau, whose influence on Sand was extensive, creates an incestuous situation at Clarens only to bring it ultimately to destruction with Julie's famous admission that incestuous equilibrium is impossible: "One more day, perhaps, and I would have been guilty!"[6] Stendhal, too, was tempted by the oedipal impulse in his novels but never fully realized it. Byron, much inspired by Chateaubriand, was the romantic most associated with incest, both in his personal life, where he cultivated sensationalism by publicizing his relationship with his half sister Augusta Leigh, and in his poetry, in which incest is linked with remorse, suffering and tragedy. In Sand's work, though, incest is the goal of the narrative and leads to a fulfilling, not fatal, end, one that has social implication beyond the interests of the characters themselves.

My reading of Sand's incest scenario also raises questions about currently prevailing opinion concerning the importance of the mother for Sand's life and work. An example of such a critical position is Germaine Brée's thesis that Sand's autobiography, *Histoire de ma vie*, as well as many of her novels, elaborates the "happy triangle" consisting of Aurore Dupin, her grand-mother, and her mother, the triangle comprising the basic family unit of Sand's childhood.[7] Brée makes a convincing case for Sand's use of this figure in her autobiography and in her fiction. Brée's arguments are not irrelevant, since the dichotomy between good and bad mother figures can be found in many of the works I treat, notably *Rose et Blanche*, *Indiana*, and *Valentine*, as well as in later novels. Yet as will be demonstrated, the plot dynamics in Sand's novels depend on a triangular relationship with the father, whereas the importance of the maternal characters is only episodic.

Aurore Dupin's unusual female family was only constituted after her father's accidental and tragic death, when she was four years old.[8] Because she was so young when Maurice Dupin died, critics and biographers have discounted his influence on her, preferring to concentrate on the battles between mother and grandmother for the daughter's affections. While *Histoire de ma vie* amply documents this aspect of Aurore Dupin's childhood, as Brée has shown, it also presents overwhelming evidence of the centrality of the father, both on the biographical and, more important, on the au-tobiographical level, for Aurore's pyschological and professional devel-opment. Sand's emphasis on the father in her autobiography provides the second reason for my identification of the father with the male figure at the end of her novels.

Like Brée, I regard Sand's autobiography as being her own version of her life story (a biography written by the self), stemming from the same imagination that created her fictional stories, and not as a factual account of her life. *Histoire de ma vie* is a very revealing psychological document. To begin with, the autobiography opens not with Sand's birth but with the history of her family, for Sand rightly felt that in order to know her, her reader had to know about her origins. This led one wag to call the book "The Story of my Life before my Birth" (*Oa* I, xxi). Part One of the work is thus called "History of a family from Fontenoy to Marengo." As Gislinde Seybert perspicaciously remarks, the family chronicled is really the paternal side, as the title indicates.[9] Aurore Dupin's great-grandfather was Maurice de Saxe, known to the French as the "Victor of the battle of Fontenoy," while her father fought with Napoleon's army in the battle of Marengo. It is true that her mother's side, not being noble or noteworthy, was difficult to trace and describe, but it is also true that Sand places great emphasis on all her paternal relatives' exploits and lives, linking them, and thus herself, firmly to France and French history. To understand her father's family specifically, in Sand's presentation, is to understand her.

In addition, she spends much time on the description of her father as a child and a young soldier, and includes excerpts—often heavily rewritten—of his letters to his mother. Little is known about Maurice Dupin outside of his daughter's account. He seems to have been a pleasant, attractive young man with a great attachment to his mother and the usual social accomplishments. He died too early to make much impact on history; what his military career would have been like during the rest of Napoleon's reign is open to speculation. Nothing in his life indicates that he would have made a great mark on the world had he lived. The fact that Sand rewrites his letters (which have been preserved at the Bibliothèque Historique de la Ville de Paris and can be compared with her versions) and substitutes her words for his shows that in her autobiography she is recreating her father according to her own image of him, indeed according to her self-image as well. Furthermore, in her version of Maurice's correspondence, she insists on the triangular nature of his relationship with Sophie and his mother and shows how Maurice definitively chose the younger woman over the older one. This father, who died when she was very young, and who even during the four years he was present in her life was often away on military duty, and precisely because he was always a distant, dashing figure, forever arrested in Aurore's memory as a handsome, delightful thirty-year-old, is clearly the focus of the first third of *Histoire de ma vie*.

These early formative years of childhood were also the time when Aurore Dupin began her first experiments with storytelling. The autobiography offers a wealth of information about this period in Aurore Dupin's life, for Sand seems to have had many early memories of childhood. She was subject to what she terms "rêverie" (*Oa* I, 467) from the time of her birth and associates this mental state with her first "artistic creation": making sounds on the brass grillwork next to her bed.

Tout cela m'est encore présent, quoiqu'il ne me soit rien arrivé de remarquable dans cet appartement: mais il faut croire que mon esprit s'y ouvrait à un travail soutenu sur lui-même, car il me semble que tous ces objets sont remplis de mes rêveries, et que je les ai usés à force de les voir. J'avais un amusement particulier avant de m'endormir, c'était de promener mes doigts sur le réseau de laiton de la porte de l'alcôve qui se trouvait à côté de mon lit. Le petit son que j'en tirais me paraissait une musique céleste, et j'entendais ma mère dire: "Voilà Aurore qui joue du grillage." (*Oa* I, 538)

All this is still fresh in my mind, although nothing remarkable occurred in that apartment, but I believe that my mind began to really function for itself there; it seems that all these objects are filled with my reveries, and that I wore them out just by looking at them. I had a particular amusement before falling asleep, that of running my fingers over the brass grillwork of the alcove door next to my bed. The little sound I drew from it seemed to me a celestial music, and I heard my mother say: "There is Aurore playing the grillwork."

At about the same time Aurore began composing endless stories while secured between four chairs so that her mother could get some work done without having the child underfoot.

Elle les [les histoires] déclarait souverainement ennuyeuses, à cause de leur longueur et du développement que je donnais aux digressions. C'est un défaut que j'ai bien conservé, à ce qu'on dit; car, pour moi, j'avoue que je me rends peu compte de ce que je fais, et que j'ai aujourd'hui, tout comme à quatre ans, un laisser-aller invincible dans ce genre de création. (*Oa* I, 542)

She declared that they [the stories] were terribly dull because of their length and the scope I gave to digressions. This is a fault I've retained, I'm told; for my part, I confess that I'm almost unaware of what I do, and that I have today the same irrepressible abandon in such storytelling that I had when I was four. (*ML*, 29)

The plot of these long "novels" is significant:

Il paraît que mes histoires étaient une sorte de pastiche de tout ce dont ma petite cervelle était obsédée. Il y avait toujours un canevas dans le goût des contes de fées, et pour personnages principaux, une bonne fée, un bon prince et une belle princesse. Il y avait peu de méchants êtres, et jamais de grands malheurs. Tout s'arrangeait sous l'influence d'une pensée riante et optimiste comme l'enfance. (*Oa* I, 542)

It seems that my tales were a kind of mishmash of everything that haunted my little brain. They were patterned after fairy tales, and the chief characters were always a good fairy, a good prince and a beautiful princess. There were few wicked beings and no great mishaps. Everything always came out right, guided by notions as happy as childhood itself. (*ML*, 29–30)

Essentially, it is the same plot retold in Sand's novels: the prince and the princess are Aurore and her father, while her mother has become the good fairy. Unlike most fairy tales imagined by girls, there is no wicked step-mother figure to bar the girl's union with the father, only a benevolent fairy. [10] Thus, literary imagination developed simultaneously with her Oedipus complex, which is not really surprising. As Peter Brooks points out: "It may be significant, as Roland Barthes notes, that the child appears to 'discover' the Oedipus complex and the capacity for constructing coherent narrative at about the same stage in life."[11]

Maurice Dupin's death put an end to this phase of Aurore's fantasy relationship with him, modified the further development of the Oedipus complex, and also changed her life in many more external ways. First, it made her his only legitimate child, and therefore the sole heiress to her grandmother's property. Hippolyte Chatiron was an illegitimate son, the result of Maurice's youthful liaison with a servant, while the baby boy Sophie Dupin had borne the previous June had died the week before Maurice. Had the father lived, he and Sophie might have had other children, displacing Aurore as only child and heiress, especially if they had had another boy. Even if they had not had more children, Maurice and Sophie would undoubtedly have given Aurore the conventional education girls received at the time; she would never have had access to the kind of financial knowledge imparted by her tutor Deschartres to the future owner of a fairly important estate. Nor would Aurore have had the kind of intellectual and physical freedom she enjoyed under her grandmother's and Deschartres's desultory supervision—carefree horseback rides, often in trousers, visits to the sick and the practice of rudimentary medicine, hours spent reading in Mme Dupin de Francueil's well-stocked library. The absolute liberty she felt while on horseback is lyrically described in a letter to Aurélien de Sèze, written in 1825: "It seems to me that we are reborn on horseback, that we come to life again" (*C* I, 212). The constraints visited upon girls, detailed in *Histoire de ma vie* in such a way as to reveal George Sand's understanding of their debilitating effects, never affected Aurore as they did her contemporaries because of her unconventional family situation.

Se priver de travail pour avoir l'oeil frais, ne pas courir au soleil quand ce bon soleil de Dieu vous attire irrésistiblement, ne pas marcher dans de bons gros sabots de peur de se déformer le cou-de-pied, porter des gants, c'est-à-dire renoncer à l'adresse et à la force de ses mains, se condamner à une éternelle gaucherie, à une éternelle débilité, ne jamais se fatiguer quand tout nous commande de ne point nous épargner, vivre enfin sous une cloche pour n'être ni hâlée, ni gercée, ni flétrie avant l'âge, voilà ce qu'il me fut toujours impossible d'observer. Ma grand-mère renchérissait encore sur les réprimandes de ma mère, et le chapitre des chapeaux et des gants fit le désespoir de mon enfance; mais, quoique je ne fusse pas volontairement rebelle, la contrainte ne put m'atteindre. (*Oa* I, 466–67)

Not to work so that my eyes would sparkle; not to run and play in the sun when God's good sun attracts me so; to wear gloves, that is, to renounce the quickness and strength of my hands; to doom myself to be clumsy and feeble; never to tire myself, when everything urges me to use up my energy; to live, in short, under a bell jar, to be neither burned, nor chapped, nor faded before

my time—such things were always impossible for me. My grandmother repeated my mother's reprimands, and the subject of hats and gloves was the
despair of my childhood; but, although I wasn't willingly rebellious, constraints
could not affect me. (*ML*, 25)

In Aurore Dupin's life, as in her novels, the social and the psychological
reinforced each other. For her, the oedipal father was also the good, heroic
father, not society's repressive, constraining father, who, according to Lacan, incarnates "the name of the father," the rule of patriarchal society that
was and is so particularly damaging to girls.[12] Maurice Dupin never became
that father because of his death, and his daughter was surely aware of this
fact, conscious on some level that her loss was also her gain in the sense
that his absence allowed her a free and unusual childhood, that essential
formative period. Thus, her novels portray the draconian father in such
characters as Delmare and Jacques, even Tristan de Mauprat, and her
heroines seek and find an alternative mate, one who is just the opposite.

At the end of Part II, chapter 5 of *Histoire de ma vie*, Sand summarizes
her father's ideas, at least as she interprets them at the time of writing her
autobiography, ideas expressed in his correspondence with his mother.

> Ainsi je le vois dès l'enfance traiter le patriciat de *chimère* et la pauvreté de *leçon*
> *utile*. Souffrant de la Révolution jusqu'au fond des entrailles et sentant sous le
> couteau sa mère adorée, je le vois ne jamais maudire les idées mères de la
> Révolution, et tout au contraire approuver et bénir la chute des privilèges. . . .
> Je le vois plus naïf, plus conséquent, plus chrétien et plus philosophe encore,
> aimer une pauvre fille enrichie un instant par un malheur plus grand que la
> pauvreté; reconnaître que son amour l'a purifiée, et lutter contre les plus vives
> douleurs pour la réhabiliter en dépit du monde. Je le vois pousser le respect
> et l'amour de la famille jusqu'à briser le coeur de sa mère et le sien propre
> plutôt que de ne pas légitimer par le mariage les enfants de son amour. (*Oa*
> I, 421)

> Thus I see him from childhood on treating the patriciate as a *chimera* and
> poverty as a *useful lesson*. Having suffered from the Revolution to the depths
> of his soul and having felt his adored mother under the threat of the guillotine,
> I see him never cursing the basic ideas of the Revolution, and on the contrary
> approving and blessing the fall of privileges. . . . I see him as even more in-
> genuous, more consistent, more Christian and more philosophical, in loving
> a poor girl enriched in an instant by a greater ill than poverty, in recognizing
> that his love has purified her, and fighting against the strongest suffering to
> rehabilitate her despite society. I see him pushing respect and love for family
> to the point of breaking his mother's heart rather than not legitimize by mar-
> riage the children of his love.

Maurice Dupin, in his daughter's description, was progressive, Republican, Christian in the broad sense, the enemy of privilege and champion of poverty—in short, the very alter ego of what George Sand herself became.

That Maurice and Aurore are one is clearly stated in *Histoire de ma vie*:

> Je continuerai l'histoire de mon père, puisqu'il est, sans jeu de mots, le véritable auteur de l'histoire de ma vie. Ce père que j'ai à peine connu, et qui est resté dans ma mémoire comme une brillante apparition, ce jeune homme artiste et guerrier, est resté tout entier vivant dans les élans de mon âme, dans les fatalités de mon organisation, dans les traits de mon visage. Mon être est un reflet, affaibli sans doute, mais assez complet, du sien. . . . [M]ais eussé-je été garçon et eussé-je vécu vingt-cinq ans plus tôt, je sais et je sens que j'eusse agi et senti en toutes choses comme mon père. (*Oa* I, 156–57)

> I will continue the story of my father since he is, without making a pun, the true author of the story of my life. This father, whom I scarcely knew, and who remains in my memory as a brilliant apparition, this artistic young soldier, has stayed wholly alive in the transports of my soul, in my constitution, in my facial features. My being is a reflection, no doubt weakened but complete enough, of his. . . . [B]ut had I been a boy and had I lived twenty-five years earlier, I know and I feel that I would have acted and felt in every way like my father.

This passage contains two key words: *auteur* and *garçon*. It is commonplace to describe one's father as "l'auteur de ma vie." Here, Maurice is the author not of her life but of her life *story*, as well as being at the origin of her book, *Histoire de ma vie*, as she indicates by commenting that she is not making a pun. His story is her story, as she says later: "For me, it is that [the story] of my father, consequently it is my own" (*Oa* I, 420), just as her story is in large part his. He is the *auctor* behind the author George Sand.

The use of the word *auteur* is clearly deliberate and can be connected with the word *garçon* used further on. George Sand is the product of Aurore Dupin and Maurice Dupin. The internalized image of the heroic father, as well as the freedom his death granted her, have combined to create this author, who, although womanly in demeanor and lifestyle, is nonetheless androgynous mentally: a woman writing, living independently, practicing a profession like a man, while not surrendering her female side. What Maurice was, so would Aurore have been had she been a boy; what she became is what he might have become had he lived, given his artistic bent. He lives on in her, while her identification with him enables her to live and write as she does. Thus the "good" father allows the girl entry into the symbolic order in a way that the traditional father representative of the law could not. There is perhaps in this equation of Maurice with Aurore a desire to assuage guilt feelings, brought on by the realization that her life has been built upon his death, so that her perpetuation of his memory, indeed his very essence, in her own life and works compensates at least partially for his loss. Rather than depending on the maternal triangle, as Brée argues, Aurore bases her identity on Maurice Dupin. In fact, it may well have been the strains of being torn between her mother and grand-mother that caused Aurore Dupin and later Sand to return in imagination to her father as role model and to find her inner strength in this identi-fication.[13]

This equivalence between Aurore and Maurice reappears in the final configuration of Sand's novels as well. The male and female members of the couple united at the conclusion exhibit similar traits; they are equals socially and morally, and in two cases they are cousins as well. The marriages at the end are unions of the same with the same, again a contradiction of Peter Brooks's thesis that "narrative is in a state of temptation to over-sameness," for oversameness is here the crowning achievement of the nar-rative. Indeed, *Mauprat* is essentially the story of Edmée's successful attempt to turn her cousin Bernard into a mirror image of herself, while in *André* the tragic ending derives from the fact that Geneviève has progressed well beyond André so that they are not equals.

Union with the father is thus also the integration of the self, the estab-lishment of a psychological wholeness essential to creation and to social happiness. George Sand's personal psychological itinerary has conse-quences beyond those relevant to her and to her biography, however. If George Sand's imaginary marriage with her good father enabled her to live in freedom and to create, then this particular kind of masculine prin-cipal should allow other women to live and create, too, unfettered by the male-dominated institutions—the church, politics, marriage—of which Sand's novels are so deeply critical. George Sand shows in her novels and in her life that there is another way, a better way, that the father, and hence society, need not be oppressive and patriarchal but may allow women and men to express themselves fully.

Let us return for a moment to the question of the mother's influence, an increasingly important theme in feminist criticism. In "Femme en voy-age," Béatrice Didier argues that in Aurore Dudevant's first surviving lit-erary work, the "Voyage au Mont d'Or," writing is associated with the mother.[14] This is so, but the association is negative. Aurore Dudevant, in seeking to write, first addresses her mother, drafting a letter whose pleading tone reveals all the wounds her mother had inflicted upon her. Rather than send this letter though, Aurore chooses instead to halt her writing for the moment because she realizes how hurt her mother would be to receive such a message. Only later does she go on to write, this time with herself as both sender and recipient, another sort of text, an autobiography. Thus, if writing is initially placed under the mother's sign, it is done so only to show the lack of connection between mother and literature rather than their affinity. Furthermore, writing is here connected with the self, and specifically with the writing of a self, the creation of a self-image, that is auto-biography.

Aurore's letter to her mother in the "Voyage" is not the first time her literary creation and her mother have been linked. Indeed, in the passage from *Histoire de ma vie* cited above Mme Dupin calls Aurore's babbled ro-mances "terribly dull" (*Oa* I, 542). Later, when Aurore was twelve and began writing for the first time, her grandmother sent Aurore's compositions to Mme Dupin, whose response was to ridicule her daughter's efforts: "*Your pretty sentences made me laugh heartily, I hope you aren't going to start talking like that.*" Aurore accepts her mother's judgment: "I was not in the least bit mortified by the reception my poetic lucubrations met. I thought she was absolutely right . . ." (*Oa* I, 808). Aurore's denial that she was mortified, a strong word, indicates on the contrary that she was indeed crushed by this tactless criticism. Significantly, her grandmother, the representative of the father's side of the family, strongly approved and supported Aurore's lit-erary essays. For a time, the mother's interdiction put a halt to Aurore's scribblings, but not permanently, for she wrote again during her convent days four years later, drafting a "novel" that returned to the fairy-tale plot of her childhood romances.[15] In any case, as Sand admits, if she stopped writing for a time, she never ceased to invent stories in her head: "I there-fore stopped *writing*, but the need to invent and to compose stories con-tinued to torment me" (*Oa* I, 808).

As Philippe Berthier points out: "The fact that her mother made fun of her first literary efforts . . . confirms that in definitively taking up writing, Aurore finally settles her relationship with her mother, breaks an old ta-boo. . . ."[16] In studying the links between Aurore, her mother, and writing, it is useful to examine the letters Aurore sent to her mother, particularly during the period when she became a writer. The letters from the years 1824–30, when Aurore Dudevant was newly married and a mother, are chatty and affectionate, filled with news of her children or requests for items not available in the provinces. Every letter written in 1830 seems to report only on Aurore's poor health, which was obviously a physical mani-festation of her unhappy mental state and worsening domestic situation. In 1831, the year she moved to Paris and began writing for the public, there is a clear change in tone. Aurore's letters are cool, commanding, more calculated. Defending herself from the calumnies her mother had heard and believed, she essentially tells her mother how to evaluate her daughter's behavior. As Sand wrote full-time and became more famous, and also as the circle of her correspondents increased, she wrote less and less frequently to her mother. At the time of her divorce (1836), she wrote to explain the facts of the case and again to prescribe Mme Dupin's behavior toward her son-in-law, Casimir.

The almost haughty tone of these letters contrasts markedly with the light and warm tone of the preceding years, but harks back to the stance Aurore had taken in 1821, when she had first defended herself to her mother against local gossip regarding her "loose" conduct. This change in tone at a crucial time in her life is obviously related to Sand's attitude toward writing, and the relationship of writing to her mother, who is now permanently excluded from Sand's inner emotions, although outwardly she will remain the dutiful daughter until Mme Dupin's death in 1837. Clearly, freedom and individuality, the two values made possible by her writing and intimately connected to her authorship, are dissociated from the mother, who, as in all the crucial times of Aurore's life, is neither supportive nor understanding, and must therefore be treated not as an ally but as a potential enemy.

Another proof of Sand's disjunction with the maternal can be found in her description, in *Histoire de ma vie*, of how she adopted her pseudonym. Not to be taken literally, this episode is another autobiographical *morceau de bravoure*. In these three pages, Sand speaks not of divesting herself of her husband's name, for by the time she began writing she had been Aurore Dudevant, not Aurore Dupin, for nine years, but of agreeing not to use her mother-in-law's name.

> "Mais est-il vrai que vous ayez l'intention d'*imprimer* des livres? —Oui, madame. —Té! s'écria-t-elle . . . voilà une drôle d'idée! —Oui, madame. —C'est bel et bon, mais j'espère que vous ne mettrez pas le nom que je porte sur des *couvertures de livre imprimées*? —Oh! certainement non, madame, il n'y a pas de danger." (*Oa* II, 138)

> "But is it true that you intend to *print* books? —Yes, madame. —Well, she cried, . . . what a funny idea! —Yes, madame. —That's all well and good, but I hope you won't put the name I bear on the *covers of printed books*? —Oh! certainly not, madame, there's no danger of that."

This amusing dialogue, most likely rearranged, or perhaps even entirely invented in retrospect, contains the word "print" twice, both times in italics. Printing books, that is, writing for public consumption, is censured by the mother-in-law, as the mother had criticized Aurore's first scribblings.

It is not the "mother's" name that would appear on book covers (Sand mentions no opposition on the part of her husband to her using his name, or even reluctance on her own part to use Dudevant), but the name invented by Hyacinthe de Latouche, who two pages further on is called her godfather ("parrain") (*Oa* II, 140). The substitute father named her after the substitute mother had rejected her, and she eventually made this name, bestowed by chance, her own and the symbol of her identity. "I and I alone made the pseudonym I was given my own, after the fact, by my labor" (*Oa* II, 140). Indeed, the name *Sand* eventually superseded *Dudevant* for her children as well; both Maurice and Solange, and later Maurice's children, took their mother's penname as a permanent name. Dudevant has now become a curiosity of history, and Mme Dudevant mère's line defunct, for she was in any case merely Casimir's stepmother, so that his children were not her direct descendants. In adopting a new name and identity, Sand broke definitively with the maternal, both natural and legal. After the above conversation with Mme Dudevant, Sand states that she never saw her mother-in-law again.

If writing and her mother are mutually exclusive, the imagined father is clearly the patron of Aurore's literary and psychological development. Shortly after recounting in *Histoire de ma vie* her early experience of writing and her mother's criticism, Sand describes another of her creations, which was never committed to paper but remained in her heart: "Corambé." Corambé is the title of a religious "novel" she imagined as well as the name of the god of her personal religion. She built an altar to Corambé, which she destroyed after it was taken for a Corpus Christi altar by a playmate, but she continued to invent stories for and about Corambé for many years, well into adulthood.

Corambé served as a focus for Aurore's imaginary characters and plots during the period when she temporarily stopped writing. Though none of her poems to him was consigned to paper, they were elaborated in her imagination. Corambé seems to be the logical extension of Aurore's earlier novels, with good characters and a charming hero. Although an ethereal, mythical creature rather than a human being, a pagan counterpart to Jesus, in many ways Corambé also resembles Sand's image of her father, particularly in his kindness and beauty. Furthermore, Corambé is androgynous, for although usually a man, he occasionally takes on the form of a woman.

Et puis, il me fallait le compléter en le vêtant en femme à l'occasion, car ce que j'avais le mieux aimé, le mieux compris jusqu'alors, c'était ma mère. Ce fut donc sous les traits d'une femme qu'il m'apparut. En somme, il n'avait pas de sexe et revêtait toute sorte d'aspects différents. (*Oa* I, 813)

And then, I had to complete him by occasionally dressing him as a woman, for up until then, it was my mother that I had loved and understood most. It was therefore with the features of a woman that he appeared to me. Basically, he had no gender, and took on all sorts of different guises.

This androgyne I would identify rather with the imagined union of Aurore with her father, where she takes the mother's place so that a new being is created. This view is supported by Helene Deutsch's explication of the name Corambé, which Sand insists is merely a pure signifier that came to her in a dream: according to Deutsch, it means *coram* (Latin: in the presence of) and *b*, the letter of the alphabet Aurore could not, or would not, say when she first learned to read. Deutsch associates this *b* (or *bé*) with the absent father, away on military business. Thus, Corambé means "in the presence of the father."[17] I would point out as well that the first syllable of *coram* also contains the initial sound of *Aurore*. Corambé, invented when Aurore was entering adolescence, signals a return to her earlier feelings for her father, as well as a further step in her artistic development, for he became the focus of her narrative energies. She herself makes explicit the link between her artistic life, Corambé, and what she terms her "spiritual life" (*Oa* I, 812).

Corambé disappeared definitively from Sand's life after she wrote *Indiana*. *Indiana*, as she describes it, was the product of a lifetime of dreams and invention, channeled at last into a specific literary form. After six weeks of feverish activity her first real novel was born, and Corambé flew away, doubtless because from then on writing would replace the mental creations of the past twenty-odd years.[18] Corambé allowed Aurore to incubate her early scenarios in her head, while in her novels and stories she would now elaborate those same plots. The conflict between form and content that ultimately drives away Corambé, whose stories are formless, is significant, for in her first novels Sand did indeed cast the same scenarios in radically different narrative forms.

That literature is the successor to Corambé and therefore renders him superfluous is evident from Sand's account of his disappearance.

> Ces chères visions [associées avec Corambé] n'étaient que les précurseurs de l'inspiration. Elles se cachèrent cruellement au fond de l'encrier, pour n'en plus sortir que quand je m'enhardirais à les chercher.
> J'aurais beaucoup à raconter sur ce phénomène de demi-hallucination qui s'était produit en moi pendant toute ma vie et qui se dissippa entièrement et tout d'un coup. (*Oa* II, 165)

> These dear visions [associated with Corambé] were only the precursors of inspiration. They cruelly hid themselves at the bottom of my inkwell, and only came out when I got up the nerve to look for them.
> I could tell much about this phenomenon of semi-hallucination which came over me most of my life and which all at once disappeared completely.

Sand's reverie, so pronounced since early childhood, dissipates immediately as she begins her career as an author. Henceforth, she will work out her visions and dilemmas in her writing, which forms a continuum with the Corambé material:

> Quand je fus dans l'âge où l'on rit de sa propre naïveté, je remis Corambé à sa véritable place: c'est-à-dire que je le réintégrai, dans mon imagination, parmi les songes; mais il en occupa toujours le centre, et toutes les fictions qui continuèrent à se former autour de lui émanèrent toujours de cette fiction principale. (*Oa* II, 166)

> When I reached the age at which one laughs at one's own naïveté, I put Corambé back in his true place, that is, I returned him, in my imagination, to my dreams; but he always occupied the center of my dreams, and all the fictions that continued to be inspired by him always emanated from this main fiction.

These later fictions, novels mostly, were written quickly and with assurance. Sand wrote with great facility and, unlike Flaubert, did not agonize over every word. However, she did correct and change her texts, often extensively, as surviving manuscripts attest. This disproves the view of Sand as an artless writer who did not craft her work as carefully as others did.[19] Sand insists that she forgot her works as soon as they were finished. "Another phenomenon appeared that I can't explain at all. As soon as I finished my first manuscript, it vanished from my memory without a trace . . ." (*Oa* II, 168). This forgetfulness, as she terms it, only increased as she wrote more prolifically, testimony to the strong ties between her work and her unconscious. It is as though Sand shifted into a special mental gear, that of the earlier reverie, to write out her scenarios, which then disappeared from her conscious mind.

In his last appearance in *Histoire de ma vie*, Corambé can also be identified with the previously elaborated image of her father, particularly insofar as social, political, and religious ideas are concerned.

> Corambé, s'il se fût mêlé de politique, n'eût pas laissé dévorer la Pologne pantelante par la Russie sanguinaire, il n'eût pas, s'il se fût mêlé de socialisme, abandonné la cause du faible à celle du fort, la vie morale et physique du pauvre au caprice du riche. Il eût été plus chrétien que la papauté. (*Oa* II, 166)

> If Corambé had gotten involved in politics, he would not have allowed bloody Russia to devour panting Poland; had he gotten involved in socialism, he would not have abandoned the cause of the weak for that of the strong, the spiritual and physical life of the poor for the caprice of the rich. He would have been more Christian than the papacy.

Thus, Sand was right that Corambé was indeed the subject of her novels; this androgyne who was at one and the same time her father and herself, the masculine and feminine sides of her being, was replaced by George Sand the writer and her numerous fictional creations.

Sand's novels are therefore the logical extension of a lifetime of invention and creation made possible by the absence, at first temporary and then permanent, of the father. All the stories described by Sand, from her first childish fairy tales through to the Corambé material and her convent "novel," even "Histoire du rêveur," one of Aurore Dudevant's unpublished short stories, resemble one another. They are "family romances," as Freud has called them, and include both the ambitious (or social) and the erotic aims Freud ascribes to these scenarios.[20] Clearly, they are the products of wish fulfillment, of a desire for the kind of wholeness and security of which Aurore Dupin was deprived.

There are differences between Aurore's scenarios and Freud's, for Freud was describing men's dreams, not women's. There is far less conflict in the woman's romance, as Freud suggests in passing, for, unlike the son, who is locked in combat with the father, the daughter, because of her gender identity with the mother, is able to conserve the mother's affection as well as win over the father. The more permeable ego-barriers that have been ascribed to women by Nancy Chodorow, in particular, show up in Aurore Dupin's romances and Sand's novels.[21] Women, although sometimes rivals, are never mortal enemies, but usually friends and sisters as well. Sand, often falsely accused as being antifeminist and cool to women in her life, depicts in her novels female support networks and sorority of a kind that the twentieth century would value highly. Thus, the character I have termed the mother figure in the novels (Noun, Silvia, Pulchérie, etc.) is always neatly eliminated by the novelist, and never by her rival character. The renounce-the-mother-to-become-like-the-father male scenario is not repeated here, for the female character can herself become the mother while obtaining the father's love. Sand attempts to create a panphilic atmosphere in which all characters live and love together as a new family, of which the *petit pavillon* episode of *Valentine* is emblematic. In fact, the friends who assemble in the pavilion are explicitly called a "famille" (*V*, 257, 281). George Sand had a predilection for small, enclosed rooms, which appear with great frequency in her novels. They are related to her secret altar to Corambé, hidden in the woods of the garden and dismantled after a young friend found it. She wanted to be alone to commune with Corambé and recreates this situation in the characters' rendezvous in private spaces. The choices Sand sets up for her female characters are not either/or but both/and. In her childhood stories and her adult novels, as in her dreams, she seeks to have it all—the love of both parents, a secure atmosphere.

The novels do differ from the earlier material in one significant way, for they contain the negative father figure, absent from the childhood tales, as well as the good one. They more fully conform to the romance genre, in which the hero must combat evil to arrive at the happy end. Again, Sand creates a female version of this genre, as will be seen more clearly in the chapters on *Indiana* and *Valentine*. The introduction of this evil element is troubling. Gislinde Seybert interprets the irascible male as an incarnation of Deschartres, Maurice Dupin's and later Aurore Dupin's tutor.[22] The portrait of Deschartres, whom Aurore loved although sometimes also feared, as drawn in the autobiography does not support this thesis. He, too, was largely responsible for her career, in that he treated her more like a male pupil, able to learn and do anything, than like a girl to be protected and thwarted. If there is any living prototype of the figure of patriarchy, it is rather Casimir Dudevant, the husband who was brutal and uncomprehending, a product of his century but also a willing participant in its laws and unwritten rules. He used, and abused, his wife's fortune, as was his right, and was an excellent example of the kind of man she described perfectly in *Indiana*:

> Savez-vous ce qu'en province on appelle un *honnête homme*? . . . Pourvu qu'il respecte religieusement la vie et la bourse de ses concitoyens, on ne lui demande pas compte d'autre chose. Il peut battre sa femme, maltraiter ses gens, ruiner ses enfants, cela ne regarde personne. (*I*, 119)

> Do you know what they call an *honest man* in the provinces? . . . Provided that he religiously respects the lives and purses of his fellow-citizens, nothing more is demanded of him. He may beat his wife, maltreat his servants, ruin his children, and it is nobody's business. (*i*, 96)

Marriage to Casimir must have been quite a shock to Aurore, for he was both an average, ordinary man, certainly not a monster or a criminal, and the antithesis of everything she had hoped for or dreamed of. In fact, she had chosen him over other suitors in large part because she saw him as a protector and friend at a time in her life when she needed both, as her correspondence and autobiography indicate (*C* I, 267, *Oa* II, 27). He was a refuge against the sexual advances of Prosper Tessier, whom she met at about the same time and who wanted her to become his mistress, not his wife. Surely this episode, in its crude betrayal of Aurore's love and confidence, figures in Sand's representation of the harsh and sexually demanding man. Casimir, to Aurore's dismay, turned out to be no different from his fellow officer. Added to her uncomfortable experience of male-dominated institutions such as the Catholic church (one thinks particularly of her overzealous confessor who sought impure thoughts where none existed), her failed marriage provided the impetus for a return to a happier psychological fantasy as well as a further complication of her original "plot."

This oppressive father figure serves a double function however; on one level, he incorporates the male society from which George Sand wanted to escape. On a deeper psychological level, though, he symbolizes her denial and fear of the very same incestuous union she sets up later in the novel. By heaping opprobrium on this paternal character and showing him to be the representative of all she disdains, Sand temporarily distances herself from forbidden desires and is then free to satisfy them with a character who is the antithesis of the scorned male. A denial in Freudian terms is an affirmation, however, so that Sand's novels in fact twice postulate a desired union with the father, first as anxious denial and then as positive fulfillment.

It is in this context that I would interpret the *polichinelle* episode recounted in *Histoire de ma vie* and discussed in support of her thesis by Yvette Bozon-Scalzitti, an exponent of the primacy of the maternal in Sand's writing. Aurore Dupin receives a Punchinello doll as a gift, which she enjoys playing with as long as her other doll is put away, for she thinks the doll in danger in the presence of the Punchinello. Aurore refuses to allow the two dolls to be together while she sleeps, and she sets the Punchinello on the stove. That night, she has a nightmare in which the Punchinello, on fire, "his hump up front" (*Oa* I, 539), pursues both her and her doll. She awakens and her sister takes the Punchinello away. The Punchinello, who resembles a soldier, "all shiny gold and scarlet" (*Oa* I, 538), the doll, and Aurore can be seen as the child's family configuration, with the Punchinello-father setting both the mother and daughter on fire (" . . . he touched us with long streams of fire") (*Oa* I, 539). Both women are objects of his desire. As Bozon-Scalzitti perspicaciously points out, the alcove where Aurore sleeps is separated from her parents' part of the room by doors with a metal grill—the same grill on which Aurore played her first "music"—so that Aurore is in a position to hear, if not see, her parents and their *secrets d'alcôve*. In refusing to allow the dolls to remain together, Aurore has tried to prevent her parents from sleeping together, and is punished by the Punchinello-father.

The follow-up to this dream is equally significant. A lamplighter, an old woman, threatens to lock Aurore up in the streetlamp.

> Il me semblait que le diable eût soufflé à cette bonne femme l'idée qui pouvait le plus m'effrayer. . . . Le réverbère, avec son réflecteur étincelant, prit aussitôt à mes yeux des proportions fantastiques, et je me voyais déjà enfermée dans cette prison de cristal, consumée par la flamme que faisait faillir à volonté le polichinelle en jupons. (*Oa* I, 539)

> The devil must have whispered to this woman the menace which would frighten me most. . . . At once, the street lamp, with its shining reflector, took on fantastic proportions in my eyes, and I saw myself already shut up in its crystal

prison, consumed by the fire which flared at the will of that petticoated Punchinello.

The connection between the two episodes is made explicit by the repetition of the word "Punchinello." Here, the daughter imagines punishment at the hands of the mother, as she had already dreamt of punishment by the father for both her illicit desires and her interference with her parents' relationship. Each incident is double-sided; both contain the desired union and fear of the union, as well as fear of punishment. Bozon-Scalzitti admits the possibility of such a reading of the Punchinello stories but chooses to reject this interpretation in favor of a mother-centered theory.

> Le lecteur freudien risque cependant de ne voir dans le cauchemar "originel" de la scène primitive, et dans ses avatars, que l'expression du désir de la fillette, inversé en angoisse, d'être, à la place de la mère, l'objet de l'amour du père. Si nous choisissons de le lire à l'endroit, . . . c'est que toute l'*Histoire de ma vie* nous y invite.[23]

> The Freudian reader might well see in the basic nightmare of the primal scene, and in its further developments, merely the expression of the little girl's desire to be the object of the father's love in place of the mother, but here turned upside down into its converse, anxiety. If we choose to read the nightmare right side up, it is because all of *Histoire de ma vie* invites us to.

On the contrary, the autobiography, as I have shown, invites the reader to seek the absent father, rather than the distant mother Bozon-Scalzitti and Brée have described. The disturbing and ambivalent aspect of Sand's scenario, seen in several of the novels, will be discussed further in the chapters on *Rose et Blanche* and *Mauprat*.

In calling upon Sand's biography and autobiography to illuminate her novels, I do not wish to reduce the latter to mere transpositions of her life story. Like all writers, Sand drew heavily on her own experience for her fiction; many characters resemble people she knew, while events of her life appeared in her work. The use of her native Berry as the setting for many novels remains one of her most original contributions to nineteenth-century literature. Yet even more interesting about Sand is the general within the particular, the way in which her writing coincides or contrasts with other women's writing, as well as its relation to men's. My point of departure is Sand's fiction, not her life, and it was my desire to explain the recurrence of a certain pattern that led me to her autobiography, also fiction of a sort, and ultimately to her biography, and not the reverse. My use of psychoanalytic theory is likewise motivated by a belief that the structure of literature is related to the structure of mind. Freud's own work, including and especially that on the Oedipus complex, was firmly grounded in literature, while his "talking cure" ultimately involves the patients' oral elaboration of their own story. The question that remains to be posed, then, concerns the extent to which the scenario that enabled Sand to live and write is applicable to other writers as well as to readers.

The author that immediately comes to mind in this context is Germaine de Staël, who was very much a model for Sand in life as well as literature. Staël's deep attachment to her father, Jacques Necker, is as well known as her rivalry with her very proper mother. Her two novels, *Delphine* and *Corinne*, depict scenarios like Sand's. In *Corinne*, two half sisters, whose link is paternal, love the same man. The younger sister marries him with unhappy results; she produces a child whom Corinne educates, as she would have her own, to be the new Corinne. In *Delphine*, a far more complex (and less successful) novel, the title character helps a younger, distant cousin financially so she can marry Léonce de Mondoville, with whom Delphine promptly falls in love. The Léonce-Mathilde marriage is also a failure; their child dies, but Delphine adopts a friend's daughter who becomes her substitute child. The two authors' scenarios are strikingly similar, although developed differently because of Staël's and Sand's different psychologies.

It would be interesting to study other women novelists, particularly those who are not overtly father-identified as was Staël, to see if comparable patterns emerge. Certainly the incestuous component reappears, particularly in such writers as Charlotte and Emily Brontë. This element may be due in part to women's greater feelings of connectedness and tendency to establish contacts with others, but, as Dianne Sadoff has shown for Charlotte Brontë and George Eliot, the father plays an essential role in the literary works as well as the lives of these authors.[24] In *A Literature of Their Own*, Elaine Showalter notes in her chapter on British women novelists of the same period: "A factor that recurs with remarkable frequency in the background of these women is identification with, and dependence upon, the father; and either loss of, or alienation from, the mother."[25]

Outside of literature, the importance of the father for the daughter's professional development has been shown by Hennig and Jardim, in their study of what they term "the managerial woman." Women executives who had reached significant positions in the business world were found to be strongly father-identified. Only or oldest children, as girls they were encouraged by their fathers to achieve beyond usual expectations for their gender.[26] Judith Bardwich has obtained similar results, which Showalter links in a qualified way with the achievements of nineteenth-century British women writers.[27] This pattern is seen in Sand's childhood in the education dispensed by Deschartres and her grandmother, who despite, or perhaps because of, her Rousseauistic bent, raised her granddaughter more like

Emile than Sophie. None of this should serve to deny the importance of the mother's influence on her daughter or to place undue emphasis on the role of the father. As stated, Sand's grandmother was in charge of her education and acted as a model of a cultivated woman for Aurore. Rather, George Sand knew, and researchers have confirmed, what appears fairly obvious today: being exposed as a girl to the physical and intellectual challenges open to boys, and having access as a woman to a world larger than the domestic sphere can have salutary effects. It seems that historically fathers rather than mothers most often supported this untraditional behavior in their daughters and, as representatives of the outside world, were the only possible models of a professional life. Sand's real father's role, as we have seen, was not that of active supporter found by Hennig and Jardim, although it would be hard to find an example of such a father in nineteenth-century France; even Jacques Necker, proud as he was of Germaine's talents, did not approve of her writing, causing her profound conflicts that Sand was spared.[28] Instead, it was the lack of paternal constraint in Aurore Dupin's life along with her positive image of her father that made her success possible.

And as George Sand she achieved great success. It is often forgotten how important a writer she was during a forty-five-year period, and not only in France. In England, Germany, Russia, and Italy readers and authors cherished George Sand the writer as well as the woman. Elizabeth Barrett Browning, George Eliot, Alexander Herzen, the Young Germans, and Giuseppi Mazzini all appreciated her work and ideas.[29] She earned—and spent—a great deal of money and was a shrewd businesswoman, as her book contracts attest.[30]

Yet, as has been the case with Victor Hugo, that other giant of the nineteenth century with whom Sand had many personal and literary affinities, her reputation has declined precipitously from the summit of critical acclaim and popular adulation she enjoyed in her lifetime. Several factors have conspired to obscure Sand's place in literary history and to consign her to the dusty shelves of unread writers. Generations of French children, much like Proust's Marcel, have read the pastoral novels and thus perpetuated the image of the *Bonne Dame de Nohant* writing stories for children, despite the very sophisticated subject matter of these novels. After her death, Sand's works disappeared from public view like those of nearly all the French women writers who had been successful in their time, a phenomenon that might be called "out of sight, out of mind." In addition, as her literary reputation waned, her legend grew in importance and weight; she was known more for her affairs with such famous men as Musset, Mérimée, and Chopin, and was accused of having had a lesbian relationship with the actress Marie Dorval. Her cigar smoking and adoption of male attire served to place the shocking image of Sand in the foreground while relegating her work to oblivion.

The centennial of Sand's death in 1976 and the burgeoning of Women's Studies have contributed greatly to the renewal of interest in her extraordinary literary production: novels, plays, short stories, essays, travel literature, and an autobiography that ranks as one of the world's best. In an era when so many literary reputations are being reexamined and the canon is being revised, it is time to look closely at George Sand and begin to acknowledge what her *oeuvre* represents for our understanding of nineteenth-century French literature. As a step toward reaffirming Sand's position among the great writers of her century, the chapters that follow will show how Aurore Dudevant became a writer and what she achieved in her early novels.

1 🐚

WRITING A SELF
From Aurore Dudevant to J. Sand

The first of Aurore Dudevant's literary texts to have survived was written when the author was twenty-three, at the request of her convent friend Jane Bazouin.[1] None of Sand's earliest attempts at self-expression was published during her lifetime, although she may have reread many of them in her later years, as notations on the manuscripts suggest; most are now available, thanks in large part to Georges Lubin's indefatigable efforts, in the Pléiade edition of the *Oeuvres autobiographiques*. Of the rest, *La Marraine* remains unpublished, and *Aimée*, the novel Aurore Dudevant brought to Paris to begin her literary career, was destroyed by her after her mentor, Hyacinthe de Latouche, termed it "wretched" (*Oa* II, 151).

The texts written by Aurore Dudevant are essentially exploratory, resembling exercises in style, composition, and characterization. Several, like "Les Couperies" or "Une Lettre de femme," are fragmentary, sketches that never became part of a whole work, whereas others, more complete, show the narrative skill of the future George Sand. In the more than half a dozen works Aurore Dudevant wrote between 1827 and 1831, there is an alternation between autobiography, the novice writer's logical source of inspiration, and fiction, as she sought to find her own voice and to attain a comfortable authorial stance. Aurore Dudevant's first compositions allow us to trace her development as a writer and chart her evolution from Aurore Dudevant to George Sand.

Aurore Dudevant's first literary effort was the delightful "Voyage au Mont d'Or" (known later as the "Voyage en Auvergne").[2] Written in the form of a journal during her stay at a spa in August 1827, the "Voyage" reveals a talent for humor, dialogue, and characterization, as well as the descriptive style for which George Sand was famous.

The "Voyage" was probably written with a real reader in mind and was later sent to a friend, most likely Félicie Molliet. Yet it is an intensely personal work, one that reveals much sadness, doubt, and searching. The opening pages contain an inordinate number of rhetorical questions, of the following sort: "Why have I come here?" "But what should I do today?" and, eventually, "[S]uppose I wrote to someone?" (*Oa* II, 503–504). It is significant that this first work should devote considerable space to the act of writing itself, as well as to Aurore Dudevant's domestic unhappiness, for her career as an author was to spring directly from her resolve to change her household arrangements by living part of the year away from her husband and the consequent need to earn a living.

She begins her journal by explaining her motivation for writing—boredom and ill humor—and proceeds to choose a *destinataire* (recipient) as well as a form. She first composes a letter to her mother, a *cri du coeur* expressing all the hurt her mother had inflicted upon her, but then rejects this option because it would cause her mother needless pain. Next, she casts about for other possible correspondents among her male and female friends, but finds none to be the ideal reader. She refuses to describe Clermont-Ferrand to her brother; "the usual obligatory travel story" (*Oa* II, 505) is not the subject matter she has in mind. She comes to realize that her journal is a form of writing but decides that it is more reflections or meditations than literature.

This preliminary consideration of writing is interrupted by a dialogue with M. Garrick, a naturalist, followed by a description of the baths, which she tours with him. Two hours remain before dinner, and Aurore decides to while them away and quiet her chagrin by writing her memoirs, which she entitles *Mémoires inédits*. After the false starts of the previous pages, she has finally found the perfect *destinataire* in herself, as well as the proper form. Her *Unpublished Memoirs* detail all the steps necessary for the production of a literary text, from the motivation for writing: "[Y]esterday's thoughts will distract me from today's," to the choice of genre: memoirs are "a genre open to everyone," and even to the structure of the work: "Shall I write a preface? Yes. I must have one" (*Oa* II, 507). She also includes the correction of the text and the redaction of a letter to a possible editor. Although summary and tongue-in-cheek, this mini-autobiography shows a literary awareness and authority in Aurore Dudevant that would develop over the following months and years into George Sand's ability to write unceasingly and in several different genres. In addition, the reader familiar with *Histoire de ma vie* will find these lighthearted *Mémoires inédits* uncanny, for they contain in drastically reduced form the outline of the later work.

The gay, playful tone of the "Voyage au Mont d'Or" reappears in *La Marraine* and *Histoire du rêveur*, Aurore Dudevant's next two literary productions, as does her preoccupation with the act of writing itself. Both were written for Jane Bazouin and contain similar dedicatory epistles, along with the tragicomic tale of a pet cricket.[3] Neither text was published during Sand's lifetime, and both manuscripts, written in notebooks, contain other, disparate texts.

La Marraine is the name given to the notebook that includes Aurore Dudevant's first attempt at writing a novel, which is not surprisingly called *Mémoires d'un villageois*. The manuscript does not begin with the novel, however, but rather with the letter to Jane, the story of the cricket, part of a recipe for plum pudding, and word games. The opening letter, presumably a response to Jane's request for a work from Aurore's pen, contains several interesting references to literature and writing. In describing her attempts to fulfill Jane's mandate, Aurore again shows a concern with the material side of the writer's craft: "What indeed was I lacking? I had Hâvre paper of excellent quality, goose quills that wrote by themselves and ink even blacker, perhaps, than that used by Monta[i]gne" (*C* I, 563). She humorously recounts the difficulties she had with structuring in a socially acceptable manner the first work she devised, which has disappeared without out a trace, if it ever existed:

> J'avais commencé par faire descendre mes héros dans la tombe au milieu des larmes de leurs proches. Ce tableau étant le plus touchant et le plus pathétique je n'avais pu résister à la tentation de le tracer le premier. Puis, j'avais donné une famille à ces intéressants personnages, mais sans songer à les conduire à l'autel préalablement, de sorte qu'un ami à qui je traçais la peinture de leur ménage, crut de bonne foi que je voulais introduire une nouvelle morale fort différente de celle observée jusqu'ici. Il se récria sur la hardiesse de l'innovation. Je me hâtai de conclure l'hymen de mes amants, et cela me faisant penser que je n'avais point encore songé à les mettre au monde, je trouvai que plus j'avançais plus il me restait à faire. (*C* I, 563–64)

> I began by sending my heroes to the grave amidst the tears of their relatives. Since this scene was the most touching and the most pathetic, I couldn't resist the temptation to paint it first. Then I gave children to these interesting characters, but without thinking to send them to the altar first, so that a friend to whom I described their family situation thought in good faith that I wanted to introduce a moral code very different from that observed until now. He criticized the boldness of the innovation. I hastened to conclude the marriage of my lovers; this made me realize that I hadn't yet thought to describe their birth, so that the more I advanced in my work, the more there was left to do.

This brief summary of her (perhaps imaginary) novel, however ironically meant, is not dissimilar to the "nouvelle morale" of *Indiana* (1832).

This letter goes on to admit that Aurore's literary baggage is skimpy, consisting as it does of a recipe for plum pudding and a laundress's bill, as well as a comic song that, she melodramatically reports, nearly got her

hanged by the proper society of La Châtre, thereby ending her career as
a poet.

> Aussi Dieu me garde de jamais me lancer dans le domaine de la poésie, dussent
> tous les lauriers du Pinde couronner mon front, dussé-je être appelée la Muse
> de mon département, titre si envié par toute femme de province qui sait lire
> passablement dans les Heures de son diocèse et qui peut écrire un billet d'in-
> vitation pour ses soirées littéraires sans faire plus de trois fautes d'orthographe.
> (C I, 563)

> Thus let God preserve me from ever entering the domain of poetry, even if
> all of Pindar's laurels should cover my brow, even if I were to be called the
> muse of my *département*, a title much envied by any woman of the provinces
> who can read passably the Hours of her diocese and who can write an invitation
> to her literary soirées without making more than three spelling mistakes.

This disclaimer to fame and literary glory manifests a sure knowledge of
the kind of provincial society Sand would later satirize in many of her
novels and also hints that whatever her writing might lead to, the last
position to which Aurore Dudevant aspires is that of provincial authoress,
queen of the semiliterates of her region.

After these preliminaries, the *Mémoires d'un villageois* begins. They turn
out to be the story of Julien, a country boy whose father, a weaver, is struck
by lightning in the second chapter of the novel. The "godmother" of the
manuscript's title is Louise, daughter of the lord of the village château and
eight years older than Julien. She sees to Julien's future after his father's
death. There is no explanation of the dual titles of the notebook and the
novel itself; the author seems undecided as to the real subject of her story.
Julien and Louise represent two plot possibilities, as well as the two social
classes that Sand would later treat. In theme and setting the work anticipates *Valentine*, although in the later novel it is the heiress to the manor
herself whom the young peasant loves.

The *Mémoires* is a rambling novel whose thirty-six chapters contain several
references to Montaigne, one of Aurore Dudevant's favorite authors at the
time, and *Tristram Shandy*; chapter 24 begins: "If you are in a hurry, skip
this chapter." Julien's first-person narrative gives way abruptly in the last
chapter to a third-person narrative that marries Julien off to Blanche, his
godmother's adopted child, and describes Louise's elopement to South
America with a Spaniard she loves. Nothing in the preceding pages has
prepared this dénouement, and one has the sense that Aurore, unable or
unwilling to continue with the plot she had developed, ended her story in
the most novelistic way she could imagine. It is significant, though, that *La*

Marraine already manifests the triangular structure of mother-daughter figures and the man to whom they are both devoted, with a final marriage between the man and the daughter.

The *Mémoires* is the work of an author already able to create characters and evoke sites. Julien, M. Lesec, the curé—a true George Sand character, kind and not the least bit hypocritical—are well drawn, as is the village where they live. Although Aurore Dudevant is on her way to mastering these skills, however, narration and plot are her weak points. Her narrative voice did not affirm itself until after the publication of *Indiana*, while a tendency toward extravagant plot devices remained in her fiction, albeit in a more moderate form.

As in Aurore Dudevant's other early texts, the narration of the *Mémoires* is even more remarkable than the story told. Julien's novel, as has been noted, is part of a larger project called *La Marraine* and is introduced because the narrator, after her letter to Jane and the tale of the cricket, is short on inspiration. She hopes that Julien will share his ideas and read the memoirs he has written at her urging; thus, Julien's work is a reflection, a kind of *mise-en-abyme*, of Aurore Dudevant's, who undertook *La Marraine* at Jane's insistence. Julien is not allowed to proceed smoothly with the reading of his memoirs, however, for there are interruptions from the cook; a discussion of the shades of meaning between *mémoires*, Julien's first title, and *souvenirs*, his second; and a consideration of the value of publishing his manuscript, before he finally gets on with his story. His dual title echos Aurore Dudevant's two titles, while the ensuing discussion shows her awareness of the importance of the title for the prospective audience: "It is important that they understand before listening what the story is going to be about" (*LM*, 29). The mention of publication, too, is significant, for it shows that Aurore is clearly contemplating writing for a wider public than just her friend, even if publication is ultimately recommended here only for the author's very few intimates and not the world at large.

Once these questions have been resolved and Julien has been given the floor, the narrator continues to interrupt, providing an editorial note and approbatory interventions. It is as though Aurore Dudevant, having chosen to write a novel with a male narrator, cannot allow him complete narrative freedom, but must constantly assert her own voice and her own control over the narrative. Why she decided to compose the memoirs of a man rather than those of a woman is a mystery. What is apparent, though, is her uncertainty over her own narrative authority. Aurore obviously felt that a male narrator was preferable, but could not totally give up the power she had had in the first pages of *La Marraine*. This conflict between male narrative authority, on the one hand, and the female voice, on the other, remains in Aurore Dudevant's early works and is resolved in *Indiana*, when she achieves narrative confidence by using an exclusively male narrator while retaining a female perspective.

In the months following the composition of *La Marraine*, Aurore Dudevant wrote her first short story. "Histoire du rêveur" is a *conte fantastique*, the tale of a traveler's mysterious adventures on Mt. Etna, which turn out in the end to have been merely a dream. "Histoire du rêveur" is a fast-paced, poetically written supernatural tale that in composition and execution is vastly superior to anything Aurore Dudevant had written until then. It is a satisfying tale of the "fantastique-étrange," in Todorov's terminology, where at the end a reasonable explanation of a supernatural phenomenon is furnished.[4] In fact, it is a fine example of the genre, worthy of such contemporaries as Nodier or Hoffmann, who combined music and the fantastic much as Aurore Dudevant does here.

"Histoire du rêveur" is a framed narrative whose first-person extradiegetic narrator, a woman, is in conversation with a certain Tricket, a magician.[5] He in turn becomes the intradiegetic narrator and recounts the story proper in the third person.[6] They appear in the beginning, again briefly in the first chapter, and finally at the end. The narrative itself is divided into four chapters. In the first, called "La Grotte des chèvres," an unknown voyager heads toward the summit of Mt. Etna to see the sunrise and all Sicily spread out before him in the light of dawn. He refuses the help of a guide, which causes the innkeeper to warn him against malignant spirits and an evil genie. The positivistic hero rejects these warnings and continues on his route. Unable to sleep at his campsite, known as *la grotte des chèvres*, he sees a frightening visage on the other side of the fire, which he soon recognizes as that of his mule. In the moonlight, he decides to press on to the summit.

In "Le Chanteur," we learn that Amédée is the traveler's name. Music, one of George Sand's most enduring themes, makes its appearance in the form of a song, heard through the forest. Amédée recognizes that the voice belongs to a trained musician but cannot decide whether the singer is a man or a woman. The song, too, is unusual; an invocation to Etna's spirits, it is "an inspired and savage poetry that bore the characteristics of an improvisation" (*Hr*, 13). Amédée answers with a song of his own and soon meets the singer, whose appearance is as sexually indeterminate as his voice. The singer mounts Amédée's mule, which promptly bolts down the mountain like an animal possessed. Amédée tries to shake his companion, who behaves like the Erlking or some other demon—in his song he had evoked Hecate, goddess of the underworld—and whose frail, girlish body suddenly shows a supernatural strength. Part two ends with the mule throwing himself and his riders down a ravine.

Part three, "L'Eruption," finds the two men on the summit and Amédée doubting his sanity. The singer denies that there had been any fall, insisting that the rarified atmosphere caused delirium. When they reach the edge of the volcano, the young man reveals himself to be a spirit and calls Etna his king. Amédée demands to join him in the seething crater. As lava flows around them, he sees his companion transformed into a woman. He follows her into the volcano, but when he kisses her he receives an electric shock and awakens in the very brief fourth chapter to discover himself on his bed of leaves at the *grotte des chèvres*.

In addition to the theme of music, "Histoire du rêveur" contains several suggestive images that link it to Sand's later texts. The most compelling is that of the androgyne, a new, literary formulation of Corambé. The singer has a voice described as "a mixture of what is most harmonious in the musical abilities of each sex" (*Hr*, 13). Amédée himself has an ambiguous name, for although it is a man's name, it ends in the feminine double *e*. The name also serves to reinforce the musical theme by its association with Mozart and E.T.A. Hoffmann. The changing gender of the singer is linked to Amédée's desire to be free of his body, a pure spirit, for it is only as the lava burns away Amédée's body that the singer becomes a passionate woman. One senses that Amédée's disembodiment symbolizes Aurore Dudevant's dissatisfactions with the constraints of her own life and the restrictions occasioned by her gender, marital status, even sexual desires. Amédée cries out: "Don't let me vegetate in real life, to which you don't seem to belong . . ." (*Hr*, 17), and exhibits a certain desperation that demands any sort of relief, no matter how drastic: "[A]ngel or devil: carry me off into this vortex that I see enveloping you already"(ibid.).[7] In fact, although the images of the last pages are potentially terrifying—as the volcano erupts, Amédée sees "the crater vomiting torrents of liquid fire . . . and throwing up to the clouds volcanic bombs whose detonnation [*sic*] was deafening" (*Hr*, 18)—he does not seem frightened. He is even able to look upon his half-consumed body without regret and to appreciate the flames that incinerated him: "[A] pure spirit, he felt the heat of the fire, not as a burning pain, but as an indescribable pleasure" (ibid.).

Amédée hopes that this purification by fire will allow him access to higher pleasures, both physical and spiritual, as well as freedom, and will afford him perfect union and harmony, for he and the woman seem simultaneously ethereal and corporeal. Yet the harmony suggested by the musical theme, as well as the chromatic scale of the third part, in which the colors red, white, and blue predominate, is unattainable. His attempt at union, in the form of a kiss, separates him from the woman and awakens him from his dream. Although "Histoire du rêveur" ends in defeat, Aurore Dudevant's dream did not, for she was soon to obtain her freedom. This story helped her both to express her unhappiness and to explore her innermost desires, while enabling her to affirm her emerging identity as a writer and perfect the craft that would support her liberation. Eventually she did achieve harmony in her own life as George Sand. Perfect union, however, remained an elusive goal.

The notebook containing "Histoire du rêveur" also includes a second part, comprising an *Avis* that warns the reader about the narrator's discursive style and forms a link between the first part and the promised, but never delivered, continuation of Amédée's story, plus "Le Grillon" and "Les Confessions."[8] Tricket is still her interlocutor, and in "Le Grillon" she again utilizes the device of the frame. This is essentially the same text that appears in *La Marraine* after the opening letter to Jane Bazouin, and in fact in both versions it is not set off from the letter in any way. The story itself is a charming tale of a pet cricket that lived in her bookcase and serenaded her at midnight. Unfortunately, the cricket was crushed in the window by a careless chambermaid, causing his friend great chagrin. This episode is a sketch, rather than a short story, and is well executed. The narration presents even more interest than the tale itself, though, for it concerns the act of telling a story and shows Aurore Dudevant's growing literary consciousness.

The narrator offers to read her tale to Tricket in the form of a long letter to Jane. This letter is quite similar to the one found in *La Marraine*, with a few notable exceptions: the laundress's bill has become a birthday greeting, and the list of material conditions necessary for writing now includes a very significant addition: money.

> J'oubliais le besoin d'argent, si c'est un stimulant utile comme je n'en doute pas. La première fois que j'écrirai pour le public je ferai des merveilles cergtainement, car je ne connais personne qui puisse s'aider comme moi de cette disposition à l'enthousiasme qui consiste à n'avoir pas le sou." (*Hr*, 20)

> "I forgot about the need for money and what a useful stimulus it is, as I don't doubt. The first time I write for the public I will certainly write wonderful things, for I know no one who can be encouraged as much as I by the disposition towards enthusiasm which comes from not having a penny to one's name."

As she wrote in this notebook, Aurore Dudevant was probably thinking more about using her pen to earn her living than of pleasing Jane. This letter is much longer than its prototype, for there are constant interruptions and digressions, in the manner of Sterne, who is mentioned by name and undoubtedly alluded to in the description of the backwards novel that begins with the death of the protagonists but never quite reaches their birth.

Thus do *La Marraine* and "Histoire du rêveur" contain two of the same

texts, somewhat altered and embellished. It is evident that Aurore Dudevant, even at this early stage, was not simply writing idly to fill time and
paper but was seriously developing her art, revising, rewriting, and re-
working to achieve the best effect. The manuscript of *La Marraine* is very
clean and is obviously a final copy, not a draft, although it does contain
one peculiarity, two versions of a brief scene, as though she could not chose
between them and decided to keep both. "Histoire du rêveur" presents an
even more interesting case, for there are three extant manuscripts of the
work, all incomplete.[9] This demonstrates that Aurore Dudevant rewrote
and recopied her text carefully and that she was already conscious of herself
on some level as an author, even if publication was still some time away.

The greater personal and narrative self-confidence she achieved through
these emendations is evident in the text that follows "Le Grillon." "Les
Confessions" is constructed in a circular fashion: the narrator begins by
speaking of her intention to write her memoirs, describes the kind of memoirs popular at the time, and gives her view of what memoirs should be
like. This discussion of autobiography reminds her of a previous conversation with another friend, "Le Bel Esprit," about Jean-Jacques Rousseau.
That exchange had been interrupted by the friend's loss of a tie pin and
the fruitless search to locate it, which is recounted in a burlesque manner,
with mordant descriptions both of the starched necktie and of an old servant's attempts to find the pin. In explaining to Tricket why she is happy
about this contretemps, which prevented her friend from destroying her
admiration for Rousseau, she proceeds to give a brief autobiographical
summary of the three stages her character had gone through in her lifetime. In so doing, she writes the memoirs that she had earlier stated she
no longer wanted to write, thereby coming full circle.

Like the "Voyage au Mont d'Or," "Les Confessions" foreshadows *Histoire
de ma vie*. Aurore Dudevant's memoirs are written with reference to Rousseau's *Confessions*. Sand's real autobiography would also be placed under
Rousseau's sign, although in the intervening years Aurore Dudevant's enthusiasm for Rousseau would be tempered by her own experience of no-
toriety. George Sand's criticism of Rousseau in *Histoire de ma vie* takes him
to task for admitting to crimes or faults that are neither edifying nor helpful
to the reader, as well as for revealing the turpitudes of his friends along
with his own. She finds that his self-accusation demeans him and stems not
from humility but from pride. Although these opinions may derive in part
from Sand's desire to avoid confessing to her own wrongs (her romantic
life is heavily censored), and may be due to self-justification as well as
conviction, it is nonetheless noteworthy that the same charge of pride is
made in "Les Confessions" by "Le Bel Esprit," her philosophical friend. In
Histoire de ma vie, the views of Rousseau attributed in the earlier text to two

different interlocutors have been synthesized and assumed by Sand as her own. The intervening years between the two texts have enabled her to express confidently and in her own name her judgment of an author who in many ways was her mentor, but for whom she did not feel unreserved admiration.

Aurore Dudevant's definition of memoirs in "Les Confessions" also resembles the rationale Sand gives years later for writing *Histoire de ma vie*: autobiography should be instructive to the reader, providing insight into the human heart that will enable others to compare their own actions and motivations with those of the autobiographer. Both projects closely follow Rousseau's, although her program is less systematic than his: where Rousseau seeks to write the first text for a course of study on human character, Aurore Dudevant/Sand hopes to interest and perhaps help the reader. Aurore Dudevant, and later Sand, does not insist on her uniqueness, as does Rousseau; rather, she is simply an example of the human condition, and her story, a true one sincerely told. Her vocabulary in "Les Confessions," with its insistence on veracity and frankness, as well as on the value of memoirs for comparative purposes, repeats Rousseau's, while her treatment of her subject parallels his.

"Les Confessions" records Aurore Dudevant's moral evolution from dependence on outside authority to confidence in the penchants of her own heart, whatever the social costs. She describes her itinerary from passivity in the face of ethical and philosophical problems to fanatical partisanship, although in both cases her opinions were derived from others. Her final and, she hopes, permanent stage was achieved by self-examination rather than the study of the writings of famous thinkers and represents the triumph of feeling and instinct over reason and systems. Aurore Dudevant's growing self-reliance, confidence in her own views, and liberation from the "anxiety of influence," as well as her imperviousness to her critics, are stated clearly in a text that in all likelihood precedes by a very short time her final break with her husband Casimir and her past.

In the early months of 1831 Aurore Dudevant moved to Paris and dramatically increased her literary production. In April or May she wrote "Jehan Cauvin," another framed narrative that was not published during her lifetime. The extradiegetic narrator uses variously *nous* or *je* and is of indeterminate gender; the frame is a traditional one, providing eleven pages of introduction and one of conclusion to a twenty-six-page narrative. "Jehan Cauvin" is a historical sketch rather than a fictional story, whose interest derives mainly from the brilliant description of the cathedral at Bourges, as well as from the burlesque opening scene in which children and ecclesiastics exchange roles in a blasphemous mass. The prose style of

George Sand is evident in the evocation of the voices resounding throughout the cathedral:

> ... [E]t les voix argentines des enfants mêlées aux longs soupirs de l'orgue allaient frapper les voûtes élevées, puis suivant la retombée des arceaux, descendaient pour remonter sous les arcades suivantes et d'ogive en ogive, de profondeur en profondeur, allaient s'éteindre en légers frémissements sous la ceinture abaissée des mystérieuses chapelles.[10]

> ... [A]nd the silvery voices of the children mixed with the long sighs of the organ struck the high vaults then, following the path of the curves downward only to rise again to the next arch and from ogive to ogive, from depth to depth, died in soft whispers under the low enclosures of mysterious chapels.

"Jehan Cauvin" describes Calvin's conversion while a student at Bourges. It concerns a crucial moment in the life of a major European figure. Yet the reader never really enters into his life. His religious doubts are told rather than shown, to use Henry James's distinction, and one senses Aurore Dudevant's disenchantment with the church more than Calvin's. The choice of subject is revealing, though, for in portraying a decisive moment in the life of a rebel and heretic, Aurore Dudevant is surely also writing about her own feelings toward society and its conventions. The reversal of the end, where Calvin's mentor Melchior Wolmar reveals himself to be a Lutheran as well, is an attempt at plot, but it is clear from Aurore Dudevant's static treatment of her topic that her ability to handle plot is still unformed. "Jehan Cauvin" is the last text written by Aurore Dudevant, for her next literary works would be signed with the temporary pseudonym J. Sand, which Hyacinthe de Latouche devised for her and Jules Sandeau.

The works written by Aurore Dudevant share many common characteristics. All, except the "Voyage au Mont d'Or," more or less take the form of framed narratives. In "Histoire du rêveur," the frame is distracting and detracts from an otherwise unified third-person narrative, while the frame in the other texts is of more interest to the student of the budding George Sand than to the reader seeking diversion, for the story-within-the-story is generally the fictional nub of the piece.

The frames and digressions are reminiscent of eighteenth-century literature, particularly Sterne and Diderot. Both "Le Grillon" and "Les Confessions," in their circuitous narration and deferred conclusions, recall *Jacques le fataliste*, where Jacques's love life somehow never gets recounted. Frames are also commonly used by authors of moral tales and fairy tales, genres familiar to Aurore Dudevant. She expressly makes reference to the latter by making Tricket a magician and by inventing a fantastic story. In addition, "Histoire du rêveur" begins with the notation "2de nuit" (*Hr*, 9), which not only implies the existence of a first night, now lost if indeed it was ever written, but, more importantly, would seem to be a reference to the *Mille et une nuits* and Scheherazade's storytelling. The choice of the cricket as a subject is also significant, for fairy tales are full of benign, anthropomorphic animal friends just like Aurore's.[11] Writing for herself or for her friends, discontinuously and in moments snatched from other pursuits, Aurore Dudevant drew on her experience of reading to provide her with models of narration.

The frame is especially useful to the novice writer, for it confers authority on the narrator and makes explicit the origin of the narrative voice. The assumption of responsibility for the narrative by a credible narrator was Aurore Dudevant's—and George Sand's—greatest difficulty in her early texts. In the "Voyage au Mont d'Or," "Le Grillon," and "Les Confessions," the narrator is a young woman closely identifiable with Aurore Dudevant herself, while the *Mémoires d'un villageois* and "Histoire du rêveur," the least autobiographical of Aurore Dudevant's writings, are narrated by a man. In "Jehan Cauvin," the genderless narrator cannot choose between a single *je* or a more general *nous*. This decentered *nous* reappears in *Rose et Blanche* as well as *Indiana*; in addition, *Indiana* is narrated by a masculine *je* who is only identified in the conclusion. In any event, after "Les Confessions," Aurore Dudevant would never again permit herself to use an exclusively female narrator, preferring to adopt a male voice along with a male name. Her first works show that the use of a male voice did not come automatically or easily, and that well before publication became a reality, Aurore Dudevant struggled with the issue of authority, so crucial to every writer, but especially to the woman writer.

The multilayered, framed form had other advantages as well, for it allowed Aurore Dudevant to pick up or drop a subject, continue or end a story as she wished, as well as to mix genres, for the truly fictional occupies only part of these texts. Aurore Dudevant's early works are autobiographical not only in that they draw in an unmediated fashion on her own life for their subject matter, as is expected in an inexperienced writer, but more importantly because they deliberately thematize the autobiographical impulse. Aurore Dudevant's two memoirs show a woman in search of herself, trying to make sense of her life and to find a direction that will make her happy. The comparison of the "Voyage" with "Les Confessions" is instructive, for the later text shows that Aurore Dudevant has made a clear moral progression from the uncertainty and suicidal despair of the "Voyage" to a calmer psychological stance based on an acceptance of her own opinions over those of others, despite possible social sanctions. She is clearly ready to begin a new phase of her life.

The presence of autobiography in Aurore Dudevant's early texts emphasizes writing in general and its material conditions as much as it does the writing of her life story; this preoccupation is seen in the letters to Jane Bazouin as well, which can also be considered autobiographical material. Aurore Dudevant can be said to be writing herself, both by using writing as a form of therapy in order to discover herself and to ease her pain, and by persuading herself that she can indeed write, that she possesses the tools, ability, and motivation necessary to be an author. She owned the pens and paper, while her motivations ranged from boredom to financial necessity to the pure desire to tell a story. Each completed text, along with Jane's pleased reactions, affirmed her identity and convinced her that she at least had potential, if not fully formed talent.

From the very first, the artist in Aurore Dudevant was struggling to appear, was questioning her craft and measuring her own ideas against those of her predecessors or contemporaries. Indeed, these initial compositions prefigure to an astonishing degree in themes, genres, and narrative voice the mature work of George Sand. Although none of her early work appeared in print, and *Aimée* was burned, Aurore Dudevant nonetheless served a valuable apprenticeship at Nohant, learning who she was and confirming that she had something to say.

2

J. SAND
Becoming a Woman Artist

Aurore Dudevant continued her literary education in Paris by writing articles, short stories, and finally a novel, *Rose et Blanche*. It was only after the publication of *Rose et Blanche* that Aurore Dudevant would truly become George Sand, with the redaction of *Indiana*. This interim Parisian period is distinguished by three characteristics. First and foremost, Aurore Dudevant's writings were published—in Latouche's *Figaro*, in the *Revue de Paris* and *La Mode*, and by the publisher Renault—unlike the works discussed in chapter 1. Second, two of these works were written with the aid of Jules Sandeau, who lent a truncated version of his name as a pseudonym. Finally, Aurore Dudevant's last writings manifest a clear preoccupation with becoming a woman artist, just as her first literary efforts described her desire to write and inscribed the writing of a confident self within each text.

The first text to appear under the pseudonym "Jules Sand" was "La Prima Donna," published in the *Revue de Paris* in April 1831. George Sand never claimed to have written the story, and it was never included in any collection of her works. Furthermore, a letter to her friend Emile Regnault, in which she refers to Balzac's complimentary note to Sandeau congratulating him on "La Prima Donna," states: "I see that the little one is well on his way to earning his livelihood as well as mine" (*C* I, 858), which implies that Sandeau alone was responsible for the story. Curtis Cate calls "La Prima Donna" a "piece of marzipan," which is a fairly accurate description of this account of a young man's silent love for a singer whose comeback appearance in *Romeo and Juliet* ends in her death on stage, followed, of course, by his.[1] The plot is absurd, and to call the style pedestrian is to be kind. Short sentences with few and clichéd adjectives mark a sharp contrast with Aurore Dudevant's already rich style, seen in the quotation from "Jehan Cauvin" in chapter 1.

Nonetheless, the last page of "La Prima Donna," where Gina makes the appearance that is supposed to restore her to health, bears the distinct imprint of Aurore Dudevant's hand. Even a casual reading of the story leaves the impression that this page was not written by the author of the preceding pages. Comparison of passages from two facing pages reveals a higher frequency of adjectives, as well as long, undulating sentences that seem to get carried away by their own rhetoric, in the page attributable to Aurore Dudevant.

"Ce n'était donc pas un songe, une vision de mes nuits agitées. Gina savait mon nom, mon amour; peut-être aussi se rappelait-elle confusément m'avoir parlé dans une de ses nuits de fièvre et d'égarement. Une rapide espérance me rendit la raison: je fis des projets comme eût pu les faire un homme dans son bon sens, je prêtai intérêt aux choses extérieures, je compris ce qui se passait autour de moi. Gina se mourait: je passai mes jours et mes nuits à songer aux moyens de lui rendre la vie. J'entendis parler d'un célèbre médecin qui venait d'arriver de Londres, et qui était descendu dans cette hôtellerie. Je vins le trouver."

. . . .

Gina s'avança à pas lents, les bras maigres, les yeux éteints et les joues caves; mais plus belle que jamais de la beauté qu'elle avait perdue, belle de ses longues souffrances, de son long veuvage de gloire, belle comme la jeune épouse qui sort de ses habits de deuil, pâle et les yeux brûlés de larmes. Mais lorsqu'elle fut arrivée sur le bord de la scène, et que, simple et naïve, elle se fut inclinée, alors, comme la bombe tombant avec fracas sur les pavés d'une ville endormie, la foule éclata tout à coup. La clarté des lumières vacilla au bruit des longs cris d'enthousiasme; les fleurs pleuvaient, les loges étincelaient de pierreries, et les écharpes blanches et roses s'agitaient dans l'air embaumé. (*PD*, 246, 247)

"It wasn't a dream, a vision born of sleepless nights. Gina knew my name, and of my love; perhaps she also remembered vaguely having spoken to me during one of her feverish and confused nights. A quick hope restored my sanity. I made plans the way a completely sane man would have, I took an interest in the outside world, I understood what was happening around me. Gina was dying. I spent my days and nights thinking of ways to restore her to life. I heard of a famous doctor who had just arrived from London and who was at the hotel. I went to find him."

. . . .

Gina advanced slowly, her arms thin, her eyes without luster and her cheeks hollow; but more beautiful than ever from the beauty she had lost, beautiful from her long suffering, from her long absence from fame, beautiful like the young wife who takes off her mourning, pale, and her eyes red with tears. But when she reached the edge of the stage, and, simple and artless, she bowed, then, like a bomb falling with a crash on the streets of a sleeping city, the crowd exploded all at once. The brilliance of the light flickered at the sound of the long cries of acclaim; flowers rained down, the boxes glittered with jewels, and the white and red scarves fluttered in the perfumed air.

The second passage contains three times the number of adjectives, and each sentence has twenty-four words on the average compared to fourteen in the first. The initial sentence of the second passage is structured in a fashion typical of Aurore Dudevant. The description of Gina refers to three parts of her body, each with a modifying adjective, while the adjective "belle" generates four phrases qualifying and capturing precisely the nature of her beauty. The word "deuil" in the last phrase inspires one more image, the decrescendo of the sentence. Aurore may also have helped edit this story, and most likely provided part or all of the plot, such as it is, but her influence is most evident in the last page.[2] Unfortunately, Balzac's praise notwithstanding, "La Prima Donna" does credit to neither of its authors and remains of purely historical interest.

In May 1831, *La Mode* published "La Fille d'Albano," signed J.S., a work Sand would later acknowledge and include in her *Oeuvres complètes*. The setting, a country village where peasants and aristocrats mingle, as well as the themes of marriage across class lines and the freedom necessary to the artist, bear Sand's hallmark. The story is essentially a dialogue between a woman artist about to marry a rich nobleman and her older brother, also an artist, who espouses the causes of art and liberty to persuade his sister that love is merely a trap for the gifted woman. Laurence is torn between her need for warm climates and artistic self-expression, on the one hand, and her love for Aurélien and the security he represents, on the other. The two desires are presented as incompatible, with the woman taking precedence over the artist where love is concerned: "The artist became a woman again, and the dreams of another, future, happiness erased the futile regrets of a lost happiness" (*FA*, 159). Her brother's contempt for her fiancé is reflected in his choice of words; he calls him a "bourgeois," "a man with a profession . . . who measures his life with compasses . . ." (*FA*, 160), the very antithesis of the bohemian artist. Carlos's arguments against her marriage are very strong and would not seem out of place in the mouth of a twentieth-century feminist. According to him, a wife is "the first servant of a family and of a husband" (*FA*, 161); marriage is a duty, slavery, imprisonment, which holds a woman captive by prejudice and custom. There is no room for Laurence's individuality, even in her dress and hairstyle, for she will have to play a role that allows for little deviation.

Carlos's imprecations against marriage, although tendentious, contain telling observations on nineteenth-century women's education and up-bringing. Women were trained for their role, tamed and accustomed to only one way of thinking and acting. Carlos realizes that he has miseducated his sister for the role she has chosen:

J'aurais taillé ton âme pour ce monde où tu veux vivre; j'aurais rétréci ton esprit, j'aurais racourci les lisières, et bientôt naturalisée dans la société qui t'attire, tu n'y serais pas comme une étrangère, gauche et timide au milieu d'un cercle où l'on ne parle pas sa langue. Il est trop tard . . . l'arbuste obéit à la main qui l'incline: l'arbre ne ploie pas, il casse. (*FA*, 166)

I would have shaped your soul for the world you want to live in. I would have narrowed your mind, I would have tightened the reins, and soon, naturalized in the society that attracts you, you would not be like a stranger, gauche and shy in the middle of a circle where your language is not spoken. It is too late . . . the bush obeys the hand that bends it, but the tree doesn't bend, it breaks in two.

For the exceptional woman like Laurence, who had tasted freedom of thought and action, as Aurore Dupin herself had, society is alien and can only destroy her. The statement that Laurence will be like a foreigner among those who do not speak her language is a central one, for women are seen as having to learn linguistic as well as social codes that are not innate. Woman's social language is not her natural one, any more than her social behavior corresponds to her true inclinations. Language is the most sophisticated of all codes, as well as the most insidious, and is, of course, that which distinguishes and characterizes human society. It is not surprising, then, that Laurence's two options present themselves explicitly in the form of language, with Carlos's impassioned speeches representing one destiny, and the language of love the other. "Where can one find a soul strong enough, skeptical enough to hesitate before the promises of love, to reject these oaths so flattering to the ear . . . ? If this soul exists, it certainly isn't that of a woman" (*FA*, 159). Carlos's arguments, along with his promise to be all the family she needs, convince Laurence that she must remain free. She leaves a note for Aurélien and departs with her brother.

"La Fille d'Albano" expresses the same anti-marriage sentiments found in later works, particularly *Indiana* and *Jacques*, for which George Sand was roundly criticized. Yet the story cannot be viewed entirely as a feminist work. Carlos plays the active role, while Laurence listens attentively to his opinions; the critique of marriage is made by him, not her, and she is essentially torn between two forms of masculine discourse. Furthermore, women are shown to be divided against themselves, with the genius who belongs to no gender at one pole and the "woman born to continue the species" (*FA*, 163) at the other. There seems to be no reconciling the two, and the married woman with children is portrayed with contempt. While this opposition of the artist and the mother may be justified by historical circumstances (the few careers open to women were made difficult, if not impossible, by demands of family and home), this explanation of the head/womb dichotomy is not sufficient, for Aurore Dudevant must have known of women who combined career and family, as she herself was well on her way to doing with the publication of this story.

The end of the story is particularly revealing. Five years after being jilted by Laurence, having recovered from the obligatory malady occasioned by that event, Aurélien takes his wife and son to Paris, where he sees a portrait of a young Italian, whom he recognizes as Laurence. The identity of the artist is not specified, but since the picture is not described as a self-portrait, we may assume that Laurence is merely the subject. The comments the painting arouses further objectify the young woman depicted.

> Quelle finesse de peau! disait-on, quelle pureté de sourcils! quelle coupe de visage! que de pensées ensevelies sous cette rêverie pieuse! de passions cachées sous cette calme méditation! Jamais Française n'eût inspiré l'idée de cette création suave et brûlante. (*FA*, 168)

> What fine skin! they said, what a pure brow line! what a shape to the face! how many thoughts are buried under this pious reverie! how many passions are hidden by this calm meditation. No Frenchwoman could have inspired the idea of this suave and torrid creation.

Laurence was the inspiration for this work, not its creator. This is not surprising, for despite references to Laurence's genius and superiority, as well as to her former life as a "poor girl making her living from her palette and her inspiration" (*FA*, 163), the most developed and lasting image of her is as model, not artist.

> ". . . [E]n moins d'un instant, tu étais représentée sur vingt toiles, comme si l'atelier avait eu vingt glaces pour te réfléchir!
>   Ah! que tu faisais palpiter de coeurs et brûler d'imaginations! Que d'âme tu prêtais au pinceau! que de vie tu versais sur la toile!" (*FA*, 164)

> ". . . [I]n less than an instant, you were represented on twenty canvases, as though the studio had twenty mirrors to reflect your image!
>   Ah! how many hearts you made beat and how many imaginations you fired! With how much spirit you endowed their brushes! how much life flowed onto the canvas because of you!"

Laurence has been liberated to become a muse, a traditional woman's occupation, and in the end she is reduced to being known as "la fille d'Albano," an anonymous, pretty face.

From September to November 1831, Aurore Dudevant and Jules Sandeau were engaged in writing *Rose et Blanche*, possibly at the suggestion of Renault, the publisher of *Le Commissionnaire*, a work that they had ghost-written.[3] Her correspondence gives the impression that she wrote the first half of *Rose et Blanche*, while Sandeau was responsible for the second, but the work itself does not bear this out.[4]

That there is much of Aurore Dudevant's personal experience in the work, particularly her travels to Tarbes and Bordeaux and her knowledge of convent life, has long been recognized. Many of the characters bear the names of people she knew; furthermore, the name of a fictional character from *La Marraine*, Blanche de Beaumont, reappears in the names Blanche and Mlle de Beaumont (Rose). It is impossible to say with certainty how much of the novel and how many of the ideas it contains are hers, since neither the manuscript nor her correspondence with Sandeau has survived. Given Sandeau's desultory work habits at this time, the large number of chapters definitely attributable to Aurore Dudevant, and the numerous themes and narrative structures that would later appear in George Sand's novels, it does not seem unreasonable to guess that she essentially wrote the novel, with Sandeau perhaps adding the spicier passages that disappeared from the second edition, which George Sand republished in 1833 under the name J. Sand.[5]

Rose et Blanche is not a good novel, although it contains some successful descriptions and several of Aurore Dudevant's mordant portraits. The basic theme of the contrasting destinies of two very different young women is well chosen, but it is poorly executed, for the authors subject Rose and Blanche to far more adventures than they could reasonably be expected to meet, even in five volumes. Many episodes are clearly included only to lengthen the work and divert the reader and were omitted from the later edition. Even so, *Rose et Blanche* resembles a serial story of the kind that Ponson du Térail would later make famous with his character Rocambole.

Inadequate characterization also plagues the novel. Aside from the title characters, who are drawn with some depth and sympathy, and a few good caricatures, like Soeur Olympie, most of the characters in the novel are figures who never come alive but are made to react to various situations without clear motivation. Horace, one of the main actors in this melodrama, is an enigma whose contradictory nature may result as much from the joint authors' gender differences as from their literary inexperience.

Horace is a pivotal figure in the novel, for he is involved with both of the women at different times of their lives and is the catalyst for most of the novel's actions. He meets Rose at the beginning of the novel, but instead of starting her on the path of libertinage her mother had chosen for her, he pays for a convent education in the hope that a religious vocation will replace her theatrical one. Later, after she has left the convent to return to the stage, he falls in love with her. His adventure with Denise (Blanche) predates the opening of the novel, while his marriage to her not only brings the earlier episode full circle but precipitates the end of the novel as well.

The Denise chapter is worth looking at in depth, for it provides the cornerstone of the plot, something Sand recognized by making it the pro-

logue to the second edition of the novel, rather than leaving it in the form
of a flashback in the first chapter of the third volume, where it was originally
placed. Briefly put, Horace rapes Denise, a beautiful idiot put in his care
by her dying father, to whom Horace owes his life. Under the influence of
wine, his nerves irritated by coffee, Horace is carried away as much by her
frightened efforts to defend herself as by her physical beauty. The next
morning, he packs Denise off to a convent, from which she will emerge
two years later as Soeur Blanche.

This episode would seem to have its literary source in two earlier texts.
The first is Kératry's *Les Derniers des Beaumanoir*, which Aurore Dudevant
had read and on which she complimented the author when she sought his
protection soon after her arrival in Paris.[6] This four-volume novel is based
on the rape of a young woman, presumed dead, by a man about to be
ordained as a priest. Clémence is not dead, only in a syncope, and gives
birth to a son nine months later. The crime, which is slowly discovered by
the other characters, although not Clémence, at least not until the end,
causes the deaths of Clémence's mother and a family friend, and finally of
Clémence herself. She marries the man, who had renounced holy orders,
on her deathbed merely to assure her son his inheritance.

The rape, which is not described, is attributable to several causes. Like
Denise, Clémence is very beautiful; like Horace, Jonathas Dermot drinks
a bottle of port during the night. Further, Jonathas is overcome by Clémence's resemblance to Mlle Morin, a woman he had loved, but who had
refused to remain faithful to him. In a way, he is punishing her through
Clémence for not fulfilling his idea of woman. Horace, too, has just been
jilted by his mistress, and publicly so. Denise becomes all women, there for
the taking, but whose conquest is made even sweeter by their fear and
protests. In both cases, the men are dominating, humiliating several women
at once, and their acts are performed on women incapable of understanding
them. Unlike Clémence, Denise does not become pregnant, for Horace
remained cool enough in his excitement to make sure of that. ". . . [H]e
suddenly regained the composure necessary to assure the tranquility of his
future" (*RB* III, 66)—a daring explanation that disappeared along with
three other pages of post-coital analysis from the second edition.[7] Afterward, both women have hazy recollections of something horrible having
taken place, without remembering precisely what. Neither seeks actively to
recall the scene, for fear of what she might discover.

The second text that elucidates the Denise chapter is Balzac's "Adieu,"
published in 1830. In her escape from Russia, Stéphanie de Vandières lost
her reason during the crossing of the Bérésina, and she now lives with her
uncle, a doctor who is trying to cure her. Her other companion is a young
woman, an idiot like Denise, of limited vocabulary and childish demeanor.

Stéphanie and Denise have many affinities. Incapable of reason, both are said to behave more like animals than humans, and are seen almost as pets by their caretakers. Neither exhibits the modesty thought to be natural to women. Stéphanie is said to have progressed when she allows herself to be dressed, for at first she remained naked, while Denise permits an artist to undo her fichu, later repeating the gesture herself, unaware of the fact that she is baring her chest. Both women possess great beauty, which, paradoxically, is made even more striking by their lack of sentience; they are beautiful statues, not real women.[8] Philippe pointedly states that fact when he says about Stéphanie: "When she was a woman, she had no taste for sweets."[9] Horace, too, makes a clear distinction between a woman of Denise's limited intellectual capacities and other members of her sex: "His wrongs toward this kind of woman could not have been the same as toward a real woman. . . . She hadn't understood the injury" (*RB* III, 65–66, 67).

The influence of "Adieu" can also be seen in the ending of *Rose et Blanche*, where Denise, now called Blanche and cured of her idiocy, relives the rape on her wedding night and dies. In both works, a repressed scene is restored to the conscious mind by the shock of seeing again circumstances too dreadful to be borne, only to kill the now fully aware woman.[10] Both deaths are ironic, for the men who caused them, though ostensibly acting for the woman's own good, are seen to be motivated purely by self-interest. Neither is content to allow the woman to be as she is but tries to make her into his vision of her and, in so doing, kills her.

Horace's attitude toward Denise poses a problem for the reader throughout the novel, as does the authors' presentation of his character. On the one hand, the rape of Denise is shown, in part at least, to be the result of intoxication and sexual attraction, compounded by a certain male cruelty elicited by Denise's attempts to defend herself. Afterward, Horace is seen to feel more fear of punishment than horror at his crime. These actions and emotions, while reprehensible, are understandably human.

Yet at the same time, Horace exhibits quite different sentiments. He was not so drunk that he was not able to ensure that Denise did not become pregnant, not for her sake, but for his own. He regards his crime as unimportant because an idiot is not really a woman, and besides, Denise was completely unaware of what happened. Later, he refers to his act as "a gross absurdity" (*RB* II, 198), "coarse and ridiculous" (*RB* II, 212), while Laorens assures him that all women would be glad to absolve him of rape. Laorens's diagnosis that Horace's remorse is really wounded pride is accurate, for, like Julien Sorel, Horace fears "le ridicule" above all else. Embarrassment alternates with guilt, with embarrassment always seeming to win out. In fact, by the end of the novel, Horace is callous and egotistical in his behavior toward Denise, and he rejects any moral responsibility for her death. He does not attend her funeral, and if he is remorseful, he is certainly not incapacitated by guilt. Although Sand dropped several pages from the rape scene in the second edition to keep the accent on Horace's feelings of unworthiness, the rest of the novel retains the same contradictory characterization present in the first version, maintaining the uneven tone.

It is tempting to ascribe the more lighthearted treatment of Horace's crime to Sandeau, while crediting Aurore Dudevant with the sections that reveal an understanding of the seriousness of the act of rape.[11] The last chapter, with its gauche references to realism and its atmosphere of conservative cynicism, as well as the fraternal conversations between Horace and Laorens, seems in particular to be attributable to Sandeau's pen. While rape appears often in George Sand's later novels, *Leone Leoni*, *Mauprat*, *Jeanne*, *Consuelo*, it is rarely seen as the completed act. Rather, it is shown to be an ever-present threat, a danger all women might have to face. In all likelihood, Aurore Dudevant created the Denise episode out of her readings of Kératry and Balzac for use as a scabrous plot device, and it was made even more piquant by Sandeau. It is difficult to draw conclusions about rape from this novel alone because it was a collaborative effort, but rape is nonetheless clearly an important and early Sandian theme, one that I will return to in later chapters.

Despite the ambiguity of Horace's feelings and the rather equivocal ending, the resolution of *Rose et Blanche* makes it clear that rape is a devastating experience that can be neither undone nor redressed. Horace hopes to reconcile his conflicting emotions of remorse and mortification by marrying Denise, thereby making up for his crime. This is not allowed to become the happy marriage that ends all comedies, however, as it could so easily have been; the tragic outcome of this ill-advised wedding, as well as Blanche's attitude toward what is in essence a forced marriage, demonstrates that Horace's fault is not so easy to repair as he had thought. Society, too, whose custom approves of such a cruel union, is castigated. The ending of *Rose et Blanche* rewrites Kératry's sentimental conclusion, in which the heroine dies of tuberculosis right after her wedding but recognizes her new husband's qualities and merit and regrets the relationship that might have been. Instead, Horace is seen by both Blanche and the narrator as a despoiler, anxious to satisfy his own needs and desires but oblivious to hers. Unlike Jonathas Dermot, who spends his life in regret and submits to Clémence's will, Horace, although generous, always gives others what he wants them to have but not what they want. Blanche is not interested in marrying her rapist and prefers to remain in the convent, just as Rose earlier had no desire to enter the fancy convent where Horace and his sister chose to send her.

Rose et Blanche is essentially the story of two women's sufferings at the hands of an egotistical man who never takes the time to get to know them as individuals. Horace sees Denise only sexually, both initially and at the moment of their marriage, while Rose is perceived solely in relation to her social class, first as a provincial actress and later as a great singer, but still a socially unacceptable marriage partner. This dim view of men as selfish and brutal, uninterested in women's needs, can only have come from Aurore Dudevant's pen and is consonant with the portrayal of men in such later works as *Indiana* and *Leone Leoni*.

The concept of romantic love also comes in for harsh criticism, for love does not seem to influence the men's conduct at all. Laorens loves Blanche but will not marry her because she has no dowry; he is unconvinced by the romantic topos that hard work and love are sufficient to create a happy, if not opulent, life and prefers to adopt the weaker but safer position of marrying an heiress. Horace quickly suppresses his love for Rose when the possibility of marrying Blanche arises, for that represents a more advantageous union morally and socially. Love is clearly not an important value for men in this novel, although it has great significance for women. In her future work, Sand will pursue this disparity between the myth of love as women perceive it and its actualization in society, linking it, as she does here, to concomitant myths of social class.

If male-female relations are shown in the novel to be exploitative and in the man's self-interest, female friendship provides a more reliable bond. As two young women alone in the world, Rose and Blanche are not only friends, but they form their own, alternative family, where, as both friends and sisters, they can give each other support and security. The portrait of their attachment is quite touching, and Rose's selfless reaction upon learning of Blanche's marriage to Horace is not unbelievable.

Friendship between men and women is also valorized as a goal to be sought, if not as one that can easily be realized. Rose alternates between feelings of love and friendship for Horace. In the first half of the novel, she recognizes that marriage between them is impossible because of the differences in social class and wishes only to be friends with him, to be acknowledged as a person whose company he might enjoy rather than simply being rejected as a woman whom it would be impossible to marry. In the letter she writes him later, after leaving the convent, she reproaches him for his coldness and for treating her as a fortune-hunter. She is hurt by his suspicions and by the fact that he never made any effort to understand her as an individual. This desire for friendship with Horace is never fulfilled, although she does fall in love with him, which is quite another thing. Her friendship with Laorens is more successful, once the initial embarrassment of their position vis-à-vis each other is resolved. He and Rose remain friends throughout the novel, getting to know and trust each other fully.

This emphasis on friendship, whether between women or across sexual lines, as well as the creation of family ties outside the usual ones, shows the beginnings of Aurore Dudevant's reflections on society and its rigid classification of people according to gender, class, occupation, marital status, or degree of consanguinity. Relationships that are freely chosen are valued over those which are arbitrarily imposed, while the one bond that requires equality and respect between the two partners—friendship—is seen to be more durable and reliable than any other. Although Aurore Dudevant does not go as far in *Rose et Blanche* as George Sand will, depicting marriage across class lines, particularly when the woman has the higher social position, she does sharply criticize those prejudices which make class divisions so absolute that not only marriage but any communication between different groups is impossible. The same postrevolutionary order that appears in Balzac's novels, where nobility and bourgeoisie intermarry to produce a hybrid class possessing both money and title, is represented fleetingly in *Rose et Blanche*, when the noble pupils of the convent admit the necessity of marrying a bourgeois if they are to marry at all, a possibility that most find not unappealing. In *Indiana* and *Valentine*, this scheme will be taken further, as Sand seeks to break down class divisions and redistribute wealth to create a more just society.

The Catholic church is another instittion that is strongly censured in the novel. The rigid rules and strict definitions covering every aspect of behavior and thought, leaving no room for individual choice, had been rejected early on by Aurore Dudevant and are here portrayed in the darkest colors. True religious belief is not denounced but only those who misconstrue religion for their own ends; indeed, Aurore Dudevant's happy days in the *couvent des Anglaises* are transposed into a positive picture of religious life. Telling contrast is made between the simple curé and the archbishop, Soeur Adèle and Soeur Scholastique, Blanche's "Jansenist" confessor, who advises her to do what she wants, and the severe ascetic, who makes her refusal to marry Horace a sin and a crime. The latter's arguments, as well as Mlle Cazalès's merciless efforts to see Horace married to Blanche and not Rose, make one wonder whether Aurore Dudevant had read *La Religieuse*, for Blanche's persecution is surprisingly similar to that endured by Suzanne Simonin.

In light of such criticisms of religion, it may seem surprising that the novel should end on a religious note and that Rose chooses to end her days in a convent, given her aversion to the cloistered life and Blanche's suffering at the hands of certain members of the community. Yet the convent, under the direction of Madame Adèle, becomes once again the locus of female bonds, as Rose renews her ties with her teacher and prepares to live in an atmosphere of supportive friendship, dedicated to God and to Blanche's memory. The penultimate chapter of the novel recapitulates all the themes sounded earlier, reiterating the undependability of romantic love and the superiority of friendship (the word "amitié" appears three times in four pages), as well as the emptiness and conventionality of society, denying transcendency even to art, which is prostituted by artist and public alike. Except for the liberty to come and go, Rose finds all she needs or desires in the convent. She has spiritual freedom and peace, the leisure to reflect, and the joy of leading a useful life, teaching young girls to sing. The last paragraph of this chapter is paradoxically serene and uplifting while expressing nonetheless the depressive bitterness that would be George Sand's personal emotional note for the next several years.[12]

There is no doubt that Rose's reclusion is meant to be seen as a positive step that allows her maximum personal and spiritual independence, not as a renunciation, for the world as she had experienced it was not difficult to abandon. The convent is seen here as it was for many centuries: the sphere in which women could realize themselves and create destinies for themselves outside of the limiting expectations of society, and not a place of repression. George Sand would, of course, not enter a convent, and her characters would find many other avenues of freedom and self-actualization. Yet in its lack of emphasis on the prisonlike quality of convent life and with its accent on friendship, leisure, teaching, fresh air, and flowers, the description of Rose's convent life curiously anticipates the kind of retired yet full existence George Sand would later create for herself at Nohant.

The young Aurore Dupin had dreamed of becoming a nun, before her grandmother put a stop to that ambition, and the dream did not die easily. Three years after her marriage, with a two-year old son, prey to an undefined depression, Aurore Dudevant spent several days in her old convent, reliving and regretting the monastic life she had left behind for marriage and motherhood. As with the "Voyage au Mont d'Or," the aforementioned chapter of *Rose et Blanche* prefigures to an astonishing degree Sand's description twenty years later, in *Histoire di ma vie*, of that last visit to the convent. A comparison of the two texts is illuminating, for they express the same positive feeling about convent life.

Je m'efforçais aussi de voir le côté sombre et asservi de la vie monastique, afin de me rattacher aux douceurs de la liberté. . . . [L]e cloître n'avait pas de terreurs pour moi. Il me semblait que je chérissais et regrettais tout dans cette vie de communauté où l'on s'appartient véritablement, parce qu'en dépendant de tous on ne dépend réellement de personne. Je voyais tant d'aise et de liberté, au contraire, dans cette captivité qui vous préserve, dans cette discipline qui assure vos heures de recueillement, dans cette monotonie de devoirs qui vous sauve des troubles de l'imprévu! *(Oa* II, 48–49)[13]

I also tried to see the dark and servile side of monastic life, so as to highlight the sweetness of freedom. . . . [T]he cloister held no terror for me. It seemed that I cherished and regretted everything in this communal life where one truly belongs to oneself, because by depending on all, one really depends on no one. I saw so much convenience and freedom, on the contrary, in this captivity that protects you, in this discipline that assures you hours of meditation, in this monotony of duties that saves you from the trouble of the unforeseen!

This section of her autobiography contains other statements that provide valuable insight into *Rose et Blanche*. In describing her alternatively somber and gay humor, Sand admits:

Mon mari . . . me jugea idiote. Il n'avait peut-être pas tort, et peu à peu il arriva, avec le temps, à me faire tellement sentir la supériorité de sa raison et de son intelligence, que j'en fus longtemps écrasée et comme hébétée devant le monde. *(Oa* II, 42)

My husband . . . considered me an idiot. He was perhaps not wrong, and little by little he managed, with time, to make me feel strongly the superiority of his mind and of his intelligence, so that for a long time I was overwhelmed and like a dolt in front of others.

For several years, Aurore Dudevant tried to conform to Casimir's opinions and repress her own, before finally gaining the self-confidence to strike out alone. Even after she was established as a writer, however, she remained shy in society and projected an image to first-time acquaintances of dullness, even stupidity. Brilliant conversation and sharp repartees were never her forte. It is the choice of the word "idiot" in the above quotation, though, that is arresting, for it is reminiscent of the diagnosis applied to Denise, although used here in a different sense. A few pages later in *Histoire de ma vie*, Sand explains that she sought in the religious life a means of quieting the agitations of her "timid soul" and subjugating a "restlessness of will that didn't seem to have an outlet" *(Oa* II, 48). This imbecilic and fearful nature suits first Denise, then Blanche, who is smart but overly timid, while Rose, worldly and strong-willed, but unsure of the arena in which her gifts will be appreciated, has been given the other half of Aurore Dudevant's character.

In *Rose et Blanche*, Aurore Dudevant evoked a period six years earlier, when her doubts about herself were strongest. Blanche's itinerary from idiocy to death shows that Aurore recognizes that she possesses intelligence but fears that to manifest it would be dangerous. Better to let herself and others believe in her stupidity. Rose, on the other hand, achieves happiness by living a more circumscribed life than is necessary, given her background and character, and exercises her talents in a rather limited sphere that is also a traditional one for women.

In painting a sympathetic portrait of Rose's monastic life, Aurore Dudevant fulfilled in a literary way her dream of becoming a nun and was able to put that behind her. More important, she exorcised many of the fears about herself that had haunted her for several years. She was not an idiot, unworthy of attention, nor would she be forced to restrict herself to a narrow range, to become a "muse de [s]on département."[14] By writing *Rose et Blanche*, Aurore Dudevant proved that she had talent and would be able to earn her living, thus to do what she wanted. Although the novel had only a modest success, it led both to her feeling self-confident enough to begin *Indiana* and to another publisher's becoming interested in her work, an essential factor for those who write for a living. Neither Rose nor Blanche, she was half of J. Sand and soon to become G. Sand, a successful writer and woman of untraditional lifestyle.

Rose et Blanche delineates for the first time in Aurore Dudevant's work the dynamic triangular relationships that will appear with regularity in Sand's subsequent novels. The central plot pairs Horace alternately with Rose and Blanche, but Laorens, a less important character, also shuttles between the two women. The initial configuration, which shows Rose destined first for Laorens, then for Horace, while Denise is the victim of Horace, gives way to a new triangle as Blanche, still in love with Laorens, is obliged to marry Horace. Her death leaves Rose and Laorens together, but his suggestion that they unite their destinies is not seriously considered by Rose, who prefers that they remain friends. Her decision to become a nun is the final transformation of all these equations, for she takes Blanche's place in the convent, even occupying her cell.

The creation and dissolution of these triangles occur in three key scenes that are mirror images of one another. The symmetry between the rape scene and the wedding night has already been discussed. Even before the rape is revealed, though, Horace relives his experience with Denise during his attempted seduction of Rose, after her mother has essentially sold her to him. As in the first case, he is intoxicated, and the woman is cold, like a marble statue. Her unresponsiveness arouses his cruelty, as he tries to bring shame to her cheeks and tears to her eyes. Rose, however, is fully aware of her situation, as Denise was not, and controls herself perfectly. Angered, yet also guilty, Horace asks her if she thinks him capable of rape. "This would not necessarily be the first" (*RB* I, 197), is her ironic answer. *Indiana* shows the same plot construction, although the latter novel is more tightly organized. In addition, these three scenes take place in enclosed, claustrophobic rooms, like the major scenes in Sand's subsequent novels.

There are differences between the evolution of the triangular relationships in *Rose et Blanche* and the structure of later novels, which again are attributable either to the joint authorship or to Aurore Dudevant's inexperience with developing what amounts to a new plot for her. *Rose et Blanche* introduces for the first time the brutal father figure, who is absent from Aurore Dupin's childhood romances but present in George Sand's novels; indeed, Horace is Denise's guardian, having been chosen by her own father on his deathbed. We therefore see the two women, here sisters by choice rather than blood, both involved, one sexually, with the same man. Unlike later novels, though, it is the wrong man, the brutal one, and thus union with him is impossible for either woman. Laorens is much more the kind of man favored by George Sand in later works, and indeed, both Rose and Blanche are attracted to him. *Indiana* shows a further permutation of this plot as Sand worked it through in her novels.

Another hallmark of Sand's scenario that appears in *Rose et Blanche* for the first time is the attempt of the "bad" mother to prostitute her daughter, although La Primerose is rehabilitated by the end of the novel. In *Indiana*, Mme de Carvajal would like to encourage her niece Indiana to form brilliant liaisons, while in *Jeanne*, the aunt is a local procuress who tries to help Marsillat obtain Jeanne's favors. Jeanne refuses this relationship, and he eventually attempts to rape her. This detail again seems to stem from Aurore Dupin's life, notably her experience while under her mother's tutelage, after her grandmother's death and prior to her marriage. In a long letter to Aurélien de Sèze, Aurore Dudevant accuses her mother of having tried to ruin her reputation.

> On eut recours au dernier de tous, celui de me perdre . . . [sic] au moins de réputation. On me conduisit dans une société légère, bruyante et dissipée, et dès le lendemain on retourna à Paris, me laissant seule, sans ami, sans guide, sans protecteur, ne connaissant les maîtres de la maison que de la veille, au milieu de jeunes gens et de militaires, auxquels on m'avait annoncée comme une personne fort inconséquente, pour ne pas dire plus. . . . Le maître et la maîtresse du château . . . me rendirent justice dès le premier jour. C'étaient des gens frivoles en apparence, mais bons, honnêtes et sensibles. (*C* I, 199)

> Recourse was had to the last of all expedients, that of ruining me . . . [sic] at least in reputation. I was introduced into a frivolous, noisy and dissipated society, and the next day I was left alone, without a friend, without guidance, without a protector, only knowing the owners of the house since the previous day, in the midst of young men and soldiers to whom I had been announced as a very flighty person, to say the least. . . . The master and mistress of the

castle . . . gave me the benefit of the doubt from the first day. They were friv-
olous in appearance, but good, honest and sensitive.

The last sentence corrects the initial characterization of this society as
debauched and is more in accord with the picture of the life at Le Plessis-
Picard drawn in *Histoire de ma vie*. However, another letter written to her
husband at the same time (*C* I, 267) gives much the same description of
the dissipated life at Le Plessis and of her mother's intentions in leaving
her there. Aurore Dupin was obviously a victim of her mother's moody
nature, perhaps even mental illness, during this period, although *Histoire
de ma vie* is in general kinder to Mme Dupin than strictly necessary, in
part, perhaps, out of filial respect and partly out of nostalgia for fairly
distant events. Aurore's letters, though, depict a woman so anxious to break
her daughter's spirit that she would go to any lengths. Mme Dupin nearly
succeeded in her plan, for it was at Le Plessis-Picard that Aurore met the
young officer, Prosper Tessier, who tried to make her his mistress. This
misadventure was probably Aurore's first contact with sexuality and taught
her that men and women do not always view "love" in the same way, as she
reveals in a letter several years after the event (*C* I, 232). She perhaps
incorporated the lessons of her stay at Le Plessis into her novels. It is also
notable that Aurore's only experience of a happy, two-parent family was
with an unusual, consanguineous couple, for James and Angèle Roëttiers
du Plessis were uncle and niece.

Structurally, then, as well as thematically, *Rose et Blanche* appears to be
almost totally Aurore Dudevant's. The systematic depiction of male brutality, the critique of the topos of romantic love on which women were
raised, the search for more egalitarian relations with men, and the positive
portrayal of a female support network bespeak the presence of the budding
George Sand. The novel details the efforts of two young women to create
lives for themselves and to express their individuality rather than their
femaleness, and shows the social restrictions a woman encounters in trying
to do so. In addition, the progressive social and religious views that George
Sand would later espouse in her fiction as well as her political writings are
contained here in a tentative, unelaborated form.

If *Rose et Blanche* looks ahead to George Sand's future, it also harks back
to Aurore Dudevant's past. As in her earliest, unpublished, texts, Aurore
Dudevant is engaged here in writing herself as well as her novel, inscribing
herself within the text while creating a new scenario to live and write by.
Each of her early writings enabled her to gain a clearer view of herself and
her opinions, adding to her self-assurance and allowing her to continue to
write. It is not a coincidence, then, that *Rose et Blanche*, like others of her
first literary efforts, depicts the act of writing itself.

Early in the novel, Rose wants to write to Horace to explain her feelings of chagrin and resentment at his treatment of her but does not, for she does not know how to spell correctly and is afraid of appearing ridiculous. Later, when she leaves the convent and is more self-confident, she does write to him, even though her spelling has not improved. The letter is not perfect, but she has had the courage to write, to communicate with Horace, and her letter has the desired effect.[15] In the same way, *Rose et Blanche*, flawed though it certainly is, represents Aurore's first full-length publication and is the final step in her apprenticeship as an author.

Rose et Blanche gives the fullest treatment of the figure of the artist of any of Aurore Dudevant's early works. Whereas the writer was present from the very first, notably in the "Voyage au Mont d'Or," "La Marraine," and "Les Confessions," the artist, either painter or singer, appears most insistently in the last of her works of apprenticeship, "La Prima Donna," "La Fille d'Albano," and *Rose et Blanche*. It is clear that in these works she is coming to terms with her feelings about practicing her art commercially and on a wide scale, not simply for herself or her friends, and she is trying to form an image of herself as a public performer.

The first artist Aurore Dudevant created was the androgynous singer Amédée of "Histoire du rêveur." This man who at a crucial moment becomes a woman possesses unusual singing ability. Since the protagonist only dreams of Amédée, or so it appears at the end of the story, the very existence of this character is called into question. Aurore Dudevant seems to be saying that perhaps her pretensions to writing are all an illusion, merely a dream.

In "Jehan Cauvin," the short story dealing with Calvin's conversion in 1529, the intradiegetic narrator is an artist, albeit an unproductive one. Théodore is a man of many talents, particularly in the domain of art and literature, but one whose laziness prevents him from ever consigning his visions to paper. Although Théodore does not record his story, the extra-diegetic narrator does, so that it is not lost. The story he tells about the cathedral of his native Bourges and its famous cleric is important for two reasons. First, Théodore is inspired to speak about Bourges by Hugo's recently published *Notre-Dame de Paris* and his celebration of the Paris cathedral. Thus, Théodore's story parallels, and perhaps even rivals, Hugo's. In addition to describing the cathedral at length, "Jehan Cauvin" also depicts a key moment in Calvin's career, that when his vocation was revealed to him. This vocation was religious, not artistic, yet it is nonetheless significant that Aurore Dudevant should be writing about vocations at a time when she herself was taking her first professional steps.

The three texts signed "J. Sand" all deal with artists. "La Prima Donna," although not written in its entirety by Aurore Dudevant, as we have seen, was undoubtedly conceived by her. The image of the singer who, having given up her career for marriage, pines for her art but dies at the moment of her greatest triumph, is certainly suggestive of Aurore Dudevant's own feelings about her career and the risks she was taking. The concept of androgyny also reappears in "La Prima Donna" in two guises; during the intermission, Gina confides to Rosetta that her voice that evening seemed different than before: "[A]nother voice than hers, a magic voice, came forth, male and full, from her expanded lungs" (*PD*, 248). This male voice in a female body is reflected in Rosetta's playing the role of Romeo, a common occurrence in early nineteenth-century opera as women replaced castrati in male roles. The woman as man, or artist as man and woman, seen as early as "Histoire du rêveur," is also meaningful in "La Prima Donna" because the same situation is repeated twice in *Rose et Blanche*.

Rose et Blanche is in part the story of Rose's itinerary from provincial actress to great singer to cloistered nun. As a child, Rose had acted because her mother chose that profession for her; significantly, the first role we see her play is that of an old man. Only later does her talent really develop. In a key scene, she sings in church and is filled with the fire of true inspiration. Her voice earns her the praise of Giuditta Pasta, the great opera star. Later, Rose has occasion to hear Pasta sing on the stage, in Rossini's opera *Tancredi*. This work, which was very popular in Paris in 1831, the year *Rose et Blanche* was written, is another opera that employs a woman in the leading male role instead of a castrato. It is important that this is the opera Rose sees, for she is unaware at first that Tancrède is played by a woman. At the end of the performance, she realizes that it is her idol La Pasta on stage and learns that a woman can play a man, can adopt a man's role through art. Again we find the presence of the artistic androgyne, the woman creating as men have always done, and we see the power of art that enables a woman to break out of her restrictive condition to reach higher levels of human consciousness.

This experience is decisive for Rose, who vows to leave the convent and devote herself to art.

> [E]lle était jeune, elle était libre; elle avait retrouvé la vie qu'elle avait tant de fois rêvée, et qui toujours avait fui devant elle, une vie enthousiaste et forte, avec ses agitations et ses émotions enivrantes. (*RB* IV, 201–202)

> [S]he was young, she was free; she had discovered the life she had dreamed of so often, and which had always fled before her, a strong and passionate life, with its tumults and heady emotions.

After leaving the theater, Rose comes across a young girl singing in the street with her mother and gives her a bit of advice: "Be poor, be miserable, be whipped by the winds and the rain; if you must, suffer from hunger, but keep your songs under the sky, your guitar and your freedom!" (*RB* IV, 207). This little scene was cut from the second edition of the novel, but it contains Aurore Dudevant's own positive feelings about the relationship between art and freedom, whatever the costs. Its language recalls that of "La Fille d'Albano," quoted above, where Laurence is described as a "poor girl making her living from her palette and her inspiration" (*FA*, 163).

The *Tancredi* episode of transvestism in the novel is followed by another, when Rose, now called "La Coronari" and a famous singer, dresses up as Tony, the supposed younger brother of a friend of Horace's, in order to test Horace's feelings for her. The plot motivation is certainly adequate, although the scene is not strictly necessary. Aurore Dudevant again shows the woman artist who can pass as a man, this time offstage. The woman artist expropriates the man's role in life as well as art. In this scene, the emphasis is on masculine behavior—not that Aurore Dudevant wanted to be a man, but she was acutely aware of certain advantages—physical and social—men had. Her unusual upbringing had allowed her to ride horseback like a boy (as "Tony" does here), had brought her into contact with country medicine, and had generally formed her into something less than a "lady" in nineteenth-century terms, although, of course, by today's standards Aurore Dudevant's exposure to the world outside the drawing room was normal and healthy. Sand is noted, indeed she has become infamous, for wearing male attire (again, like "Tony"). This habit began during those adolescent horseback rides and became useful in Paris to allow her the freedom to walk easily and to go wherever she pleased. What for decades was seen as a scandal has today become a commonplace, as women wear pants for the same reason Sand did: "feminine" clothes are still impractical for free movement. Her view of woman's ability to incorporate both masculine and feminine qualities, as defined by society, is clearly shown, physically, mentally, artistically, and socially in all these scenes of cross-dressing.

La Coronari eventually gives up her brilliant social position to return to the convent and teach the students to sing. As I have argued, this ending is not a defeat but simply a rejection of the noise and superficiality of "le monde" in favor of the quiet, intellectual freedom of the convent. Aurore Dudevant had tasted the world Paris had to offer: she had visited its theaters, worked for its newspapers, even felt the sting of the censor for one of her articles. Yet unlike Balzac, and myriads of her contemporaries, she did not thrive on Paris, did not need its quick pace or its adulation in order to feel alive and creative. She remained a provincial, but in the positive sense, all her life, preferring to visit Paris but to live at Nohant. She became not a provincial artist, a "lady novelist," but a great writer who celebrated her native Berry. Rose's choice is clearly in some sense Aurore Dudevant's, too, her acknowledgment of the kind of artist she was and of the arena in which she would exercise her talents.

The recurrent presence of the artist in her early works is thus evidently tied to her own self-image as the fledgling writer perfecting her craft and trying her literary efforts out on the public. This self-image is androgynous, as I have shown, and it is also at this point uncertain, apprehensive. The singer in "Histoire du rêveur" perishes in a volcano and is then said to be merely a figment of Amédée's imagination; the Prima Donna dies of her art, while Laurence, "La Fille d'Albano" becomes merely a model, absent from the story. "La Fille d'Albano" is particularly important, for it contains George Sand's feminist social program, but expressed by a man. She cannot yet imagine a successful woman artist who speaks in her own voice. Laurence survives, unlike others of these artist figures, but not as a creating subject. These texts display a fear of public performance, of exposure to others, of the vulnerability associated with publishing one's ideas for the world to read and criticize. Aurore Dudevant is suffering not from the "anxiety of influence," but from its converse, the anxiety occasioned by the lack of a tradition relevant to her situation.[16]

What models could a young woman writer turn to in 1831? Christine de Pisan was the first French woman writer to live by her pen in the fifteenth century, but it is doubtful Aurore Dudevant would have known much about her. Lafayette, one of Sand's sources in *Indiana* and *Valentine*, was very much a part of court society and did not write for a living. The many eighteenth-century woman writers also led decorous lives, for the most part, and lived in a period propitious to women's intellectual activity. Riccoboni, Genlis, the irreproachable "gouverneur" of the future Louis-Philippe, Souza, Elie de Beaumont—none of these women had left their husbands and children to earn her own living by writing. The only likely model for Aurore Dudevant was Germaine de Staël, and she represented an ambiguous one at that.

Free, independent, Staël had many lovers and bore children who were not fathered by her husband, as Aurore Dudevant had already done. She wrote influential books, and not only fiction, and was known and admired worldwide. Staël was also persona non grata in France, the archenemy of Napoleon, and ridiculed as much as praised for her literary and political activities. Staël, for Aurore Dudevant, must have symbolized the dangers as well as the glories of female authorship and personified the social risks she was taking in choosing to become a writer. It was too late to emulate the eighteenth-century writers she knew and loved, both for personal and political reasons. As Germaine Brée points out in what remains one of the only general studies of French women writers, after Napoleon, "literary and social circles no longer reinforced one another in the same way. This conjunction affected the woman writer's position adversely: social respectability and literature parted company."[17] Staël, for better or for worse, was Aurore Dudevant's model, and later became the standard by which Sand was judged. Perhaps for this reason, Sand would always keep a certain distance from Staël, preferring, understandably, to be known and appreciated for herself.[18]

Becoming a woman writer, alone and self-sufficient, was thus a risky undertaking. Aurore Dudevant expresses her unconscious anxiety in all her early texts, depicting women artists but not yet able to imagine the free and transcendent artist of *Consuelo*. Consuelo herself would be born of Sand's own positive experience as an author, but well after Sand had established her voice and her reputation; significantly, though, *Consuelo* is set in the eighteenth century, not Sand's own era. Despite her uncertainties, however, Aurore Dudevant persisted with her writing. Publication, the warm reception from the public, and the encouragement of her friends evidently helped her to exorcise her fears, for shortly after her return to Nohant in January 1832 she began *Indiana*.

Aurore Dudevant's apprenticeship was complete. In Paris, she had gained practical experience with publishers and a budding reputation as an author. In the four years since the redaction of the "Voyage au Mont d'Or," Aurore Dudevant had made great strides in characterization, composition, and narration. *Rose et Blanche* is a far cry from *La Marraine*, begun only two years earlier. George Sand was at last ready to make her appearance on the literary scene.

3 🍂

INDIANA

Heroic Romance and Bourgeois Realism

Barely two months after the publication of *Rose et Blanche*, Aurore Dudevant began work on a novel that would become *Indiana*, this time without the intervention of Sandeau. She composed the novel in a relatively short time, for it was revised, printed, and distributed within three and a half months. *Indiana* appeared in May 1832 under the name G. Sand.

It is important at this juncture to consider how Aurore Dudevant acquired her final pseudonym. In *Histoire de ma vie* (*Oa* II, 138–39), Sand explains that her editor Dupuy wanted her to publish *Indiana* under the name Sand because that name was already known by the public. She refused to use J. Sand, since Sandeau had had no part in writing *Indiana*, and Latouche is again credited with solving the thorny question of naming by decreeing that Sand should remain, but with a new first name. Sand recounts that she chose George because it was synonymous with "Berrichon." Much the same story appears in a letter to Charles Duvernet that accompanied a gift of the newly published novel in May 1832: "I am *Georges Sand, Jules Sand* is my brother" (*C* II, 89). How much truth there is to these accounts is hard to determine. What is certain, though, is the progression in first name from J. (or Jules) to G. to Georges to George, which takes over definitively in Sand's correspondence in May 1833, exactly one year after the publication of *Indiana*.

It is clear from the conversation with her mother-in-law discussed in the introduction that Aurore Dudevant was determined from the beginning of her literary career not to use her real name for publication. *Rose et Blanche* displays not only an anxiety about identity but a serious concern with naming, a closely related concept. The idiot Denise becomes Soeur Blanche, while Rose Primerose is called Mlle de Beaumont at the convent, La Coronari on stage, Tony briefly, and finally Soeur Rosalie. All these name changes that accompany personal and professional developments in the lives of the characters reflect the evolutions in Aurore Dudevant's own life: Aurore Dupin had become Aurore Dudevant, and was becoming known as J. Sand, a name of convenience that she must have considered temporary. As she wrote her first novel in 1831, she was evidently preoccupied with finding an appropriate name to go with her new life as an author.

It seems probable to me that Sand did not immediately chose Georges as a pseudonym (with an *s*, as in the letter to Duvernet), but rather that Dupuy proposed putting G. Sand on the cover of *Indiana* on the theory that J. Sand and G. Sand *are* different, as Sand insisted, but not so different that the public wouldn't in fact think they were the same person and buy the book. The G. then had to be fleshed out, and Sand at that point chose Georges. Therefore, Georges is derived from G., and not the other way around, as she implies. What makes Georges a typically *berrichon* name, her stated reason for picking it? Georges Lubin speculates that the association was with the land and agriculture, for the Berry was essentially an agrarian province. Perhaps Sand also had in mind Georgeon, that fantastic devil of her province. Indeed, what was Georges Sand, and later George Sand, but a mythical figure? Half of a male-female team, then a woman writer with a man's name, married yet free, womanly although occasionally attired in men's clothes, Georges Sand was a creature unlike other humans. Georgeon seems as likely an inspiration as agriculture for this chimerical writer, particularly since in her autobiography she characterizes the artist as "[l]'homme oiseau" (*Oa* I, 18), and attributes to birds non-gender-specific behavior in marriage. Authorship, androgyny, and fabulous beings are irrevocably linked for Sand.[1]

Sand admits in *Histoire de ma vie* that had she known she would become famous, she might have chosen another name entirely, particularly as Karl Sand was already notorious for having assassinated the German dramatist Kotzebue. Unfortunately, she did not have a real say in the matter, for as J. Sand she had already achieved a modest success. However, although the name G. Sand was a fortuitous acquisition and must be attributed to Dupuy, she made the best of it, making it truly hers by eventually adopting George as her first name. The dropping of the *s* has been attributed to Sand's anglophilia, but it would seem rather to stem from a desire for individuality, and a return to the same-but-different model on which the choice of the name G. Sand was originally based. George is not the usual French spelling and thus stands out. Georges and George are homonyms, for the *s* is silent, so they are the same aurally, but different graphically. George Sand is a unique name in France and designates she who is a woman, but a woman writer. George without *s* is the sign of her difference, and the final *e* aligns the name with French words that are generically feminine. George Sand is not simply a male pseudonym, then, but another example of the creative union of male and female in Sand's life and art.[2] In her literature, she would use a male voice but a female perspective, while in her correspondence she would mix genders, signing George but writing in both the masculine and feminine.

In July 1832, Sand wrote to Laure Decerfz, *"In Paris Mme Dudevant is dead. But Georges Sand is known as an energetic old fellow"* (*C* II, 120). This death notice, italicized in the text, signals the demise of that social construct, Mme Dudevant (and not the woman Aurore Dupin Dudevant), and the birth of a new phenomenon, the woman writer with a male name. The final question regarding Sand's pseudonym is the one she does not even raise herself in her explanations of the origin of her name, a curious omission. This question concerns her choice of a male first name. Even if the name G. Sand was imposed by Dupuy, why could she not have adopted one of the many female first names that begin with G, for example, Gabrielle, the first baptismal name of her daughter, Solange? There was no tradition of male pseudonymity among French women writers, although anonymity was not unknown. Seventeenth- and eighteenth-century women were known by their last names with Mme as title: Mme Riccoboni, Mme de Genlis, Mme de Staël. In this, as in so many other domains, Sand was an innovator, for French women writers like Marie d'Agoult (Daniel Stern) and Delphine Gay (Vicomte de Launay) imitated her by choosing male pseudonyms. She was even more influential in England, where not only the Brontës and Marian Evans followed Sand's example, but a whole later generation as well.

Artistic creation for Sand was a male identified activity, as we saw in the last chapter. It is not that a woman could not become an artist. On the contrary, Sand was very familiar with both French and English women writers of previous generations, as her writings and her library attest.[3] But becoming a woman writer in the public sphere in 1832 was a gamble and entailed adopting a male role, at least to a certain degree. Society frowned on the practice of any profession by women of a certain class; actresses, those other public performers, were by definition *déclassées*. The Civil Code made it impossible for a woman to keep or manage her own earnings. Moreover, the strictly feminine role assigned to women, who were supposed to be passive and delicate, was foreign to Sand, who had long ago developed a more balanced, androgynous self-image. A male name both coincided with her view of herself and enabled her to be more easily accepted as a writer by society. Although George Sand's identity as a woman was an open secret in Paris from the beginning, unlike George Eliot's or Currer Bell's, the male name with the unusual spelling invited a certain confusion as to her gender and posited her from the outset as a writer who was unconventional. By erasing Mme Dudevant from the literary registers and replacing it with George(s) Sand, she made sure that she was not treated as a "lady novelist," but rather as a serious artist. As Musset wrote after the publication of *Lélia* (and before their liaison), "You are George Sand; otherwise, you would have been madame so-and-so writer of books."[4] In adopting a pseudonym, she escaped the fate of all other French women writers before Colette and her twentieth-century successors, that of being called Mme Dudevant where her male contemporaries are known just by their last names: Balzac, Hugo, etc., a turn of events that would have pleased her. George Sand remains different from both men and women writers of her time, distinctive.

Sand intended *Indiana* as a serious portrait of everyday life, "bourgeois realism," as she called it (*C* II, 46), without the frivolity, coarseness, and diffuseness that characterized her and Sandeau's previous novel. While *Indiana* is a much more realistic work than *Rose et Blanche*, especially as concerns characterization and plot, it is best described as a romance, to use Northrop Frye's term.[5] More specifically, *Indiana* belongs to that mode which Fredric Jameson has called the "art romances of the Romantic period."[6] In her first long, independently written work, conceived and executed with an eye toward publication, Sand turned to one of the oldest literary genres, adapting and changing it for her own purposes.

Frye describes the quest romance as "the search of the libido or desiring self for a fulfillment that will deliver it from the anxieties of reality but will still contain that reality" (Frye, 193). He has identified in the romance six phases that "form a cyclical sequence in a romantic hero's life" (Frye, 198), as well as numerous characteristics particular to the genre, which all appear in *Indiana* with certain salient exceptions.

The most obvious difference between *Indiana* and Frye's examples concerns the reversals occasioned by the gender of the protagonist, who is a heroine rather than a hero, and who acquires at the end not a bride but a bridegroom. Nor is the reversal completely symmetrical, for Indiana does not rescue Ralph, as the hero does the lady, although he has the same psychological link to the oedipal father as the bride has to the mother. Indiana's quest is also far more spiritual than concrete and contains fewer physical adventures than the romances Frye describes, even though she does cross the ocean alone in a last, daring effort to be united with Raymon. This lack of external adventures has at least as much to do with Indiana's gender and women's circumscribed life as it does with the author's desire to relate a simple and natural story.

Indiana contains all the phases noted by Frye except the first, the birth of the hero(ine), which is not exceptional. Indiana's innocent youth (II) is described twice, by her and by Ralph, as an idyllic time spent in the pastoral setting of l'île Bourbon and characterized by the chaste love she and Ralph felt for each other. Her quest (III) involves the search for happiness and freedom and leads ultimately to self-knowledge, while her enemy is society and its laws, particularly those governing marriage, which allow women no voice in their own destiny. While Raymon at first appears to be the villain, especially in his more sadistic and diabolical moments, he is best seen as the catalyst that enables Indiana to understand the workings of French society and to appreciate the kind of alternative represented by Ralph.[7]

The fourth phase requires the "maintaining of the integrity of the innocent world against the assault of experience" (Frye, 201), and corresponds to Indiana's attempt to justify Raymon and his cowardly action in letting her leave France, rather than analyzing his behavior and recognizing that she and he have vastly divergent views of love and its consequences.

The fifth phase is complementary to the second in that it represents an idyllic, erotic world, but one where experience is comprehended rather than yet to come (Frye, 202). This phase encompasses Ralph and Indiana's voyage back to the île Bourbon, along with their moments at Bernica, where Ralph reveals his true self and Indiana understands the error of her choice of Raymon. This is also the point of epiphany, coming as it does at the top of a waterfall[8] and invoking a mysterious spiritual intervention that even the positivistic Ralph prefers to ascribe to an angel (*I*, 349).[9] This moment of truth leads to the sixth and final phase, where Ralph and Indiana establish their own, separate household and withdraw as much as possible from the rest of society. The cycle renews itself, however, as Ralph recounts their story and describes their life to a young man whom they incite to follow their example, should society reject him. There is a potential sequel in this disciple's adventures in society that might lead to a similar, contemplative retreat; at the very least, Ralph and Indiana's experience is repeated in the young man's narration of the story.

By viewing *Indiana* as part of the romance tradition, we are able to demonstrate the unity of the novel as well as the necessity of the conclusion to the whole. The last chapter, which in the original edition was simply numbered 15, was later called "Conclusion. A Jules Néraud," and dedicated to the friend who had taught Sand so much about l'île Bourbon. Wladimir Karénine and Pierre Salomon both assert that this chapter was added after the novel had been completed, but before publication, either to avoid an unhappy ending or to lengthen the novel (*I*, v–vi). Neither suggestion is valid. George Sand would end her next two novels with the death of the protagonists, while *Rose et Blanche* did not have a happy ending, so she was not averse to tragic conclusions if necessary. As for the length of the novel, without this conclusion the two original volumes contain about the same number of pages (volume I fills 342 pages, volume II, 362, or 333 without chapter 15), so that the argument that the second volume was too short simply does not hold.

Rather than seeking external reasons for the ending of *Indiana*, we should examine the internal logic of the narrative. Seen from this perspective, the île Bourbon becomes the locus of the fulfillment of the desires that occasioned the story. Neither the real world, symbolized by France, particularly Paris, nor a fantasy world, l'île Bourbon is a French colony where French life is duplicated, but inexactly, so that the freedom to live differently than in French society exists. As is the case with its prototypes, *Indiana* ends in a rebirth that is also a reintegration, but on a different plane: at the end, Indiana is part of a couple, as at the beginning, only that couple is more genuine, being based on choice rather than coercion.[10]

This concluding chapter has a further structural function, for it provides the origin of the narrative and reveals the identity of the narrator. Throughout the novel, the narrator has been a mysterious figure. First-person interventions reveal him as well as his unknown narratee to be a man (*I*, 105), while his many tentative comments show that he is not omniscient but is occasionally underinformed as to all the circumstances of his tale. The conclusion allows us to understand the narrator's hesitancy, for he is merely repeating the story as he heard it from Ralph. This ending underlines the cyclical nature of the narrative as well, for it is only after the narrator has met Ralph and Indiana that he can tell their story, yet this meeting comes at the end, not at the beginning of the novel. Thus, *Indiana* ends where it properly should begin.

The discovery of the narrator's identity does not resolve all the ambiguities of the narrative, however. There are passages in the novel that seem clearly attributable to Sand herself, while others, especially those which express uncertainty about particular events, reveal the viewpoint of an outsider, the narrator. In Gérard Genette's terms, we can distinguish between "who sees?" (a female) and "who speaks?" (a male).[11] As noted in chapter 1, the use of a male narrator did not come easily to Aurore Dudevant. On some level, she felt from the first that narration was a male task, not a female one, or at least that a male narrator was more credible, while nonetheless continuing to assert her own voice. The alternation between "je" and "nous" in *Indiana*, as previously in *Rose et Blanche* and "Jehan Cauvin," shows Sand's continued unwillingness to create an authoritative narrator who assumes complete responsibility for his narrative. However, there is a clear distinction between *La Marraine* or "Histoire du rêveur" and *Indiana*, in that the earlier works contain a male intradiegetic narrator and a female extradiegetic narrator who in some sense controls the text, whereas in *Indiana* the male narrator dominates. The female voice is still present, but it is harder to detect, for it has gone underground.

Although Sand systematically utilized a male narrator, she left gaps in all her texts where the female voice comes through—in perspective, in partial narration, as in *Lélia* and *Leone Leoni*, or in the inclusive "nous." The male narrator, like the male name, hides but imperfectly the female presence behind it. In revising her novel, as we know she did (*C* II, 46–48), Sand must have chosen to distance herself from the narrative, perhaps on account of its controversial content, perhaps because of earlier notions regarding male narrative authority, by interposing a separate narrator who, because of his gender and background, could not be assimilated to the author. This was accomplished by adding a final chapter, which served further to give more balance to the novel's plot. The "Conclusion" is therefore a positive and significant addition to the novel, and not the appendage it has been taken to be.

In addition to encompassing six phases, the romance is also characterized by a dialectical form (Frye, 187): the hero, symbol of light, combats the dark enemy, with all the other characters divided along similar lines. This binary opposition appears in *Indiana* on many different levels; it is found in the style, structure, and thematics of the novel.

The contrast between light and dark, white and black, is not seen in the characters, for the major ones all possess both good and bad traits, with only Mme de Carvajal and Delmare appearing predominantly negative and Mme de Ramière positive. Rather, the opposition is represented in a more sophisticated manner, both stylistically, in the black and white imagery that pervades the novel, and in the counterpoint that is set up between the enclosed, dark interiors of France and the open-air spaces of the île Bourbon. The structure of *Indiana* depends less on the four parts into which the novel is divided (Sand's primitive plan having been "four volumes about four characters" [*C* II, 47]) than on a series of interior scenes that are all variations on a theme. This structure has already been discerned in *Rose et Blanche* and discussed in the preceding chapter. *Indiana* presents a more elaborate version of this method of composition.

The novel begins with a tightly composed scene painted in chiaroscuro, worthy of a Dutch miniaturist. Three immobile figures are seated in front of the hearth. A few pages later, a description of the fire, which crackles and dies, illuminating some objects while plunging others into shadow, gives an eerie, Gothic effect, particularly when Delmare is said to resemble a ghost as he paces back and forth. Clearly, something unpleasant is about to happen.

This claustrophobic atmosphere is repeated in the key scenes of the novel, which all take place in dark, confined spaces; even Indiana and Ralph's suicide attempt is set in the narrow gorges of the Bernica, during the night. Only the final discussion between Ralph and the narrator takes place in a fully light and open area, the garden. Significantly, the landscapes for which George Sand is famous and which had already appeared in *Rose et Blanche* are nearly absent from *Indiana*, as Sand herself admitted (*C* II, 48). The Brie countryside, Paris, Bordeaux, are barely evoked except for salient monuments (L'Institut, les Quinconces) and summary descriptions and appear more as names than as identifiable places. Only the interiors, where the action is played out, count. Although l'île Bourbon is carefully described, as befits the scene of a childhood paradise lost as well as an adult paradise regained, no important action takes place there until the very end of the novel.

The second crucial scene in *Indiana* is the one that inspired Musset's famous poem to Sand, which begins:

> Sand, quand tu l'écrivais, où donc l'avais-tu vue,
> Cette scène terrible où Noun, à demi nue,
> Sur le lit d'Indiana s'enivre avec Raimond?
> Qui donc te la dictait, cette page brûlante
> Où l'amour cherche en vain d'une main palpitante
> Le fantôme adoré de son illusion? (*I*, 87)

> Sand, as you were writing the novel, how did you imagine this terrible scene where Noun, half nude, intoxicates herself in Indiana's bed with Raimond? Who dictated this burning page to you, where love seeks vainly with a trembling hand the adored ghost of its illusion?

The scene still makes a powerful impression on the reader today, charged as it is with eroticism, voyeurism, and energy.

After crossing the garden, a study in black and white, Raymon reaches Indiana's circular room, accompanied by Noun. Here, the same vacillating light as in the beginning creates strange shadows and blinds Raymon momentarily, while the mirrors seem to fill the room with ghosts, as Noun, dressed in Indiana's clothes, is reflected as both herself and her mistress. The light of the room contrasts with the dark of the night outside, while the virginal whiteness of Indiana's bed becomes the scene of debauchery. This episode is painful, for the reader sympathizes with Noun and her love of a man who, at the height of passion, is thinking of another woman. Like Musset, one feels impelled to ask how Sand imagined this scene, so disturbing in its depiction of a sexual act that is almost perverted.

This scene is repeated, and corrected, in Indiana and Ralph's suicide attempt at Bernica. It is dark when they begin their vigil, and only the white water is visible. The mist it gives off creates an atmosphere of mystery, and in the darkness, the ordinarily beautiful site becomes a frightening abyss. The moon rises, lighting the way, and after confessing his love for Indiana, Ralph picks her up in his arms "and carried her away [l'emporta] to hurl her with him into the torrent . . ." (*I*, 338; ellipses in original). The verb recalls that used in the earlier scene, when Raymon "entraîna sa créole échevelée" (carried off his disheveled Creole)(*I*, 86). The next day, in the more prosaic light, both men fall to their knees on the spot of their acts of passion, Ralph to thank God, and Raymon, in a rather unrealistic tirade, to beg Indiana's pardon for having profaned her bed and, by extension, her person.

The frankly sexual nature of both these scenes is reflected in the imagery Sand employs to describe their settings. In the first, Indiana's closed, circular room is reached by traversing dark corridors, described elsewhere as a "labyrinth" (*I*, 36). As Stirling Haig has perspicaciously noted, this room is a "veritable hermetically sealed Venusberg."[12] Its inaccessibility and secrecy are reminiscent of the invisibility of much of the female sexual anatomy. The female genitals are also discernible in the description of Indiana's bed, "this little bed half-hidden beneath the muslin curtains . . ." (*I*, 82), "narrow and virginal" (*I*, 83), which is appropriately adorned with a very male palm branch. The identity of the woman and the bed is made explicit in the narrator's comment that Raymon "shuddered with desire at the thought of the day when Indiana herself would open its delights to him" (*I*, 83). Raymon is never able to possess Indiana, who remains for him virginal and unavailable like her bed. His orgy with Noun, who had set out fruits "which coquettishly presented their rosy sides . . ." (*I*, 82), a metaphor for a woman ready for a sexual encounter, leads to tragedy precisely because she is the wrong woman in a forbidden place.

There is a different emphasis in the imagery of the gorges of Bernica. The most explicit description of the site comes fifty pages before the suicide scene. Here, the gorge is decidedly female, whereas the waterfall is a male image.

C'est un lieu pittoresque, une sorte de vallée étroite et profonde, cachée entre deux murailles de rochers perpendiculaires, dont la surface est parsemée de bouquets d'arbustes saxatiles et de touffes de fougère.

Un ruisseau coule dans la cannelure formée par la rencontre des deux pans. Au point où leur écartement cesse, il se précipite dans des profondeurs effrayantes, et forme, au lieu de sa chute, un petit bassin entouré de roseaux et couvert d'une fumée humide. (*I*, 251–52)

It is a picturesque spot, a sort of deep and narrow valley, hidden between two

perpendicular walls of rock, the surface of which is studded with clumps of
saxatile shrubs and tufts of ferns.

   A stream flows in the narrow trough formed by the meeting of the two sides.
At the point where they meet it plunges down into frightful depths, and, where
it falls, forms a basin surrounded by reeds and covered with a damp mist. (*i*,
231)

This setting represents sexual union, which for Ralph and Indiana is successful.[13]

   The original scene between Noun and Raymon is replayed by Indiana
and Raymon, with Noun's ghost haunting the room, not Indiana's. As Noun
had worn her mistress's clothes, so does Indiana disguise herself as Noun
to ascertain the truth about the servant's relations with Raymon. The action
is prepared by the same white/dark imagery as earlier, with the trees hidden
by fog and mist. Raymon is happy to leave the dark and eerie park, filled
with memories of Noun's suicide, for the illumination of Indiana's room,
but there he meets the by-now familiar vacillating light. The cruelty Raymon
had shown toward Noun by using her to express his desire for Indiana in
the previous scene is mirrored here as Indiana attempts to shock Raymon
and force a confrontation between them. However, Raymon turns this scene
to his advantage and tries deliberately to dominate and humiliate Indiana.
Like its prototype, this encounter changes his love into hatred. Unfortunately for Raymon, this scene is interrupted by Delmare's arrival, as the
first one was shattered by Indiana's entrance, and Raymon is not able to
complete his seduction of Indiana.

   This episode marks a turning point in the presentation of Raymon's
character. From a daring young man-about-town, open to all romantic
adventures, he becomes sadistic and egotistical, interested only in breaking
Indiana's spirit and making her his slave. Like Laclos's Valmont, he carefully calculates his discourse and his letters so as to tell her what she wants
to hear. He renews his attempt at seduction some pages later, when Indiana
takes refuge in his room, expecting him to save her from having to accompany Delmare to l'île Bourbon. Unlike Indiana's room, Raymon's has no
fire, and one imagines Indiana sitting in the cold and dark, awaiting Raymon's return. Their exchange is ended, as in the past scenes, by the arrival
of daylight, which floods the apartment and brings with it Indiana's enlightenment. Raymon's rhetoric is similar to that which he had employed
in the previous scene, while he uses the same physical insistence that stops
just short of rape. In this case, though, it is Raymon himself who puts an
end to the scene, saying to Indiana: "Come, madame, it is time for you to
leave" (*I*, 214).

   These final words are reproduced textually in the last scene in Indiana's room, when Laure de Nangy, now married to Raymon, says to Indiana, "Kindly leave" (*I*, 302). After having been sent away by Raymon from his room in Paris and accompanied out by his mother, she is definitively told to leave his room at Lagny by his wife. Indiana's home is no longer her own, and she has nowhere to go but a "lodging-house," which, curiously, is seen, like her room, as a refuge from an "inextricable labyrinth" (*I*, 305).[14] Yet the hotel room is not the white arena where virginal dreams are played out. On the contrary, "a dull, hazy light creeps regretfully over the smoky ceilings and soiled windows"(*I*, 304) of this anonymous room. Indiana's itinerary of lost illusions has shown her a somber, tarnished side of life that she had never imagined in her light, girlish room, where the travel books and etchings of Paul and Virginie's pastoral *amours* did not reveal the existence of grimy hotels and lovers such as Raymon.

Despite her despair, Indiana does not die in this dismal hotel room, as she so romantically imagines she will. She is rescued by Ralph and comes eventually to live happily with him in a traditional colonist's home, described earlier as "diaphanous" (*I*, 257) when compared with European houses. It is open and airy, without the dark, winding corridors and claustrophobic interiors she had known in France. The final scene of the novel corrects the opening one, where three people are seated silently in the dark: at the end, Indiana, Ralph, and the narrator converse in the outdoors.

The binary structure of the romance evident in the stylistic contrast between black and white imagery reappears on a thematic level in the opposition of ignorance and knowledge, which also represents a black and white dichotomy. Up until the end of the novel, Indiana is trapped in a conspiracy of silence and rhetoric: silence on the part of those who do not want her to know the painful truth about certain events, and rhetoric from those who tell her what they think she wants to hear. As the heroine of a woman author's romance, Indiana must undergo months of suffering and tests that consist not of slaying dragons but of understanding and combatting the society in which she lives as well as learning to know herself. This she does by listening to the language of men and evaluating the systems they represent. The male values expressed through language that Indiana must learn to recognize and reject pertain to love, politics, religion, and the military. Initially ignorant, she becomes enlightened, less in an intellectual sense than in a moral sense, and leaves sophistry behind for a world where she and Ralph mean what they say and say what they mean.

Love as defined in the novel is a verbal game whose rules both sides understand, although men created the rules first, and each side knows the possible moves open to it. Raymon is an expert at this game, for he is both a writer of political brochures and a persuasive speaker. His oratorical capabilities are shown in the novel not in a political forum, however, but

rather in his love scenes with Noun and Indiana. Raymon is conscious of
playing a role as he woos a woman; he elaborates speeches based on previous models of a lover's discourse. He tells women what they are condi-
tioned to want to hear, and they respond accordingly. "[H]e knew that the
promises of love did not involve honor, happily for society. Sometimes,
too, the woman who had demanded these solemn oaths had broken them
first" (*I*, 136). Indiana, however, is a stranger to French society and does
not even know that these games exist, much less how to play them. It is
not insignificant that she is a Creole, descended from a Spanish father and
brought up on an island far from her new home. Indiana is doubly an
outsider in French society: she is a foreigner as well as a woman in a man's
world.[15] Raymon is aware of this, and she is not.

> Et, quand il vit qu'elle ne se rendait pas, il céda à la nécessité et lui reprocha
> de ne pas l'aimer; lieu commun qu'il méprisait et qui le faisait sourire, presque
> honteux d'avoir affaire à une femme assez ingénue pour n'en pas sourire elle-
> même.
> Ce reproche alla au coeur d'Indiana plus vite que toutes les exclamations
> dont Raymon avait brodé son discours. (*I*, 186–87)

> And when he saw that she did not surrender, he yielded to necessity and
> reproached her with not loving him; a commonplace expedient which he de-
> spised and which made him smile, with a feeling of something like shame at
> having to do with a woman so innocent as not to smile at it herself.
> That reproach went to Indiana's heart more swiftly than all the exclamations
> with which Raymon had embellished his discourse. (*i*, 167)

Indiana is "[i]gnorant like a true Creole" (*I*, 164), not only of history and
geography but also of the social realities of her time. Like Emma Bovary,
for whom Indiana served as a model, she learned about love in books.
"Where did you dream about love? in what novel intended for chamber-
maids did you study society, I beg you?" asks Raymon (*I*, 210). It is ironic
that he should accuse Indiana of acting according to the prescriptions of
novels, for his own language is precisely that of fiction and is a fiction she
takes seriously. When one compares Raymon's rhetoric of love with Indiana's concept of love, derived from novels rather than experience, one
finds many parallels.

Raymon's view of love is sadistic and of the "blame the victim" variety.
Love remains on the periphery of his actions, separate from the rest of his
life, as was the case with the men in *Rose et Blanche*. This is apparent first
in his affair with Noun, which he sees as a lark, and later in his attitude
toward Indiana's possible return from l'île Bourbon, which he intends to
use as the occasion to take her as his mistress, not his wife.

Indiana accepts this sadistic concept of love. "She knew society so little that she made a tragic novel out of life . . ." (*I*, 71). When she receives Raymon's letter, she reacts mechanically to his call.

> Tel était son enthousiasme, qu'elle craignait de faire trop peu pour lui. . . . Elle eût donné sa vie sans croire que ce fût assez payer un sourire de Raymon. . . . (*I*, 275)
> . . . L'Amour, c'est la vertu de la femme; c'est pour lui qu'elle se fait une gloire de ses fautes, c'est de lui qu'elle reçoit l'héroïsme de braver ses remords. Plus le crime lui coûte à commettre, plus elle aura mérité de celui qu'elle aime. C'est le fanatisme qui met le poignard aux mains du religieux. (*I*, 281)

> So great was her enthusiasm that she feared that she was doing too little for him. . . . She would have given her life, with the idea that it was too small a price to pay for a smile from Raymon. . . . (*i*, 254–55)
> . . . Love is woman's virtue; it is for love that she glories in her sins, it is from love that she acquires the heroism to defy her remorse. The more dearly it costs her to commit the crime, the more she will have deserved at the hands of the man she loves. It is like the fanaticism that places the dagger in the hand of the religious enthusiast. (*i*, 260)

Pierre Salomon, in a note to his edition, attributes these sentiments to Sand herself and calls them "a way of hiding an unpleasant reality under an honorable mask . . ." (*I*, 281). However, Sand is not so much justifying Indiana's conduct (or her own, for that matter) as explaining its source. Love, for Indiana, means sacrifice of self and others for the beloved. It is this sort of love that is found in novels and preached by Raymon. Just as he held her responsible for his unhappiness and frustration, so does she accept this responsibility.

> [E]lle n'agissait point en vue d'elle-même, mais de Raymon; . . . elle n'allait point à lui pour chercher du bonheur, mais pour lui en porter, et . . . dût-elle être maudite dans l'éternité, elle en serait assez dédommagée si elle embellissait la vie de son amant. (*I*, 281)

> [S]he was no longer acting in her own interests but in Raymon's; . . . she was going to him, not in search of happiness, but to make him happy, and . . . even though she were to be accursed for all eternity, she would be sufficiently recompensed if she embellished her lover's life. (*i*, 260–61)

In her study of women's moral development, Carol Gilligan concludes that women are taught to be self-sacrificing and to place the needs of others ahead of their own. Indiana's thoughts are not an expression of bad faith, as Salomon implies, but rather represent a typical female viewpoint, one that Sand both depicts and exposes as deleterious to woman's existence.[16]
Raymon and Indiana's sadomasochistic relationship might actually have

succeeded, had their reunion not been interrupted by his wife, who arrives before Raymon can hide Indiana, as he had earlier planned to do. For once, Raymon the orator is speechless. "But Raymon answered nothing; his admirable presence of mind had abandoned him" (*I*, 301). Shocked by Indiana's return, he speaks only eleven words in three pages. His verbal spell over Indiana is broken, and her *amour romanesque* will soon fade, to be replaced by another, more genuine love.

If Raymon is reduced to silence, Ralph becomes more eloquent as he and Indiana return to their childhood home with the intention of committing suicide. "His words were marked by his feelings, and for the first time, Indiana knew his true character" (*I*, 315). As she learns to know Ralph, Raymon disappears from her heart. His words, too, have a powerful effect on Indiana, as they await death by the waterfall, but far from being the artificial rhetoric of Raymon, Ralph's discourse is the exact reflection of his thought. There is a correspondence between the signifier and the signified in his speech that is lacking in Raymon's. Ralph speaks as the moon rises, and his vocabulary repeatedly uses words of light: "brille," "feu," "lumière" (*I*, 318). It is a moment of truth, of honesty, when everything hidden is brought into the open. The authenticity of Ralph's love, the revelation of his character, show Indiana that she has been mistaken in both her appraisal of Ralph and her choice of Raymon. Ralph's love is genuine while Raymon's was just talk. Ironically, had Ralph revealed his real feelings earlier, Indiana would never have fallen for Raymon's lines. Yet the narrative structure of *Indiana* requires the characters' ignorance for the novel to continue: if Indiana had truly understood Ralph, if she had been apprised of the real cause of Noun's suicide, if Raymon had told her and Delmare of Ralph's love, there would have been no novel.

The end of the novel, with its insistence on transparency and candor and the image of the veil that is finally lifted, has a Rousseauistic ring. Raymon is shown to be a false love object, a mere "héros de roman," while Ralph, unremarkable as he is, is Indiana's true companion. When the narrator meets Ralph and Indiana, he remarks significantly: "Neither of them was particularly brilliant" (*I*, 346). Their words express their feelings and are the more powerful for their simplicity. Sand gives Indiana a chance that is denied to Emma Bovary, that for happiness outside of the novelistic world she had created for herself and men like Raymon had fostered. Like Rousseau before her and Flaubert after, however, she repeats the paradox of criticizing novels within a novel; she uses fiction to show a "realistic" alternative to fiction based not on rhetoric, ignorance, and illusion, but on truth and understanding.

In addition to love, politics is another one of the men's verbal games that are illustrated in the novel. Political discussions as well as the recounting of specific political events of the era occupy a large place in this novel and serve to situate it in the precise time frame of October 1827–January 1832. This places the novel astride the major political crisis of the romantic age, the revolution of 1830. Indiana is noticeably absent from the heated discussions between Delmare, Raymon, and Ralph, each of whom represents a different political perspective. It is not surprising that she does not join in these debates, for all three systems supported by the men exclude women from political participation. Her lack of partisanship, attributed by the men to her ignorance, has a deeper meaning, for she develops her own political ideas, formulated outside of the received ideas that the men had assimilated as part of their education. Her condition as outsider, unfettered by previous socialization, again allows her to see more clearly the positions defended by the men. Her questions are "naïves," her spirit "neuve et ingénue" (*I*, 164), only in relation to male society's expectations and conventions.

Through these discussions, Indiana learns that political systems are less the expression of indisputable truths than the codification of existing power structures. They consist merely of the "interests of civilization constituted into principles . . ." (*I*, 164). Indiana's political ideals, on the other hand, depend on "the straightforward ideas and simple laws of common sense and humanity . . ." (*I*, 164), and derive from a Rousseauistic opposition between civilization and nature, although she is more optimistic about humanity's inherent goodness. These views contrast sharply with both Delmare's Napoleonic dreams and Raymon's monarchistic opinions, which are twice designated by the narrator as "utopies" (*I*, 158, 165) and are therefore not in conformity with political reality. Significantly, Ralph's republican ideal, which, with certain important modifications, is at the base of Indiana's opinions, is not ridiculed as impractical or unrealistic.

Delmare and Raymon become fast friends, despite their political differences. In fact, by the end of the novel, Raymon feels more loyal to Delmare than to Indiana. "He was too much Delmare's friend, he owed too much consideration to the confidence this man had in him to steal his wife; he had to content himself with seducing her" (*I*, 212). This expression of male solidarity would be funny if it were not made at the expense of Indiana, who has no idea that men can be more faithful to the principles of male bonding than to the women they love. Raymon's concept of marriage is quite similar to Delmare's despite his superior education and manners. He assures Indiana that, had she been married to him, ". . . you would have blessed your chain" (*I*, 75). The word *chaîne* appears several times as the metaphor for her marriage to Delmare, along with the word *esclavage* (slavery), and it is therefore significant that it recurs in Raymon's discourse. Ralph and Indiana, on the other hand, once they have left French society behind, use their money to free the slaves of Bourbon. Furthermore, they are not married according to civil or religious law but simply live together, unfettered by socially defined ties.

Religion is another area in which Raymon and Indiana have opposite views. Hers are expressed in a letter to Raymon.

[J]e ne sers pas le même Dieu, mais je le sers mieux, et plus purement. Le vôtre, c'est le dieu des hommes, c'est le roi, le fondateur et l'appui de votre race; le mien, c'est le Dieu de l'univers, le créateur, le soutien et l'espoir de toutes les créatures. . . . Vous vous croyez les maîtres du monde; je crois que vous n'en êtes que les tyrans. (*I*, 242)

[I] do not serve the same God, but I serve Him more loyally and with a purer heart. Yours is the god of men, the king, the founder and the upholder of your race; mine is the God of the universe, the creator, the preserver and the hope of all creatures. . . . You deem yourselves the masters of the world; I deem you only its tyrants. (*i*, 224)

This letter contains the clearest formulation of the dichotomy between male and female values in the novel and links male institutions all together in one mutually supportive system: religion is used to justify government and society, to create and perpetuate oppression. Indiana is fully aware that her life is ordained not by God but by men. She follows her husband because to refuse him would mean being rejected by all other men, as Raymon has already proven, and would leave her without any means of survival.

Indiana only arrives at her concept of religion during the course of the novel, as can be seen in her explanation of her two suicide attempts. At first she rejects suicide because it is forbidden by God, and she justifies her walk into the Seine by the fact that she was unaware of her actions. Her second attempt is deliberate, for she is by then convinced by bitter experience that the usual image of an intolerant God propagated by society is not the only one. "Unhappiness, in entering my life, gradually taught me another religion than that taught by men" (*I*, 311). In religion, as in love and politics, Indiana learns to reject men's views for her own. It is important to note, however, that *Indiana* does not condemn men, but male institutions and those men who seek to perpetuate them. Both Delmare and Raymon are shown to be products of their society and, by implication, eventually changeable.

Indiana is not only a romantic heroine but the heroine of a romance as well. Sand set her novel in the France of her time but structured it in an ageless fashion, updating the form to suit her needs. She utilized five of the six phases of the romance and reproduced its ordinarily repetitive structure (the hero undertakes several quests, meets with several obstacles, etc.) by organizing the novel around one key scene that is reprised and modified until a successful outcome is obtained. Furthermore, Sand integrated the oppositions central to the romance into the thematics and the imagery of the novel, thereby retaining a key element of the form without being forced to present the one-dimensional characters usually found in the genre. The plot of the novel remains the same as that of the romance, for Indiana learns to recognize and conjure the evils of male social and religious conventions, ultimately emerging victorious from her struggle.

In a provocative article, Leslie Rabine asserts that Sand reproduced in *Indiana* the nineteenth-century ideology of the passive and chaste woman. That is not the case. Although Rabine is partly correct in stating that Indiana's "independence is contained in her dependence on a man . . . ," Indiana still achieves a major spiritual victory over society, one that is transmitted by the novel and is reproducible by the reader.[17] Laws, attitudes, and social customs have changed dramatically in the last 150 years, so it is easy for us to forget just how radical *Indiana* really was. Feminists today study male discourse and analyze patriarchal institutions, as Sand did, and they draw the same conclusions. Sand was not the first to criticize women's condition in society through her fiction. Graffigny's *Lettres d'une Péruvienne* (1747) did so overtly, particularly attacking women's insufficient education, while novels by all women did so covertly. Sand goes further than her predecessors both in demonstrating that religious, social, and political systems combine to oppress women and in locating their power in language. She posited a difference between men's and women's language in "La Fille d'Albano," and in *Indiana* she proves it.

It is instructive in this context to compare *Indiana* with Hugo's *Notre-Dame de Paris*, published the previous year. Esmeralda is also victimized by the church, the law, and love, represented by Claude Frollo, Jacques Charmolue, and Phoebus de Châteaupers. She goes to the scaffold without ever realizing that she has become a sacrifice, a scapegoat.[18] Critics of the time, almost all of whom were male, reacted positively for the most part to Sand's castigation of society, although it is doubtful they understood just how subversive her program was. Charles Rabou, who wrote: "Let us make the author of *Indiana* give up her professorship in Social Economics and reduce her to being merely a powerful painter of passions," was one who did recognize the extent of Sand's rebellion and wanted it suppressed.[19] Women did heed her message, not only in France but in Europe and America, and hailed her as their champion. The fact that Rabine can criticize Sand for not going far enough shows how great a distance women have traveled since 1832.

Sand used a traditional narrative genre to depict contemporary mores and problems. More important, *Indiana* proposes solutions to the insuffi-

ciencies of the society Sand criticizes, thereby fulfilling the didactic function of the romance and its related forms, the folktale and the myth. One
of these solutions has already been described as representing the sixth or
penseroso phase of the romance, that of contemplation and retirement,
where the intimate desires that occasioned the story are realized within an
idealized version of the real world, in this case l'île Bourbon. Sand also
presents a more pragmatic solution to the social ills she diagnoses, one that
is applicable to the France of her time. This solution becomes evident when
we consider the evolution of the triangular configurations formed by the
lovers in the novel, as in *Rose et Blanche*.[20]

At the beginning of *Indiana*, there are three people seated in the salon
at Lagny—Indiana, Delmare, and Ralph. Indiana and Delmare are married, although in name only, and Ralph is Indiana's cousin and childhood
companion, who is now the friend of the couple. Soon we are introduced
to Noun, Indiana's *soeur de lait* and servant, and Raymon; these two are
having a secret affair. This initial configuration gives way to a brief, transitional triangle consisting of the two women and Raymon. His attempts to
romance them both quickly fail, and Noun's suicide removes her forever
from an infernal game she was unprepared to play.

Raymon and Noun's love scene, commented on above, is the moment
when the Indiana-Noun-Raymon triangle gives way to the central triangle
of the novel, that of Indiana, Ralph, and Raymon. After the revelries of
the previous night have passed, and daylight brings Raymon to his senses,
he notices a covered portrait of Ralph in Indiana's room, and is incensed
that this man is, figuratively at least, allowed to see Indiana every hour of
every day, in all her most intimate moments. He later learns that Ralph
has literal access to her room as well. The thought of Ralph's privileges
incites Raymon's jealousy and deepens his desire for Indiana. This becomes clear in the hunt scene that soon follows. Raymon sees Ralph kiss
Indiana on the lips, although presumably in a purely fraternal spirit, and
he later becomes envious that Ralph has the pleasure of buying a horse for
Indiana. Moreover, this episode reveals to Raymon that Ralph's feelings
for Indiana go beyond friendship. He witnesses Ralph's attempt at suicide
when Indiana has been reported killed, and recognizes the depth of Ralph's
love for her. The *désir triangulaire* described by René Girard, in which a
man's desire for a woman depends on another man's love for her, deter-
mines Raymon's courtship of Indiana, for it is Ralph that Raymon con-
centrates on in his seduction, not Indiana herself.[21]

First, Raymon wants to replace Ralph in Indiana's room and in her affections, and to claim her even more completely than Ralph, for Raymon
knows that Indiana's relationship with her cousin is merely platonic. Second, he wants to prove his own superiority to Ralph himself, by eluding

his vigilance on the way to Indiana's room. Finally, he tries to show Indiana that his politics are superior to Ralph's, less because he is convinced of the divine right of monarchy than because he is humiliated that dull Ralph's opinions should carry more weight than his brilliant arguments. In his desire to best Ralph, of course, his feelings for Indiana get somewhat lost, and even she herself senses that his political orations are not really aimed at her. "In those moments, it seemed to Indiana that Raymon was not paying attention to her at all . . ." (*I*, 166).

By contrast, Ralph's jealousy functions very differently. In his hatred of Raymon, he never loses sight of Indiana, her needs and desires. Rather than trying to crush his enemy, he is courteous and generous toward him, so that Indiana will not be hurt. Unlike Raymon, who demands that Indiana relinquish everything for him, Ralph explicitly tells her: " . . . [I] don't want such a sacrifice, I will never accept it. Why should my life be more precious than yours?" (*I*, 311). Ralph's jealousy does not obscure his love, and he does not participate in the same way as Raymon in this triangle.

The passage from this central triangle to the final configuration is made via two ephemeral triangles: that of Indiana, Delmare, and Raymon, where Indiana is torn between love and duty, and the Raymon, Indiana, and Laure de Nangy triangle, which parallels the earlier Raymon, Indiana, Noun relationship and is even more short-lived.

The end of the novel mirrors the beginning, but in a more stable and acceptable way. Indiana and Delmare's paternalistic, chaste marriage has become M. Hubert and Laure's father-daughter relationship, with Raymon occupying the third place in the triangle as Laure's husband. This arrangement provides a more normative family picture and replaces a marriage that was ill-assorted on several levels with one that is a partnership of equals. In addition, the illicit, morganatic relationship between Raymon and Noun is replaced by Ralph and Indiana's unsanctified marriage. Moral as well as social equals, they find the love and spiritual contentment that elude Laure and Raymon.

Just as the debonair Raymon is the contrary of the stiff, quiet Ralph, Laure de Nangy is the opposite of Indiana. Worldly, sensible, able to identify and protect her interests, Laure has no illusions as to what the future holds for an heiress like herself. "[S]he had too much good sense, too much knowledge of contemporary society, to have dreamed of love when two millions were at stake" (*I*, 293). Although Laure is a minor character, the contrast between her and Indiana is made explicit in two key scenes, one at the beginning and another toward the end of the novel, where each woman is shown against the same background, the eighteenth-century decor of the salon at Lagny. Indiana is overwhelmed by this setting, seated as she is under the mantel of a "huge white marble fireplace inlaid with gilt copper."[22] She is compared to a "flower born yesterday and forced to bloom in a Gothic vase," where "gothic" means old or outdated (*I*, 25). The description of the decoration of the room reinforces her passivity, for the sculptures are "tortuous" and far too complicated for the eye to follow with any success. Laure, however, is able to understand this room well enough to do a pastiche of it. She controls her surroundings, changing them at will, while Indiana is dominated by them.

> C'était une chose charmante que cette copie, une fine moquerie tout empreinte du caractère railleur et poli de l'artiste. Elle s'était plu à outrer la prétentieuse gentillesse de ces vieilles fresques; elle avait saisi l'esprit faux et chatoyant du siècle de Louis XV sur ces figurines guindées. (*I*, 288)

> The copy was a fascinating thing, a delicate satire infused with the bantering yet refined nature of the artist. She had amused herself by exaggerating the pretentious sweetness of the old frescoes; she had grasped the false and shifting character of the age of Louis XV on those stilted figures. (*i*, 266)

In her study of *Indiana*, Clotilde Montaigne calls Laure a "cold and dominating woman" and compares her to Balzac's Foedora.[23] Yet although Laure is totally unlike Indiana, I would argue that she is not meant to be a negative character, any more than Raymon is. She is simply an appropriate partner for Raymon. Both are products of their society. They are equal in rank, intelligence, and experience of the world. Laure's legal inferiority with respect to her husband is counterbalanced by her superior "cleverness" (*I*, 293). The final image of her is one of strength, whereas Indiana cowers on her knees before Raymon and Laure. In this scene Laure speaks, while Raymon is silent, and she identifies herself as the owner of the property: "You are in my house, madame" (*I*, 302).

Both final pairings are better socially and emotionally than those at the outset of the novel, but neither is perfect. Ralph and Indiana live outside of society on an island paradise that is an escapist's dream. While they try to change that society by purchasing slaves, their efforts are limited by their financial resources and do not attack the roots themselves of law and convention. In addition, Ralph and Indiana's relationship borders on the incestuous. Ralph not only is Indiana's cousin but during her youth served as her father, while during her marriage he acted as a protective older brother. His confession to Indiana before their suicide attempt repeatedly uses different words of kinship: "I made you my sister, my daughter, my companion, my pupil, my world" (*I*, 322); "My kisses were those of a father . . . "(*I*, 324); "I swore . . . to never forget my role as your brother . . . " (*I*, 331); and, finally, "It is now I who am your brother, husband, lover forever more" (*I*, 336).

This overdetermined union is in accord with the romance tradition, though, for the bride won by the hero after his quest has a "psychological connection with the mother in an Oedipus fantasy . . . " (Frye, 193). Here, as throughout the novel, the roles have been reversed, and Ralph represents the father. Indiana has gone from marriage to an overt father figure, an older man, to union with a covert father figure. L'île Bourbon, then, represents a double return to the past for Ralph and Indiana. They go back not only to the physical setting of their childhood but to its emotional climate as well, repeating the close relationship that they had had in their youth while adding to it a sexual component. This is indeed the realization of a girl's oedipal fantasy.[24]

Indiana shows a further development of *Rose et Blanche* in that two women are involved with a man who turns out to be the wrong man, but the situation is righted in the end as Indiana discovers that Ralph is her ideal partner. The scene between Raymon and Noun, where Raymon imagines he is making love to Indiana, touches a raw nerve because of its oedipal content: the women are more than rivals in love, they are mother-daughter figures loved by the same man. That is why the scene disturbed Musset and continues to carry a strong erotic charge.

Raymon is a necessary transitional figure on two levels: he is the catalyst both in the romance plot, enabling Indiana to identify concepts inimical to her happiness, and in her relationship with Ralph. As the initial triangular situation was set up, Indiana never would have recognized Ralph's qualities, nor would Ralph ever have indulged in a relationship with Noun. In order for Indiana to turn from Delmare to Ralph, she has to pass through Raymon. This arrangement can be seen as a flaw in the novel, for Ralph's true personality and the depth of his love are kept hidden from Indiana until the end. His characterization relates to the problem of point of view and narration, for Ralph is essentially presented as Indiana saw him and not in an objective way, which gives rise to certain inconsistencies. Sand compressed her scenario further in subsequent novels, eliminating this intermediate figure and refining her presentation.

On the other hand, Laure and Raymon remain within the confines of society and conform to its rules. Theirs is not a love match but a marriage of convenience. Yet inasmuch as the solution of the île Bourbon is the stuff of romance and wish fulfillment, so is Lagny the site of contemporary social realism. Laure and Raymon are the ideal couple of 1830, and their marriage is of the kind often portrayed by Balzac, for it represents the union of bourgeois fortune and noble blood. Unlike Balzac, however, Sand is not interested in the source of these recent fortunes, but rather in their use.

George Sand's awareness of the economic realities of her time appeared discreetly in *Rose et Blanche*, where money and its ability to buy almost anything informs the plot in a significant way. Horace buys Lazare a boat as a recompense for having saved his life; later, after his rape of Denise, Horace pays her a pension and places her in a convent. He also resolves to pay for Rose's education in order to protect her from being forced to supplement her income through prostitution. Money, or lack of it, prevents Laorens from marrying Blanche, while the power money bestows helps Mlle Cazalès to bring pressure on Blanche and coerce her to marry Horace. As already indicated, the alliance of the nobility with the wealthy bourgeoisie is touched upon comically, as the girls in the convent stoically envisage the possibility of marriage with the heir to an industrial fortune as the only alternative to remaining single. In *Indiana*, economics forms an integral part of the plot as well. Sand describes in detail the financial situation of the characters and, like Jane Austen, gives specific figures.[25] This orientation is not surprising from a woman who was raised to run an important estate and who, as we have seen, was an astute businesswoman, both where Nohant and her book contracts were concerned.[26] Ralph has "fifty thousand francs in private income" (*I*, 108), while Laure de Nangy possesses "two millions" in capital (*I*, 293). Delmare is described as the "proprietor of a comfortable manor with its dependencies, and, what is more, a manufacturer fortunate in his speculations . . . "(*I*, 24).

In fact, Delmare's factory provides the underpinning of the plot. When caught climbing the wall of Delmare's property, Raymon does not admit that he is Noun's lover but rather explains that he came to spy on Delmare's manufacturing techniques. This excuse gains him entry to the factory, and his visit enables him to see Indiana again while kindling his relationship with Delmare. Delmare's commercial enterprise is soon threatened, however, due to the bankruptcy of a Belgian firm, and he must leave for Antwerp to ascertain the damage to his fortune. His absence from Lagny allows Raymon access to Indiana, while his unexpected return prevents Indiana's seduction. Indiana and Delmare are ruined by the Belgian failure and must sell Lagny to pay their creditors. The property is bought by M. Hubert, a wealthy industrialist who had adopted Laure after the death of her father, the former owner of the château Hubert had bought to invest his money. She therefore combines aristocratic blood with a bourgeois upbringing and a commercial fortune, making her an especially attractive partner. This background suits Raymon perfectly, for he seeks a wife of both rank and assets.

> Il appartenait à une haute et rigide famille qui ne souffrirait point de mésalliance, et pourtant la fortune ne résidait plus avec sécurité que chez les plébéiens. Selon toute apparence, cette classe allait s'élever sur les débris de l'autre,

et, pour se maintenir à la surface du mouvement, il fallait être le gendre d'un industriel ou d'un agioteur. (*I*, 263)

He belonged to a family of high rank and unbending pride which would brook no mésalliance, and yet wealth could no longer be considered secure except in plebeian hands. According to all appearance that class was destined to rise over the ruins of the other, and in order to maintain oneself on the surface of the movement one must be the son-in-law of a manufacturer or a stock-broker. (*i*, 243)

Raymon resolves to marry Laure in order to acquire this fortune, and she accepts him. This marriage precipitates the end of the novel, as Indiana at last acknowledges Raymon's true character and subsequently learns to understand Ralph.

The end of *Indiana*, then, posits two distinct options: one can either try to accept the new bourgeois society or withdraw completely from it. The latter solution is more valorized emotionally, although it is also recognized as the less feasible, while the more realistic solution is shown to be the way of the future.

[I]l faut trop d'énergie pour rompre avec le monde, trop de douleurs pour acquérir cette énergie. . . . Allez, jeune homme, poursuivez le cours de votre destinée; ayez des amis, un état, une réputation, une patrie. . . . Ne rompez point les chaînes qui vous lient à la société. . . . (*I*, 353)

[T]oo much energy is required to break with society, and too much suffering to acquire that energy. . . . Go, young man, follow the course of your destiny; have friends, a profession, a reputation, a fatherland. . . . Do not break the chains that bind you to society. . . . (*i*, 327)

This dual conclusion is typical of the art romance, as Jameson has defined it: "Romance as a form thus expresses a transitional moment, yet one of a very special type: its contemporaries must feel their society torn between past and future in such a way that the alternatives are grasped as hostile but somehow unrelated worlds" (Jameson, 158).

George Sand, like others of her contemporaries, particularly Stendhal and Hugo, is using this form as a symbolic attempt "to come to terms with the triumph of the bourgeoisie and the new and unglamorous social forms developing out of the market system" (Jameson, 158), with the important difference that she welcomes rather than fears these changes. Charles Rabou was absolutely right in comparing Sand to a professor of Social Economics.

Sand is at a crucial point in the development of her social thought. On the one hand, she promotes the new order of intermarriage between classes even before it becomes fashionable to do so.[27] On the other hand, she is far from suggesting the radical class modifications portrayed in some of her later works. The resolution of the novel's romantic entanglements produces not only emotional stability but traditional class conformity as well. Both members of each couple are of equal social rank, whereas the initial couples represented less socially acceptable alliances.[28] Despite the reestablishment of more normative unions, there is a clear *embourgeoisement* in the lifestyle of both couples and a willing acceptance of the end of *ancien régime* social practices. Sand is above all pragmatic, here as in most of her novels, in her economic vision; she knew that total abolition of class distinctions was utopian and unrealistic, whereas her proposed marriages were not, as the nineteenth century was to prove.

The requirements of the art romance narrowly correspond to those of Sand's family romance, and she has brilliantly cast her own, special scenario in an original literary form. She has made the quest romance accessible to a heroine, while giving it a purely psychological and social dimension and eliminating the physical adventures. Sand created the kind of novel Hugo envisioned, a contemporary amalgam of idealism and realism: "After the picturesque, but prosaic, novel of Walter Scott, there will be another novel left to create, more beautiful and more complete, in our opinion. It is the novel that is both drama and epic poem, picturesque but poetic, real, but ideal, true, but great, which will combine Walter Scott with Homer."[29] The review of *Indiana* that appeared in the *Journal des Débats* on July 21, 1832, uses similar language in describing the novel as "pages both ideal and true that only a woman could have written. Let us all thank her for having dared to do so."[30] The synthesis forged in *Indiana* was an impressive achievement both for Sand and for the nineteenth-century novel.

4 🐌

VALENTINE
Tristan and Iseut in the Berry

George Sand turned again to the romance for her second novel, *Valentine*. Written shortly after *Indiana* and published in the same year, this work contains an adaptation of a well-known literary tradition from the Middle Ages that has had far-reaching influence on French literature: the tragic love story of Tristan and Iseut.[1] Sand did not repeat the Tristan story literally but rather recast it by retaining salient features and episodes of the legend while transferring the action to her era and her province. In so doing, she demonstrated that the ancient story lost nothing of its impact in the translation.

The parallels between *Valentine* and the Tristan story are striking, both in plot and in thematics.[2] In addition, the fundamental structure of the Tristan romance, which involves not only the Tristan-Iseut-Mark love triangle but subsidiary triangles, as well as doubles and repeated scenes, corresponds to that of *Valentine* and is especially suited to the exigencies of Sand's creative imagination. As with *Indiana*, in *Valentine* Sand combines an established form with her own contemporary social vision, making the novel another example of what Jameson has termed "the art romances of the Romantic period" (Jameson, 158).

Blond like Iseut, Valentine meets with Bénédict through music, as in the case of Tristan and Iseut in Ireland. Music continues to be an important motif in the development of their love. The relationships in both the legend and the novel begin as friendship, for each woman is already betrothed to another when she falls in love; in each case, illicit love predates marriage and continues afterwards. Furthermore, these marriages are arranged and are designed to do more than simply unite the partners. Mark hopes to bring peace with Ireland by marrying Iseut, while M. de Lansac expects to pay his debts with Valentine's property.

Bénédict, an orphan like Tristan, is raised by an uncle and aunt. Both

he and Valentine, like their counterparts in the legend, have obligations
to their families that would prevent their marrying, even if the difference
in their social conditions were not an obstacle. Bénédict and Tristan owe
debts of loyalty to their uncles—Bénédict for his education and upbringing,
Tristan because he originally sought Iseut to be Mark's bride—while Valentine and Iseut must obey their mothers' wishes. Sand has kept the uncle
figure in M. Lhéry, who is Bénédict's uncle and foster father, as was Mark
to Tristan, although M. Lhéry is not also Valentine's husband. This pattern
is also repeated in the Bénédict-Valentin relationship, where Bénédict acts
as a foster father to Valentine's nephew. Valentin becomes the child Bénédict and Valentine never have and prefigures Valentine II, the child of
Athénaïs and Valentin, who is herself a double of Valentine.

Both works show a similar oscillation between sexuality and abstinence,
desire fulfilled and controlled. Tristan and Iseut, having drunk the love
potion, give in to their desires. In order to fool Mark into thinking his
bride a virgin, they ask Brangien to substitute for Iseut on the wedding
night. By contrast, Bénédict and Valentine do not consummate their love
until late in the novel. Valentine remains virgin until then for she spends
her wedding night apart from her husband, who leaves soon thereafter on
business. She does spend the night chastely with Bénédict, however. As in
Indiana, Sand has again reversed the gender of the protagonist, for instead
of a substitute bride, we find in *Valentine* a surrogate bridegroom.

This scene is a key one in the novel, as in the romance. It marks a turning
point in Valentine and Bénédict's relationship, for under the influence of
opium, taken to help her sleep, Valentine admits her love to Bénédict for
the first time. Valentine has had recourse to the drug because her faithful
servant Catherine had forgotten to prepare her mistress's usual sleeping
potion. The substitute bride(groom) scene, then, in both cases depends on
the servant's carelessness, and in both is attributable to a potion. Like Brangien, Catherine continues to serve her mistress during Valentine's affair
with Bénédict.

The mystical nature of this night is underlined by Bénédict's thoughts:
"Alone at her feet, in the solemn nocturnal silence, protected by her artificial
sleep that it was not in his power to interrupt, he felt he was fulfilling a
magic destiny" (V, 192). Valentine responds unconsciously to Bénédict's
caresses, and for a short time thinks that she has married him instead of
Lansac. Bénédict's love for Valentine is shown to be eternal and extraordinary. His love is spiritual as well as physical, and in spending this night
with Valentine, he has possessed her completely, more fully than if he had
slept with her.

Love and death are inexorably linked in this scene, as they are when
Tristan and Iseut drink the love potion.[3] Valentine even dreams of death:

" 'Let us die together!' she said to him" (*V*, 194). Death even more than love brought Bénédict to Valentine's room in the first place. Originally, he had intended to kill her husband, then himself, but he missed the opportunity. He subsequently resolves to kill either Lansac or Valentine to preserve her from the indignities of the wedding night. Once he is reassured that Lansac has left the château, he envisions a murder-suicide as the only answer to his dilemma. Love and death struggle for preeminence as Bénédict loses the courage to kill first Valentine, then himself, but refrains from giving in to his desire to possess her physically after learning that she in fact does love him. He decides at last that the best solution is to kill himself. In a foreshadowing of the conclusion, the attraction of death prevails over desire, and Bénédict prepares to shoot himself after leaving Valentine a farewell letter.

Against all odds, Bénédict survives his suicide attempt. After regaining consciousness, he still insists that he would prefer to die and be followed by Valentine, for he knows that the news of his condition has made her ill. The doctor mandates that they be brought together, to cure each other; like Iseut, whose healing powers twice cure Tristan, Valentine becomes not only Bénédict's nurse but the very balm that makes him well again.

After their recovery, Valentine and Bénédict spend fifteen idyllic months together in a *petit pavillon* on Valentine's property that she has arranged as a quiet retreat for them and their intimates; this period corresponds to Tristan and Iseut's perfect love in the forest. Like the original pair, Valentine and Bénédict pass their time with music and reading, in a setting that is described as the "Elysian fields" (*V*, 249), just as the legend's forest scene represents Adam and Eve's earthly paradise.[4] "It was like an enchanted island in the middle of real life, like an oasis in the desert" (*V*, 250). Both husbands penetrate this world but, for their own private reasons, ignore the indications of the lovers' affair. Mark leaves signs of his presence so the lovers will know that he has been at their cave. Similarly, Lansac uses the pavilion to inform Valentine about the financial transactions that would take place the next day. She infers from his tone and his conduct that he knows everything about her situation vis-à-vis Bénédict, who overhears the entire conversation.

Valentine undertakes to enlist Lansac's help in resisting her love for Bénédict. This interview owes much to Lafayette's celebrated avowal scene from *La Princesse de Clèves*.[5] Lansac, like King Mark, does nothing to end Valentine's relationship with Bénédict; in fact, he turns his back on her when she implores his protection. "You see me about to fall into a chasm that I detest, and, when I beg you to hold out your hand to help me, you push me over the edge with your foot" (*V*, 288). Having practically given her his blessing, Lansac leaves for Russia, and Valentine and Bénédict continue to see each other, as did Tristan and Iseut upon returning to the court. It is at this point that Valentine and Bénédict consummate their affair.

Once Tristan and Iseut return to court from the forest, their affair cannot proceed as before, and their separation is inevitable.[6] It is likewise clear from the moment Lansac returns that the idyll Valentine and Bénédict have known in their secret world is over. "Yes, madame, we were happy, but we won't be any longer!" exclaims Bénédict (V, 271). The end of the novel arrives quickly and inevitably, as Valentine and Bénédict succumb to their passion but must separate temporarily after her property is sold to satisfy Lansac's debts. Valentine goes to live with the Lhérys, where Bénédict dies just as Valentine has learned that Lansac's death in a duel has freed her to marry her lover.

Bénédict and Tristan both die because of a misunderstanding fueled by jealousy, deliberate in the one case and inadvertent in the other. Tristan's death is attributable to Iseut aux Blanches Mains's lie about the color of the sails on the boat bearing Iseut to cure him of a poison wound. Bénédict is mortally wounded not by a lance but by a pitchfork, because Georges Simonneau had told Pierre Blutty that Bénédict was seeing Pierre's wife, Athénaïs; neither knows or suspects that Valentine is the object of Bénédict's love. Tristan's wound was obtained in a fight to help another regain his captured lady, a situation that is reversed in *Valentine*, where Simonneau and Blutty join forces to ambush the man they take for the seducer.

Iseut and Valentine die of grief and are united with their lovers in death. On Tristan and Iseut's tomb grow an intertwining rose and vine, symbol of their inseparability.[7] Bénédict and Valentine's double grave is covered with primroses. The romance model, in which death accompanies love from the time of drinking the love potion and ultimately triumphs, prefigures the ascendancy of death over love in *Valentine*.

Death haunts Bénédict and Valentine even after the wedding-night scene, as he repeatedly threatens to kill himself either alone or with Valentine so that they may at last be united and their misery ended. Love in *Valentine* is neither happy nor pleasurable; rather, it causes the utmost pain and suffering, so that death would be a release. Bénédict prays to God to deliver him from the torments of his love: "Take pity on me . . . ; recall my soul to your kingdom, snuff out this devouring breath that consumes my lungs and tortures my life; do me the favor of allowing me to die" (V, 303). Valentine, too, sees their love as fatal and speaks of succumbing to her *destinée* (V, 226, 287) in such a way that the word means not simply fate, but doom. An affair that is described as "a perpetual combat, a storm always recommencing, a pleasure without end and a hell without escape" (V, 305) cannot and will not lead to a happily-ever-after ending. Union in death is all Valentine and Bénédict expect from their love, and that is what they obtain.

The role of Louise finds its complement in the Tristan story as well. Louise is the figuration of Iseut aux Blanches Mains. Her function in the text is like that of Iseut II, whom Tristan chose second because she reminded him of the original Iseut, but whom he did not love despite her passion for him. The identity of the two Iseuts, manifested in their bearing the same name, is repeated in the kinship of Valentine and Louise, who are half sisters. Louise loves Bénédict, who initially was attracted to her before his meeting with Valentine; later, he merely wants to be her friend. Louise, however, continues to love him. She nurses him after his suicide attempt, as Iseut II cares for Tristan at the end of the story, and insists she loves him more than she does Valentine. Jealousy dictates her behavior, as it motivates Iseut II's fatal lie. "In an instant, friendship, compassion, generosity, all noble feelings went out of her heart; she could not find a better vengeance than to humiliate Valentine" (*V*, 233).

Valentine and Louise's encounter after Bénédict's death parallels the two Iseuts' confrontation over Tristan's deathbed. Here, though, it is Louise who berates Valentine, whereas in the original, Iseut does the talking. In a sense, Louise's speech represents what Iseut II might have said, had she been given the opportunity.

> "Ainsi . . . c'est vous qui l'avez tué! . . . Vous ne savez pas comme je l'aimais, cet homme qui est mort! mais vous lui avez jeté un charme, et il ne voyait plus clair autour de lui. Oh! je l'aurais rendu heureux, moi!" (*V*, 329–30)

> "Thus . . . it is you who killed him! You don't know how I loved the dead man! but you put him under a spell, and he couldn't see clearly around him. Oh! I would have made him happy!"

Like Iseut aux Blanches Mains, Louise survives the death of the lovers.

In *Valentine*, the recurrence of the theme of fatal love, as well as the basic plot of the Tristan story, is uncanny. The underlying structure of the romance also corresponds to that of *Valentine*, for both are generational sagas based on triangular relationships. The central romantic triangle is accompanied by several others. All evolve via a series of substitutions, of which the substitute bride(groom) is the most important. There is more than a suggestion of incest in the permutations of this figure, as in the Tristan story; at the very least, the kinship relations are all overdetermined.

The number and complexity of relationships depicted in *Valentine* are extraordinary. The novel opens with a geometric configuration (3 + 2) similar to that found at the beginning of *Indiana*. Athénaïs is engaged to her cousin Bénédict, who is attracted to Louise de Raimbault, while Valentine is engaged to M. de Lansac. Upon meeting Valentine, Bénédict soon forgets Louise. Louise has recently returned to the area in secret after a long absence caused by her having been sent away after she had borne an illegitimate child. This child, called Valentin, was the result of Louise's affair with a man who was at the same time her stepmother's lover and whom Louise's father killed in a duel. Louise is enough older than Valentine to have been like a mother to her younger sister. The Valentine-Louise-Bénédict love triangle, then, repeats Louise's original triangular relationship with her stepmother and their lover, and Bénédict's death in the end repeats that of the earlier lover. The deaths of both men, as Louise herself points out, are attributable to a member of the Raimbault family.

Bénédict also breaks his engagement with Athénaïs, who in many ways is the double of Valentine. They are approximately the same age and were brought up together as friends. Although Athénaïs is the daughter of peasants, and Valentine the daughter of a count, it is Valentine who has simple tastes and humble aspirations, while Athénaïs wears fancy clothes and amply fulfills her parents' ambitions for her social success. Still in love with Bénédict, Athénaïs weds Pierre Blutty on the day that Valentine goes through with her marriage to Lansac, despite her feelings for Bénédict. In the end, Pierre Blutty's continued jealousy of Athénaïs's affection for Bénédict results in the latter's death. Thus, Bénédict participates simultaneously in two different triangles: Bénédict-Valentine-Lansac, and Bénédict-Athénaïs-Pierre Blutty. Similarly, Tristan is involved both with Mark and Iseut, as well as with the two Iseuts.

Athénaïs later becomes engaged in a new triangle, for, as her marriage to Pierre becomes less happy and her love for Bénédict turns into friendly affection, she is more and more attracted to Valentin, Louise's son. This relationship is simultaneously innocent and guilty and also hints of incest. Athénaïs and Valentin start out as friends. When they meet, Athénaïs is only seventeen and already married, Valentin, a mere fifteen and still practically a boy. Athénaïs treats him like a younger companion as they spend much time together in the pavilion. Their childish games soon become serious, and both are strongly attracted to each other. Their initial fraternal relationship turns into marriage, for Pierre Blutty's death one year after Bénédict's frees Athénaïs to wed Valentin.

This marriage, which does not take place until several years later, after Valentin has finished his studies and become a doctor, mitigates the tragedy of Bénédict and Valentine's death by uniting them symbolically in the persons of Bénédict's cousin and Valentine's nephew. It also makes concrete the spiritual survival of the lovers implicit in the intertwining branches on the grave of Tristan and Iseut, or the primroses on Bénédict and Valentine's tomb. Again, Sand has adapted her model, creating a new and positive ending with important social implications.

Valentin and Athénaïs's marriage differs from those of *Rose et Blanche* and *Indiana* in that it combines aristocratic blood and title with peasant wealth rather than bourgeois fortune. Valentin is not simply an idle aristocrat, however, for despite his title and Athénaïs's money, he practices medicine in the region, another sign of Sand's middle-class ideals introduced in *Indiana*. Valentine, too, although nobly born and raised, shares none of her mother's class prejudices. Sand presents in *Valentine* an unusual view of the peasantry for her time, emphasizing the money, education, and social aspirations peasants had acquired since the Revolution. "You don't want to believe that today everyone in France is educated! These people are rich; they have helped their children develop their talents," Valentine's grandmother informs her incredulous daughter-in-law (*V*, 86). The difference between the Lhérys, rude peasants who had earned their fortune by hard work, and their daughter, whom they raise like a lady, shows the increased blurring of social distinctions in Restoration France.

Money and class play as great a role in *Valentine* as in the author's previous two works. Sand again gives the kind of specific figures that allow the reader to follow the evolution of the characters' financial status. Bénédict has "five hundred pounds in private income" (*V*, 140), which he doubles over the course of the novel. Athénaïs inherits 200,000 francs from an uncle. Valentine insists she would be happy with "twelve hundred francs in private income" (*V*, 273). Lansac owes nearly 500,000 francs, an enormous sum that he expects to pay by selling the property Valentine has brought to the marriage; this sale reduces her to a capital of 20,000 francs. In fact, *Valentine* is as much the story of the Raimbault property as it is that of the Raimbault sisters.[8]

The estate, which had been sold during the Revolution as "biens nationaux" (national property), had been bought back by the count de Raimbault with the dowry of his second wife, "mademoiselle Chignon, daughter of a rich manufacturer . . ." (*V*, 74), a situation that recalls M. Hubert's in *Indiana*. This marriage, the narrator goes on to say, had been blessed by Napoleon himself, who "loved to unite old names and new fortunes . . ." (*V*, 74), and is typical of the Empire, in which classes mingled more easily than before, or after. The successful result of the alliance of title and bourgeois fortune, the reconstitution of the former splendor of the château and lands of Raimbault is brutally destroyed by the sale of the property to satisfy the debts of Lansac.

The comte de Lansac is an example of the decadent aristocracy, a man who has run up debts beyond his own income and who marries purely for money. His wife's happiness is of little consequence to him. During the engagement he plays the role of the deferential fiancé but intends to maintain his freedom after marriage by leaving Valentine in France while he pursues his career—and his mistress—in Russia. Lansac's death in a duel, an illegal but quintessentially *ancien régime* practice, seems a fitting end to a lifestyle that the French could no longer afford to support.

It is the Lhérys who eventually buy the Raimbault property and recreate Mlle Chignon's dream of restoring its grandeur. They go even further, however, for they are good and charitable, whereas Valentine's mother was selfish and unpleasant. The château becomes not only a showplace but the seat of hospitality as well, as the Lhérys share their good fortune with the community. These peasants move several rungs up the social ladder, from the cottage they inhabit in the beginning to the château they possess at the end. Their daughter acquires a title with her marriage, and their granddaughter will have a much easier life than they did. Yet the Lhérys are not ambitious in the way Mlle Chignon was; unlike her, they do not sacrifice their daughter's happiness to their own political aspirations. They merely hope to enjoy the fruits of their labors and offer their family a better life.

Like *Indiana* before it, *Valentine* ends with two different social and romantic options. Valentine and Bénédict have been reduced to equal economic status by the sale of Valentine's property; in fact, Bénédict is now slightly richer. Despite this newfound equality, Valentine and Bénédict do not marry and live happily ever after in their thatched cottage, as Bénédict dreams they will when he learns of Lansac's death. They die to make way for another couple, which is paradoxically both conventional and nontraditional.

Valentin is an illegitimate son, yet he is the comte de Raimbault, while his wife is a rich and cultivated peasant. Theirs is at once a morganatic marriage and the marriage of complementaries, each bringing different assets to the union. Although less radical than a Valentine-Bénédict marriage, where the woman is of higher social rank, Athénaïs and Valentin's marriage repeats those of the Napoleonic era (that of the comte de Raimbault and Mlle Chignon, for example) while breaking down class divisions even further. Their daughter, the new Valentine, will have all the social advantages of her great-aunt and more: she will grow up in a loving home, with parents who are each able to teach her different skills and values. The repetition of the name and character of the novel's heroine underscores the cyclical nature of the story, with the difference that the younger Valentine will have the guidance and care that her great-aunt lacked and therefore, presumably, a happier life. Personally as well as socially, this resolution produces beneficial results.

The final configurations of the novel reenact those of the beginning, recalling those of *Indiana* as well. Where the Lhérys cottage contained two parents and their daughter, along with her cousin/fiancé, the Raimbault château shelters Valentine II and her parents, along with their parents, Louise and the Lhérys. This group (minus Valentine II) divides up along the same lines as that of *Indiana*: a parent/child relationship plus a happy, equal couple. Louise, Valentin, and Athénaïs reproduce M. Hubert, Laure, and Raymon's arrangement, while the Lhérys recall Indiana and Ralph. "Are we not the same age, you and I? has that made us any less happy?" asks Mme Lhéry of her husband (*V*, 332–333). In both novels, the parent figures are firmly fixed in their role at the end without the ambiguity and sexual equivocation that reigned at the beginning: M. Hubert is Laure's (step)father whereas Delmare was Indiana's fatherly husband; Louise is Valentin's mother and Valentine II's grandmother, and not the sexual rival she was for Valentine. The triangle has become a threesome. At the end, the potentially unstable arrangements have come to a stasis, and there is no confusion in relationships or bloodlines. Yet, paradoxically, the very insistence on the purely parental role of Hubert and Louise betrays an anxiety on Sand's part about the possibility of a parent who is more than just a parent.

In *Indiana*, I have argued that the Ralph-Indiana couple forms an oedipal union that is successful and productive. The case is quite different in *Valentine*. Why is the oedipal relationship, that of Bénédict and Valentine, short-circuited in the later novel? The explanation of their failure to marry lies in the continued presence of Louise, the mother figure. Noun, Indiana's rival, commits suicide and is no longer a threat to her mistress. Louise, however, remains in the novel and continues to love Bénédict. Her jealousy of Valentine is frequently underscored. Louise is a literal mother figure as well as a half-sister to Valentine. " 'Why are you using the formal *vous*?' asked Louise; 'Are we not sisters?' 'Oh! It is because you are also my mother!' responded Valentine" (*V*, 60–61). In this scene, as throughout the novel, they insist on the mother-daughter aspect of their relationship. Furthermore, as described above, the Louise-Bénédict-Valentine triangle reproduces the very bizarre earlier triangle composed of Louise, her stepmother, and their mutual lover, just as Aurore Dupin's family repeated the Maurice-Madame Dupin-Sophie triangle Sand insists upon in *Histoire de ma vie*. The rivalry of mother and daugther for the same man constitutes the oedipal situation. My reading of both these triangles therefore posits them as oedipal in nature, even though Bénédict is not otherwise described as a father figure. Thus, for Valentine and Bénédict to marry while Louise is still alive would be an impossible occurrence because the daughter's fantasized union with the father presupposes the disappearance of the mother. As Louise's previous experience has shown, the presence of the mother in this kind of situation leads to tragedy, not fulfillment:

> "Mon amant immolé par mon père; mon père lui-même, abreuvé de douleur et de honte par ma faute, cherchant et trouvant la mort quelques jours après sur un champ de bataille; moi, bannie, chassée honteusement du toit paternel, et réduite à traîner ma misère de ville en ville avec mon enfant mourant de faim dans mes bras! Ah! Valentine, c'est là une horrible destinée!" (*V*, 236)

> "My lover sacrificed by my father; my father himself, sick with suffering and shame through my fault, looking for and finding death a few days later on a battlefield; I, banished, shamefully thrown out of my father's house and reduced to dragging my miserable self from city to city with my child dying of hunger in my arms. Ah! Valentine, that is a horrible fate!"

The solution to this explosive triangle (since Valentine and Bénédict are lovers, after all), is the union in death of Valentine and Bénédict and their replacement by Athénaïs and Valentin; since the mother remains, the daughter is sacrificed, whereas in *Indiana* the opposite was the case. At the end of *Valentine* there is no rivalry between Athénaïs and her daughter or between Athénaïs and Louise. Louise, the disapproving, sexually competitive mother, becomes the doting grandmother who has clearly withdrawn from the romantic arena: "The time for passion is behind her; a shade of religious melancholia has spread over her everyday thoughts" (*V*, 334).

Athénaïs and Valentin essentially repeat the Valentine-Bénédict relationship within difference, for Bénédict and Athénaïs are cousins and Valentine and Valentin are aunt and nephew; their daughter, Valentine, bears the same bloodlines that the child of Bénédict and Valentine would have had. Therefore, in some sense Sand nonetheless fulfills her oedipal dream indirectly, for the younger Valentine represents the offspring of the oedipal Bénédict-Valentine relationship. Perhaps for that reason Valentin and Athénaïs's early relationship is shown to be somewhat incestuous, although in a different way, since it is a fraternal friendship that has been sexualized. Like Valentine, and Indiana before her, Athénaïs achieves this kind of union only after an initial marriage to a brutal, uncomprehending man. Furthermore, the similarity of the names Valentin-Valentine establishes a special link between father and daughter. Valentin himself is the result of the original oedipal triangle involving Louise and her stepmother, thus accentuating this incestuous means of reproduction. The potential is established for another oedipal couple in the future, even if the present denies such a possibility. *Valentine* thus doubly asserts the kind of relationship it seeks to repress.

The final picture of life in the Raimbault château mirrors George Sand's fantasy of what her own childhood should have been like. A grandmother, loving parents, and a granddaughter live in a château, as Nohant was called according to a different sense of the word. The son, although illegitimate, has noble blood, as did Maurice Dupin. Even though Sand's father was the offspring of a lawful marriage, the paternal side of her family was noted for its illegitimacy, as she herself acknowledges in her autobiography:

> . . . [S]i, de ce côté [paternel], je me trouve d'une manière illégitime, mais fort réelle, proche parente de Charles X et de Louis XVIII, il n'en est pas moins vrai que je tiens au peuple par le sang, d'une manière tout aussi intime et directe; de plus, il n'y a point de bâtardise de ce côté-là. (*Oa* I, 15–16)
> . . . [(I]f, on this [paternal] side, I find myself in a real, if illegitimate, way, to be a close relative of Charles X and Louis XVIII, it is just as true that I am linked to the popular classes by my blood, in the same intimate and direct way; in addition, there is no bastardy on that side of the family.

The daughter-in-law, a commoner, is a widow, but she falls in love with her second husband while still married to her first husband. Sophie Dupin was purportedly widowed during the Revolution and the mistress of a fellow soldier when Maurice fell in love with her. She was older than Maurice, as Athénaïs is older than Valentin. Both women have faults stemming primarily from an incomplete education, which are corrected by an indulgent husband. "Athenais was good, she was happy; her husband, endowed with Valentine's excellent character and reason, easily dominated her and corrected many of her faults" (*V*, 333). Happy and beautiful, their daughter is the object of her grandmother's affection. "Her greatest joy is to raise her blond and fair granddaughter . . ." (*V*, 334). The girl is given a family name, as Aurore Dupin had received that of her grandmother and great-great-grandmother.

Sand had experienced a similar family arrangement for two months, from July to September 1808. Maurice's untimely death brutally disrupted this happy situation. Sand's subsequent years of childhood, torn between her mother and her grandmother, are well known. She did not choose to record this situation in her novel but instead depicted her dream of the perfect family life. As in *Rose et Blanche*, Sand realized her most intimate wishes in a literary way by putting herself in the place of Fate, who had ruled that her parents not live happily ever after.

Or was it simply fate that Maurice Dupin died so unexpectedly in an accident? Did his daughter perhaps have guilt feelings about causing his death, as is common in children? In the novel, Louise accuses Valentine of having killed Bénédict and Valentine fully accepts that responsibility. She then dies herself. Sand has compensated in *Valentine* for her wishes that were destructive to the family unit by eliminating the daughter and reestablishing the proper family configuration, thus denying both her forbidden desires and her father's death. *Valentine* therefore ends Sand's scenario differently from *Indiana*, and the two novels can be read as a diptych, with the earlier work showing a positive outcome and the later novel a negative one to the same basic situation.

   Valentine is for many reasons a less successful novel than *Indiana*. Although it was well received by the contemporary press as a worthy successor to *Indiana*, particularly as far as its arguments against conventional marriage were concerned, *Valentine* simply does not have the incisiveness of Sand's first novel. Valentine is not the kind of inspirational heroine Indiana was, nor does she analyze her experiences of society as Indiana does. Rather, it is up to the reader to deduce Sand's admittedly trenchant commentaries on marriage, which becomes nothing more than an economic transaction that leaves women powerless to prevent their own despoliation. Otherwise, as a feminist work, *Valentine* is surprisingly thin compared with *Indiana*. Only in its social and financial program does *Valentine* match and even surpass *Indiana*. Sand's literary innovations are also more circumscribed than previously. She has made the medieval epic contemporary and given it a new ending, which satisfies her own plot but contradicts the death theme both of the legend and of the novel.

   Ultimately, *Valentine* is a work that in many ways is less than the sum of its parts. In her article "Eléments pour une lecture de *Valentine*," Mireille Bossis asks two penetrating questions, whose answers are neither evident nor simple: "First, is it a novel that ends well or badly? What is its message?" In essence, *Valentine* is a novel that ends happily despite its tragic plot, even though that ending is made possible only after four characters die violently, as Bossis points out.[9] George Sand has imbued the novel with her own phantasms to such an extent that the purely fictional aspect of the work suffers, as demonstrated by the fact that after 334 pages the reader cannot decide how to evaluate the ending. The novel is unfocused, so that it is difficult to know exactly whose story is being told; the title could just as easily have been *Louise*, *Bénédict*, or even *Athénaïs*. This ambiguity and lack of correlation between the title and what appears to be the main character will reappear with increasing frequency in Sand's novels and is symptomatic of the psychological needs that underlie her work. *André* is really Geneviève's story, *Jacques* concerns Sylvia and Fernande as much as Jacques, and *La Petite Fadette* devotes considerable space to the twins Landry and Sylvinet.

   A look at the *Notice* to the novel, written in 1852, sheds some light on what Sand herself was trying to express in this curious work, even though the introduction was written twenty years later and cannot be taken literally.

> Je retournai dans le Berri en 1832, et je me plus à peindre la nature que j'avais sous les yeux depuis mon enfance. Dès ces jours-là, j'avais éprouvé le besoin de la décrire; mais, par un phénomène qui accompagne toutes les émotions profondes, dans l'ordre moral comme dans l'ordre intellectuel, c'est ce qu'on désire le plus manifester, qu'on ose le moins aborder en public. . . .
>
> . . . Tout cela n'avait de charmes que pour moi, et ne méritait pas d'être révélé aux indifférents. Pourquoi trahir l'*incognito* de cette contrée modeste . . . ? Il me semblait que la vallée Noire, c'était moi-même, c'était le cadre, le vêtement de ma propre existence. . . . (V, 1–2)

> I returned to the Berry in 1832, and I enjoyed painting the natural beauty I had beheld since childhood. Since that time, I had felt the need to describe it; but, by a phenomenon that accompanies all deep emotions, moral as well as intellectual, it is that which one wishes to reveal most that one dares least bring up in public. . . .
>
> . . . All of this held fascination for me alone, and did not deserve to be revealed to those who were indifferent. Why should I betray the incognito of this modest province . . . ? It seemed to me that the Black Valley was me, was the frame, the dress of my own existence. . . .

In speaking of the natural beauty of her native province, Sand also describes herself. She makes the parallel explicit when she states that "the Black Valley was me." Although the object *la* of the second sentence refers to *la nature* ("j'avais éprouvé le besoin de la décrire"), it could also, logically and grammatically, refer to *mon enfance*. What she felt the need to describe was her childhood as much as her province. In point of fact, Sand did not evoke the Berry in *Valentine* to quite the extent she alleges in this *Notice*, at least not in the way she would integrate the province, its people and customs, into her later novels; except for a few touches of local color ("la bourrée," "les traînes"), *Valentine* could be set anywhere in rural France. She did, however, portray her childhood, albeit in an indirect way. Consciously, she was describing her region. Unconsciously, she was playing out the drama of her intimate desires.

This *Notice* shows that the novel was written under the sign of repression. Sand admits herself that "it is that which one wishes to reveal most that one dares least bring up in public." Just as her province had significance for her alone, so did her innermost thoughts and desires. Yet, as she revealed or, to use her apt word, "betrayed" the identity of her province, she also manifested her own secret emotions and dreams, which were really the subject she wanted to treat. Since her childhood was so closely associated with the Berry, writing about the one automatically meant unveiling the other, but in such a way that no one, not even herself, would discern the subtext. Indeed, in the decade following *Valentine*, Sand again lavishly documented her province in what have become known as the *romans champêtres*: *La Mare au diable*, *François le Champi*, and *La Petite Fadette*, all of which contain the familiar oedipal scenario. *Valentine*, despite its shortcomings, marks an important step in Sand's creative development.

5 🐚

LÉLIA

Both *Indiana* and *Valentine* firmly established Sand's reputation as a writer. The beauty of Sand's prose was hailed, and her criticisms of men, marriage, and society, tolerantly approved. She was, after all, a member of the iconoclastic romantic generation that had brought new and daring themes to French literature. *Lélia* received a very different reception from that of the first two works. The reaction was sharply mixed, with Capo de Feuillide writing a particularly vituperative attack on the novel that led Sand's friend Gustave Planche to fight a duel with the critic.

Although there was almost universal agreement that the style of *Lélia* was beautiful—"Otherwise, in no other of her novels has the author shown more magic and charm of style"[1]—the form and the ideas were either lauded or castigated. Planche, who had had a strong influence on the evolution of the novel, assured readers of the *Revue des Deux Mondes* that *Lélia* "will begin an explosive revolution in contemporary literature and will give the death blow to purely *visible* poetry" (*L*, xxxvii). Musset, in a review he never published, denied that *Lélia* would produce a revolution;[2] however, he found the novel original and praised it highly in a letter to Sand as a work that defined her as an author, not a lady novelist.[3] Sainte-Beuve wrote a fairly balanced review for *Le National* and concluded that writing *Lélia* was a courageous act for Sand. "Whatever you might think, *Lélia*, with its faults and excesses, is a book that largely deserved to be written. If the reports of the moment are against it, the very violence of this clamor is enough proof of the audaciousness of the enterprise" (*L*, 594).

The negative critics did not mince words in excoriating Sand and her novel. *Le Petit Poucet* called *Lélia* a "work of lewdness and cynicism" (*L*, 589), while the relentless Capo de Feuillide wrote that the novel contained "the prostitution of soul and body."[4] Both he and Léon Gozlan felt that *Lélia* was not a work to be read by women, for it would contaminate them. Since Sand herself was a woman, the implication in these criticisms is that she was somehow corrupt. In fact, Capo de Feuillide compared her to Sade!

The question of the author's gender intervened in the critique of *Lélia* in a different way than in the past. Early critics knew for the most part that G(eorge)(s) Sand was a woman, although some thought they could discern male and female hands at work in *Indiana*, probably because they were aware of her former collaboration with Sandeau. Sand's gender did not play a large role in the evaluation of *Indiana* and *Valentine*; if anything, the fact of her being a woman brought her sympathy or was seen as the cause of her sensitivity to certain issues. With *Lélia*, the situation changed. *Le Petit Poucet* doubted that the author of such a novel could be a woman. The *Journal général de la littérature française* ascribed *Lélia* to a male author and thought that the work would perhaps not be of interest to women (*L*, 586). On the other hand, Planche felt that women especially would find in *Lélia* their own history and see the novel as an apologia for their suffering and helplessness, not an accusation against them. Jules Janin published a long article in *L'Artiste* in 1836, reprinted in other periodicals as well, in which he attributes male and female genders to Sand and describes *Lélia* as the work of a woman against women:

> Cette fois, George Sand quittant ce chaste manteau viril dont elle s'était en-veloppée avec tant de courage et d'énergie, a voulu se montrer plus qu'une femme, c'est-à-dire dans sa pensée, deux fois plus qu'un homme, et elle est tombée dans les plus graves excès. . . . George Sand, redevenu une femme, dans ce livre qui est écrit contre les femmes, devait ainsi porter la peine de ce déguisement.[5]

> This time, George Sand, taking off the vast virile coat in which she had en-veloped herself with so much courage and energy, wanted to show herself more than a woman, that is, in her thought, twice as much as a man, and she has fallen into the gravest excesses. . . . George Sand, having gone back to being a woman, in this book which is written against women, should thus pay the penalty of this disguise.

Sainte-Beuve also devotes fully one-third of his article in the *National* to the question of women authors, whom he applauds for their efforts to win more respect and less idolization for their sex, at least as long as women do not enter en masse into writing as a profession. "We especially like to see a noble effort on the part of women to enter into a more equal intellectual partnership with men, to handle all sorts of ideas and to express themselves when necessary in more serious language" (*L*, 591).

A woman's book, a novel that would corrupt women, a young man's scorn of life—is *Lélia* any of this? How could readers come to such diverse views of the same work? What exactly was *Lélia*, and how can we read the novel today?

Lélia was original in form and ideas. Both "roman" and "roman-poème," as Sainte-Beuve called it (*L*, 593), *Lélia* was and is difficult to classify. It has no conventional plot, particularly as compared with the elaborate plots of Sand's previous work. As Shelley Temchin points out, certain events occupy a disproportionate amount of space, while others are glossed over, so that narrative time (*Erzählzeit*) and time narrated (*erzählte Zeit*) stand in strange relation to each other.[6] *Lélia* is not narrated by one narrator. As in a classical play, each character is allowed several monologues, while the dialogues become *dialogues de sourds*.

The novel is divided into five parts. Part I is mostly an exchange of supposed letters between Lélia and Sténio, with occasional third-person narration. Part II contains a conversation between Magnus and Sténio and more exchanges between Lélia and Sténio. The last two "chapters" or sub-divisions of this part are again narrated in the third person and describe Bambucci's ball and Lélia's meeting with Pulchérie. In Part III, Lélia speaks almost exclusively while Pulchérie listens. Part IV is the shortest and consists of third-person narration and letters between Lélia and Sténio. Part V contains the most sustained third-person narration. In *Lélia*, the female character speaks extensively in her own name, for the first time since Aurore Dudevant's early works, and is given responsibility for her own story. Although the first-person narration and minimal novelistic form and content make it easy to identify Lélia with Sand, it should be remembered that however much Lélia derives from her creator, she is a fictional char-acter. As Sand wrote to Sainte-Beuve while the novel was in progress: " . . . [D]on't completely confuse the man [*sic*] with his suffering. . . . [I]n reality, the man is often less than his pain and thus less poetic, . . . and less damned than his demon" (*C*, II, 277).

Part prose-poem, related to the epistolary novel, philosophical medita-tions, gothic novel—*Lélia* is all this and more. Sand's sources were many: Byron is mentioned by several critics; Anne Radcliffe, whom she had read in the convent, is indubitably present; Sénancour and Nodier, as Pierre Reboul exhaustively (and exhaustingly) documents, formed the backbone of her novel. Staël's *Corinne*, which Reboul mentions in passing (*L*, 11), was surely a greater influence than has been imagined. Yet *Lélia* resembles none of the works Sand drew upon; she did not improve on any one form, but melded several into a wholly new book whose discontinuous, fragmentary form mirrors its raw emotional content.

Like Corinne, Lélia is an artist. Her family and origins are mysterious, as are Corinne's. There is an explicit comparison between the two women established during the ball scene early in the novel: "The dying Corinne must have been plunged into this same mournful attention when she heard her last poems being declaimed at the Capitol by a young girl" (*L*, 46). In form, there is also a similarity between the two novels, for *Corinne* is itself an original work, part travelogue, part traditional *récit*. The long epistolary monologues of *Lélia*—if one can so describe the passages, much more than letters, where each character speaks in turn—are reminiscent of Corinne's descriptions of Rome's antiquities.

Corinne's art is clearly defined, if imperfectly portrayed; she is an *improvisatrice* whose oral, spontaneous poetry is by its very nature ill suited to reproduction in a written work. It is always difficult to depict a writer convincingly in a literary work, for unless the author is particularly adept, the character's work can be hard to judge. For three hundred years, critics have been arguing over whether Oronte's sonnet in Molière's *Misanthrope* is a good or bad poem. In *Lélia*, the song Sténio declaims in "Le Vin" has been attributed to Musset, Sainte-Beuve, Ajasson de Grandsagne, or another of Sand's friends. Pierre Reboul also diplomatically states that the verses are not so good that they couldn't be attributed to Sand herself, for she had written occasional poems in the convent, but she seems to have lacked true talent in this literary genre alone. Sand has cleverly avoided the problem of *showing* Lélia's artistry (to use James's term) by simply calling her an artist without being more precise; the number of times the word "poète" appears in the text, as well as the fact that Lélia writes to Sténio, makes it a likely assumption that Lélia was a writer, if not literally a poet. Lélia is an Artist, a woman artist who represents all forms of artistic endeavor and all exceptional women whose gifts put them sometimes above, often below, the rest of humanity, but surely outside of the usual social circles.

As has been recognized since the novel's publication, *Lélia* owes much to Byron. Planche calls the novel a cross between *Manfred* and Plato's *Phaedo* (*L*, 587). Musset found certain pages as beautiful as *Lara*, while Chateaubriand wrote to Sand that she would be the Lord Byron of France (*L*, 595). Lélia is a female Byronic hero, a Byronic heroine. She is larger than life, a type, rather than a mimetically *vraisemblable* character, as Reboul insists too often in his edition. She stands alone, unique and exceptional in a changing, disappointing world. She is hypersensitive and, being capable of much, desires more. "Poetry had created other faculties in me, immense, magnificent, and which nothing on earth could satisfy" (*L*, 167). Like the Byronic hero, too, Lélia is possessed of "heroic Satanism," in Peter Thorslev's phrase.[7] From the very first page of the novel, Sténio asks Lélia if she is an "angel or a demon" (*L*, 7), a nonhuman creature. In Part IV, he damns her as diabolical for having united him with Pulchérie.

If Lélia derives from Byron's creations, as well as from Faust, with whom she compares herself (*L*, 100–101), she is also firmly fixed in a well-known line of specifically French heroes, the romantic sufferers of the *mal du siècle*, particularly René, Obermann, and Nodier's characters. *Lélia* is a *roman de l'individu*, a personal cry of despair from one who does not fit into society and who sees no way out of her dilemma. Just as Lélia is the first French Byronic heroine, *Lélia* represents the first time the French *mal du siècle* is expressed by a female character. Although Staël was the first woman author to describe the malady of melancholy in *De la littérature* and depicted Oswald as its victim in *Corinne*, neither Corinne nor Delphine really embodies the *mal du siècle* except in the sense that all women were excluded from society and power, and many felt keenly their status as outsiders, unable to act or participate fully in the world. Sand, of course, does insist sharply on this aspect of Lélia's problem, but she does so in a work in which, as in *René* and *Obermann*, the voices of the individual characters and philosophical themes take precedence over fictional plot. Staël's aims were clearly different from Sand's in *Lélia*, even if *Corinne* did serve on several levels as a model.[8] Sand thus arrogated the major theme of both the first and second generation of romantics to herself and to women, and the greatness of *Lélia* lies in its dialectic of general, human despair and that specific only to women. Furthermore, *Lélia* integrates all the separate causes for dissatisfaction, adding literal physical impotence to the spiritual and social powerlessness evinced by previous heroes.

Lélia returns to *Indiana* in its criticism of love, religion, and society as oppressors of all, but of women especially. Sand's portrayal of love in *Lélia* does not differ substantially from that in her previous works. In *Lélia*, though, Sand has made bold to put her critiques in the mouth of a female character, rather than showing her opinions indirectly through the plot or narration.[9]

Lélia speaks specifically of what is known today as "romantic love," that form of passion invented by the post-Rousseau, romantic generation.

> "C'est pourquoi nous cherchons le ciel dans une créature semblable à nous, et nous dépensons pour elle toute cette haute énergie qui nous avait été donnée pour un plus noble usage. Nous refusons à Dieu le sentiment de l'adoration. . . . Nous le reportons sur un être incomplet et faible, qui devient le dieu de notre culte idolâtre." (*L*, 55)

> "That is why we seek heaven in a creature like ourselves, and we expend on this creature all that high energy we've been given to use more nobly. We refuse God the emotion of adoration. . . . We transfer it to an incomplete, feeble human being who becomes the god of our idolatrous cult." (*l*, 36)

This god is always revealed to be a false god and is overthrown, broken, only to be replaced by another, and yet another. When she recalls her first love, Lélia tells Pulchérie that the beloved became the focus of all her energies: "[I] carried over onto him the enthusiasm that I had had for the other creations of the Divinity" (*L*, 166). She goes on to describe a particu-

larly female way of loving, one that is reminiscent of Indiana's tortured
and misguided love for Raymon.

> "C'était un état inexprimable de douleur et de joie, de désespoir et d'énergie.
> Mon âme orageuse se plaisait à ce ballottement funeste qui l'usait sans fruit et
> sans retour. . . . Il lui fallait des obstacles, des fatigues, des jalousies dévorantes
> à concentrer. . . . C'était une carrière, une gloire; homme, j'eusse aimé les com-
> bats . . . ; peut-être l'ambition de régner par l'intelligence, de dominer les autres
> hommes par des paroles puissantes, m'eût-elle souri aux jours de ma jeunesse.
> Femme, je n'avais qu'une destinée noble sur la terre, c'était d'aimer." (L, 170)

> "I experienced an inexpressible state of sadness and joy, of despair and energy.
> My afflicted soul took pleasure in this ill-starred tossing that consumed me
> fruitlessly. . . . I demanded obstacles, fatigues, devouring jealousies to re-
> press. . . . This was a glorious career. Had I been a man, I would have loved
> combat. . . . Perhaps in my youth I might have sought to reign by intelligence
> and to dominate others by powerful speeches. As a woman, I had only one
> noble destiny on earth, which was to love." (l, 110)

Love is woman's only vocation, whereas men can choose combat or power;
men can produce but women merely waste their energies. When Lélia in
the monastery imagines death near, she sees it as a "death worthy of heroes
and saints" (L, 198), a glorious end, not a servile one. In particular, men
can dominate by their words, a poignant admission that she does not see
her own writing as having the same impact as a man's. Indeed, although
Sand was enormously influential, even outside of France, her force would
not be felt for several years, since she had only been writing for the public
for a year and a half. Yet Sand might already have felt that her first two
novels were too well received, that male critics were patting her on the head
rather than helping put into effect her program of social reform.

Woman in love is masochistic and self-effacing; she cannot assert herself
in the relationship. "I know that I have used up my strength in devotion,
that I have abjured my pride, effaced my existence behind another's" (L,
171). Further on, she states: "The more he made me feel his domination,
the more I cherished it, the greater pride I took in wearing my fetters" (L,
173), the word fetters (chaîne) being the one that appears in Indiana as the
synonym for marriage both with Delmare and (potentially) with Raymon.
As in Indiana, too, Lélia discovers that her masochism is scornfully received
by men and not appreciated, so that she derives neither personal satisfaction
nor outside regard for her self-abnegation. The flaw in this model of woman's submersion in her lover and suppression of her own self stems from
the inevitable resurfacing of what Lélia calls egotism, but what more properly might be termed self-love, as opposed to selfishness. This self-love is
not limited to women but applies to both sexes. ". . . [H]uman egotism is

ferocious, it is indomitable . . ." (*L*, 172). Lélia articulates the dialectic of love as defined by the culture, in which the needs of the self are at war with the demands of the other: "[I] felt that one could both love another, to the point of submitting to him, and love oneself, to the point of hating him who subjugates us" (*L*, 172). For women, no equilibrium between these conflicting urges is thought necessary or desirable by society.

Woman's needs extend beyond the spiritual to the physical, as anyone who has ever heard of *Lélia* knows, for the scandal surrounding the novel was due largely to its sexual frankness. While literature had portrayed women as sexual beings before (Corinne is a perfect example of a sympathetic character who is evidently sexually experienced), Lélia is the first woman to speak of her sex life and, what is more, to do so in a critical way. Lélia launches two accusations against men's bedroom technique. Men are brutal, interested only in their own pleasure, and do not hesitate to engage in what today is called "conjugal rape" to satisfy themselves. "But he would pursue me, and claimed that he did not want to have been awakened for no reason. He savored his fierce pleasure on the breast of a woman who had fainted and was half dead" (*L*, 175). This last image recalls that of the idiot Denise, attacked by Horace in *Rose et Blanche*. *Lélia* expresses the same fears of male sexual power and physical force as *Rose et Blanche*. Once, when Sténio abandons his passive stance and takes Lélia in his arms, forcing her to kiss him, Lélia pushes him away and says: "Leave me alone, I don't like you when you are like this!"(*L*, 90). Later, after Sténio's death, Lélia recalls the past and her feelings for him. "I would have liked to be your mother and be able to clasp you in my arms without awakening in you a man's desires" (*L*, 319).

The corollary of male crudeness is the lack of sexual pleasure and fulfillment felt by women. "When he was asleep, satisfied and gratified, I remained immobile and dismayed at his side" (*L*, 174). It is not that women do not feel desire, nor is it their fault that they cannot respond sexually; rather, men are indifferent to women's needs. This is the crucial distinction between Lélia and Balzac's Foedora, with whom Reboul compares Lélia. Balzac criticizes Foedora's coquetry and coldness; she makes a virtue out of her frigidity and uses it as a weapon against men. This image is that of the man-eater and man-hater, common in our culture. Sand shows a woman who wants to feel sexual pleasure but to whom it is denied and who therefore loses all hope of ever finding satisfaction. Surely Sand's negative depiction of men's lack of sensitivity and inability to please women must have insulted and infuriated the French male critical fraternity, who prided themselves on their prowess in love and contributed heavily to the excoriation of the novel and its author.

By the end of the novel, Sténio has come to much the same conclusions as Lélia regarding woman's condition. In the "Don Juan" section of Part V, he expresses his disillusionment with debauchery and with women; yet in accusing woman of being merely a figment of man's imagination and of having the potential to be as unfaithful as man, he nonetheless repeats Lélia's earlier arguments about the conflict between masochism and self-love in woman's soul. Sténio points out that don juanism is based on the man's eternal conquest of a willing victim and insists that woman's own desires and demands will not remain repressed but will eventually burst forth. He apostrophizes Don Juan:

> "Avais-tu lu quelque part dans les Conseils de Dieu que la femme est une chose faite pour le plaisir de l'homme, incapable de résistance ou de changement? Pensais-tu que cette perfection idéale de renoncement existait sur la terre et devait assurer l'inépuisable renouvellement de tes joies?" (*L*, 292–93)

> "Did you read somewhere in the Counsels of God that woman is a thing made for man's pleasure, incapable of resistance or change? Did you think that this ideal womanly perfection of renunciation existed on earth and would assure the inexhaustible renewal of your joys?" (*l*, 203)

Sténio has discovered the other side of Lélia's dilemma, namely that if masochism is untenable, so is sadism. Just as Lélia was not grandiose in her self-denial, as Pulchérie tells her, but merely foolish, Sténio and his ilk are not heroes and conquerors, but merely libertines who are rightly condemned. Although Sténio's words have a further structural function in the novel, they complete the portrait developed by Sand of love as total misunderstanding between the sexes.

Because of her lofty talents and unusual sensibility, Lélia cannot find refuge in the kind of love available in the culture. Nor is prostitution the answer, although Pulchérie finds her own justification as a courtesan. Like Lélia the artist, Pulchérie the courtesan is presented without elaborate explanation. We see her at the ball, surrounded by admirers, and later in her villa; although the ignominy and opprobrium attached to prostitutes are alluded to, they are never shown in the novel. Pulchérie simply *is* a courtesan and is neither castigated nor punished. Unlike Manon Lescaut, who paid for her profligate ways with her death, or Hugo's repentant heroines such as Marion Delorme, Pulchérie neither dies nor repents but simply lives her life as she knows how, doing good where she can and taking her pleasure, physical and spiritual, when possible. This positive, unembarrassed, and nonjudgmental depiction of the courtesan departs sharply from those of prostitution before or after, at least until Colette, whose Léa of the *Chéri* novels is as unsentimentally and unapologetically drawn as Pulchérie.

Sand's perspective differs from the male viewpoint, in which the courtesan is a danger to society and the family and must be neutralized, either through repentance, death, or social exclusion; her creation of Pulchérie contributed not a little to the controversy surrounding the novel.[10]

The traditional distinction between "good" women and "bad" does not exist in *Lélia*. In a phrase that anticipates Proudhon's famous dictum "housewife or courtesan," but in an entirely opposite spirit, Pulchérie assimilates lovers, mothers, and courtesans, "three conditions of woman's destiny that no woman can escape, whether she sells herself to a man as a prostitute or as a wife, by a marriage contract" (*L*, 153). Pulchérie even goes so far as to suggest that the prostitute is superior to the mother, whom society reinforces in her choice of career while the prostitute is an outcast despite the fact that her profession is utilized, even made necessary, by that same society. It is as outsiders that Pulchérie and Lélia find their spiritual as well as real sisterhood, for neither is accepted by proper society. Pulchérie, though, has created a fulfilling life for herself within her own sphere, and like Trenmor, the other character of the novel who has found peace and equilibrium by circumscribing his life, serves as both conscience and reproach to Lélia, who will not bend and cannot compromise, and thus is consumed with regret and impotence. Yet it is clear that it is not Lélia's fault, but society's, that the exceptional woman cannot find an acceptance of her gifts and a match for her soul; the narrator states that the crowd at Spuela's ball was offended by Lélia's independence (*L*, 48). The courtesan, the mother, and the lover, whatever the hardships of their lives, are happier than the woman artist.

Like love, religion offers little solace to women, for the church is a profoundly misogynist institution, as *Rose et Blanche* and *Indiana* had already shown. On her supposed deathbed, Lélia is refused absolution by Magnus, who denies her a place in heaven or hell. In any case, Lélia does not believe in the trappings of religion and thus cannot accept Pulchérie's suggestion that she enter a convent if she cannot make a life for herself in the world. It is a measure of the gulf between the two editions of *Lélia* that in the later one, Lélia becomes an abbess. Magnus, the priest maddened by his lust for Lélia, calls her the enemy and strangles her while repeating words of exorcism, convinced she is Satan. In Magnus's tortured mind, Lélia is a temptress and the test of his faith, a test he fails every time, to the point of doubting the existence of God. Magnus presents Lélia as a "hideous monster, a harpy" (*L*, 83), and imagines her as a succubus who entices him in his bed. This depiction of woman as the source of evil and sexual debasement is an old one in the church, going back to Saint Paul. While a clear criticism of the effects of priestly celibacy, which is openly reproved by Lélia in Part V, *Lélia* also demonstrates how women are blamed by religion for the effects they produce in men and condemned by these same men as unnatural.

Sténio, too, sees Lélia as a monster. When she describes the monster of the Apocalypse, the Whore of Babylon riding a hydra, Sténio exclaims, "Are you not this unfortunate and terrible apparition?" (*L*, 117). Lélia tells Trenmor that for Sténio, she is a "monstrous exception" (*L*, 123), who enables him to believe in his own dreams as normal and usual.

Viewed as an oddity by Magnus and Sténio, Lélia becomes a monster in her own as well as in society's eyes. She makes the connection explicit in Part III, where she describes her stay in an abandoned monastery, ornamented with "these monstrous sculptures with which Catholicism used to adorn its places of worship" (*L*, 181). Like her in her impotence, these grotesques are imprisoned in stone, images of desire and fury unable to move or act.

> "Au-dessous de moi, ces bizarres allégories allongeaient leurs têtes noircies par le temps et semblaient comme moi se pencher vers la plaine pour regarder silencieusement couler les flots, les siècles et les générations. Ces guivres couvertes d'écailles, ces lézards au tronc hideux, ces chimères pleines d'angoisses, tous ces emblèmes du péché, de l'illusion et de la souffrance, vivaient avec moi d'une vie fatale, inerte, indestructible. . . . [J]e m'identifiais avec ces images d'une lutte éternelle entre la douleur et la nécessité, entre la rage et l'impuissance." (*L*, 181–82)

> "Beneath me these bizarre allegories stretched out their heads, blackened by time. They seemed to stretch toward the plain and silently to watch the flow of waves, centuries, and generations. These fantastic scaly serpents, these lizards with their hideous bodies, these chimeras full of anguish, all these emblems of sin, illusion, and suffering lived a life that was inert and indestructible. . . . [I] identified myself with these images of eternal struggle between suffering and necessity, between rage and impotence." (*l*, 116–17)

Lélia, in her song in Part II called "A Dieu," asks God why he created her a woman, only to turn her to stone. The image is a tragic inversion of Galatea's transformation from Pygmalion's stone sculpture into a live woman. In *Lélia* a woman becomes frozen, useless to others and herself; in *André*, Sand will create a further variant of this legend, the awakening of a woman who becomes not her creator's equal but his superior. Sténio evokes Pygmalion directly in Part V, when he asks: "Why should I henceforth bend my knee before this marble idol? Even if I had Pygmalion's burning glance and the gods' assent to animate her, what would I do with her?" (*L*, 255). Reboul sees the word "stone" as an allusion to Lélia's "frigidity" (*L*, 99), but it is wrong to limit Lélia to a mere reference to sexual dysfunction in this passage, as she so obviously places her insufficiencies in a social and artistic context.

Lélia speaks specifically of her soul, not her body: "Is that what is called a poet's soul? . . . O life, o torment! to aspire to everything and to grasp nothing, to understand everything and possess nothing!"(*L*, 100). She longs to feel, but she also wishes to act, to be able to use her gifts. She does not know why she has been chosen to suffer. "If this is the fate of the chosen, let it be sweet and let me bear it without suffering; if it is a life of punishment, why have you inflicted it on me?" (ibid.). Her invocation to God is followed by a section entitled "Dans le Désert," in which Lélia, who has become a female Christ figure, a prophet of doom who is unheeded, paints a dismal picture of civilization. The world is old and exhausted, and its population does not become better with progress. "The arts, industry and science, the whole scaffolding of civilization, what are they if not the continued effort of human weakness to hide its evils and cover its misery?" (*L*, 114). Man and nature are in conflict, with man despoiling beauty and creating chaos out of God's order. ". . . [W]e couldn't spend three days here without spoiling the vegetation and polluting the air. . . . You would call it making a garden" (*L*, 109). Lélia foresees the results of the Industrial Revolution in the pollution and destruction of nature: ". . . [T]his wild valley . . . blossoms beautiful and proud without dreaming that in a single day the plow and the hundred-armed monster called industry could rip open its breast to steal its treasures . . ." (*L*, 119). This is not the picture of lush nature, either on the île Bourbon or in the Berry, and of unconventional marriages breaking down class barriers and creating new wealth and prosperity; rather, it is an apocalyptic vision of a world beyond redemption. Again the word "monster" appears alongside the image of the rape of nature perpetrated by progress.

Decidedly, Sand's imagination was obsessed with the unnatural while she wrote *Lélia*. The world as she described it is filled with horrible creatures and suffering; even the warm, meridional regions commonly thought to be paradisiacal are ruled by ferocious, bloodthirsty animals. Humans are themselves compared to animals, and their anxieties described as grotesques. Not only do people pillage their environment, but they flay animals to use the skins and feathers for clothing and covering. In a passage that might have influenced Baudelaire and that anticipates Freud's work on neuroses and the unconscious, Lélia characterizes the poet's imagination as necrophilic, teratogenic:

"Ce que les peintres et les poètes ont inventé de plus hideux dans les fantaisies grotesques de leur imagination et, il faut bien le dire, ce qui nous apparaît le plus souvent dans le cauchemar, c'est un sabat de cadavres vivants, de squelettes

d'animaux, décharnés, sanglants, avec des erreurs monstrueuses, des superpositions bizarres, des têtes d'oiseau sur des troncs de cheval, des faces de
crocodile sur des corps de chameau; c'est toujours un pêle-mêle d'ossements,
une orgie de la peur qui sent le carnage et des cris de douleur, des paroles de
menace proférées par des animaux mutilés." (*L*, 112)

"The most hideous things poets and painters have invented in their grotesque
fantasies also appear most often, it must be said, in our nightmares. We dream
of witches' sabbaths of living corpses, animal skeletons, emaciated, bloody, with
monstrous deformities and bizarre superpositions—bird heads on horse
trunks, crocodile faces on camel bodies; there are heaps of bones, it is an orgy
of fear that smells of carnage and the cries of suffering, the threats proffered
by mutilated animals." (*l*, 71)

Lélia describes what can be termed the collective unconscious detailed by
artists and dreams:

"Croyez-vous que les rêves soient une pure combinaison du hasard? Ne pensez-
vous pas qu'en dehors des lois d'association et des habitudes consacrées chez
l'homme par le droit et par le pouvoir, il peut exister en lui de secrets remords,
vagues, instinctifs, que nul ordre d'idées reçues n'a voulu avouer ou énoncer
et qui se révèlent par les terreurs de la superstition ou les hallucinations du
sommeil? Alors que les moeurs, l'usage et la croyance ont détruit certaines
réalités de notre vie morale, l'empreinte en est restée dans un coin du cerveau
et s'y réveille quand les autres facultées intelligentes s'endorment." (*L*, 112–
13)

"Do you think that dreams are a pure combination of chance? Don't you think
that outside of the laws of association and the habits that man endows with
right and power, there can exist in him secret, vague, instinctive remorse which
he has not wanted to admit rationally and which reveals itself through the
terrors of superstition or the hallucinations of sleep? Although customs and
belief have destroyed certain realities of our moral life, the imprint remains
in a corner of the brain and awakens when the other intelligent faculties sleep."
(*l*, 71)

In *Histoire de ma vie*, Sand pursues this syncretic thought when she asks:
"Is the life of the individual not the summary of the life of the species?"
(*Oa* I, 535). Here, the collective life is the terrifying underside of the mind's
capacity. The woman artist not only is a monster; she creates monsters in
her language, in her imagination; her work, by extension, must also be
seen as monstrous. Sand, like her British and American contemporaries,
fits the pattern discerned by Sandra Gilbert and Susan Gubar of the social
and self-image of the woman writer as monster giving birth to unhealthy
progeny.[11]
    Lélia thus repeats in radically intensified form Aurore Dudevant's doubts

about her career as an artist, expressed in her very first works. Despite the acclaim awarded to *Indiana* and *Valentine*, Sand obviously did not feel successful herself. She felt vulnerable and insecure, without a niche in society or a clear identity, social or sexual. The first line of the book, significantly a question, raises the issue explicitly: "Who are you?" (*L*, 7). As Pulchérie tells Lélia: "[I] only saw that you had a problematic life as a woman" (*L*, 154). *Lélia* posits again Sand's androgynous self-image as man-woman even as it explores her uncertainties concerning her vocation and explicitly links the two in a way the earlier works did not because Lélia speaks for herself. The artist as man and woman appears twice in *Lélia*, for both Lélia and Sténio are artists and androgynous figures. It should be noted also that Lélia's name is a pseudonym, and that Pulchérie is called La Zinzolina by her friends, so that the same connection between name and identity is made in *Lélia* as in *Rose et Blanche*.

Pulchérie and Lélia share a crucial scene in the novel that specifically asserts Lélia's male side. Pulchérie describes her sexual and social awakening as an adolescent thanks to Lélia, a confession that has no previous literary model, as Reboul rightly points out (*L*, 156). Pulchérie reaches the stage where she is able to perceive herself as other, to differentiate herself from her sister and to break out of her own narcissism. The use of the mirror shows Pulchérie's evolution; at first, she only looks at herself and wants to kiss her own reflection, but after her dream, she finds her sister more beautiful because Lélia resembles a man. The adolescent Pulchérie moves from self-love (and love of the same—the mother) to love for a man, the usual path of female development, while Lélia does not. When Lélia looks into the water, which functions as a mirror, she does not recognize her own beauty or appreciate her androgyny; it is as though the mirror remains empty for her. The young Lélia has no self-image, or at least not the traditional one, and cannot develop like Pulchérie. Lélia specifically states that nothing happened for her that day, whereas Pulchérie's life was changed. Later, Lélia does assume her androgyny, appearing early in the novel in a man's costume at Spuela's ball, as Sand's first heroines had played male roles in the theater.

The scene between the two sisters, which has sometimes been interpreted as a lesbian confession, instead continues Sand's self-portrait not only as androgynous but as the alter ego of her father.[12] It is significant that Pulchérie dreams first of a man, "a man with black hair" (*L*, 156), and then sees Lélia, on whom she projects the description of her dream lover, and not the other way around. Lélia is described as a man by Pulchérie: her skin is tanned, her arms hairy, her expression masculine. "I thought you resembled this beautiful black-haired child of whom I had just dreamed, and, trembling, I kissed your arm" (*L*, 158). There is again constituted a

triangle consisting of the two women and a man, with an equivalence established between the man and Lélia as doubles.

This dream triangle prepares the next one, where Lélia and Pulchérie
switch roles so that Sténio makes love to Pulchérie when he thinks he is
with Lélia at last. Even though *Lélia* is as far from Sand's previous works
in plot and narrative form as possible, the novel nonetheless presents the
same kind of structure as its predecessors: two sisters are involved with the
same man, one briefly and sexually, while the other is eventually united
with him, in this case in death. The first triangle resembles this one in that
sexuality is also present, if only in fantasy: Pulchérie and her imaginary
lover exchange a kiss. Pulchérie insists that she has become Lélia by possessing Sténio, while Sténio has nonetheless consummated his relationship
with Lélia through Pulchérie. Pulchérie is therefore the link through whom
Lélia and Sténio achieve oneness, just as earlier it was through her that the
identity of the dream man and Lélia was created.

After this encounter, Sténio becomes explicitly Lélia's double and equal.
Earlier, he had been a younger version of Lélia, a poet, too, but one who
had not yet produced. He was optimistic, whereas she was disillusioned.
In his farewell letter to Lélia after his discovery that he had spent the night
with her sister, he uses language that repeats Lélia's earlier formulations.
"But God set me higher or lower than the rest of them" (*L*, 225). The fifth
part of the novel makes the equivalence between Sténio and Lélia even
clearer. Sténio, too, is physically impotent; he rejects his model Don Juan,
the way Lélia had repudiated romantic love, as we have already seen. He
has also become an outsider; even as he shares the orgies with his supposed
friends, they mock him. Like Lélia, Sténio has become "sceptical and cold"
(*L*, 258). Unable to find any meaning in his life, Sténio commits suicide.

Lélia joins him in the grotto where his body has been laid out, another
of the enclosed spaces dear to Sand's imagination. There, she is called "the
corpse's worthy fiancée" (*L*, 313); further on in the text, she imagines their
reunion with God at some future point and says, "Perhaps then we will be
equals, perhaps we will be lovers and siblings" (*L*, 320). Their imagined
union is incestuous, as was overtly stated by Lélia after Sténio's night with
Pulchérie: "Be just my brother and my son, and let the thought of any
marriage appear incestuous and bizarre" (*L*, 233). Their union takes place
sooner than Lélia dreams, for Magnus, now mad with remorse over Sténio's
death and with desire for Lélia, strangles her. Although Magnus clearly
represents many things in the novel, he most symbolizes physical desire
and is in many ways a foil for Lélia, who also desires but in a more
metaphysical way, without achieving satisfaction. Here, Magnus incarnates
the forbidden, wild desire that allows Lélia and Sténio to come together.
Their marriage in death is made concrete in the image of the two meteors

that Trenmor sees on the surface of the lake: "He spent the entire night watching those inseparable lights, which sought and followed each other like two souls in love" (*L*, 325).

Lélia and Sténio's union is that of two androgynes, rather than the marriage of a woman and a man; if Lélia is shown as androgynous, so is Sténio depicted as a young girl as well as a young man, at the beginning, where Trenmor describes Sténio as a child, feminine in appearance, and at the end, where Magnus takes the cadaver, dressed in a white winding-sheet and wearing a crown of flowers, like a bride, for that of a woman. Lélia prefers this nonvirile Sténio to the sexually avid, demanding lover he became at times.

> Lélia se rappela les jours où elle l'avait aimé le plus. C'était lorsqu'il était plutôt poète qu'amant. Dans ces premiers temps de leur affection, la passion de Sténio avait quelque chose de romanesque et d'angélique. . . . Plus tard, son oeil s'était animé d'un feu plus viril, sa lèvre plus avide avait cherché et demandé le baiser, sa poésie avait exprimé des transports plus sauvages; c'est alors que l'impuissante Lélia s'était sentie effrayée, fatiguée et presque dégoûtée de cet amour qu'elle ne partageait pas. (*L*, 318)

> Lélia remembered when she had loved him most. It was when he was poet rather than lover. In those first days of their affection, Sténio's passion had a romantic, angelic quality. . . . Later his eyes would grow animated with a more virile fire. His greedy lips would seek and demand kisses. His poetry would express more savage outbursts of feeling. Then the impotent Lélia had felt frightened, fatigued, and nearly disgusted with this love she did not share. (*l*, 224–25)

Lélia's fear of the kind of brutal virility described in Part III as well as here leads to a desire for a more maternal, less threatening relationship with Sténio and perhaps sheds some light on Sand's own penchant for younger men whose pattern of sexual behavior was not yet fixed, and thus open to modification by her.

The final couple in *Lélia* is thus similar to those of *Indiana* and *Valentine*. Both partners are equals and, furthermore, they resemble each other. The man is not the patriarchal father figure, but a gentle, kind friend. In *Indiana*, Ralph and Indiana were an explicitly oedipal couple whose incestuous bonds were alluded to throughout the novel. The case in *Lélia* is much more subtle and, as in *Valentine*, relies on internal, structural evidence. Yet in addition to the triangular relationships I have defined as oedipal, *Lélia* seems obsessed with secrets and with the dead to such a degree that this theme must be taken into account when dealing with the novel's oedipal content.

We have already looked at Lélia's evocation of monsters and cadavers as forming the basis of the dreams of poets. With an admirable prescience, Sand distinguishes between two categories of dreams: those which are healthy and allow the soul to renew itself through sleep, and those nightmares which reveal troubles with which the dreamer cannot cope, the "secret remorse" (*L*, 113) of the unconscious that surfaces in sleep.

> "Mes rêves ont un effroyable caractère de vérité; les spectres de toutes mes déceptions y repassent sans cesse, plus lamentables, plus hideux chaque nuit. Chaque fantôme, chaque monstre évoqué par le cauchemar est une allégorie claire et saisissante qui répond à quelque profonde et secrète souffrance de mon âme." (*L*, 128)

> "Instead, my dreams have a frightful character of truth. The ghosts of all my disappointments pass continually back and forth. Each phantom evoked by nightmare is a clear, gripping allegory that responds to some deep, secret suffering in my soul." (*l*, 81)

She then recounts a dream of her own, in which she pursues her sister, whom she thinks dead (this is before her meeting with Pulchérie); as she follows what she thinks is her sister's form, another ghost appears, described as "some hideous object, an ironic demon, a bloody cadaver, a temptation or a remorse" (*L*, 129). There is again set up a triangular situation with the two women and this horrible phantom, seen as both temptation and guilt.

Cadavers and the "living dead" reappear constantly in *Lélia*. Lélia's account of her year spent in the deserted abbey gives two very revealing examples of Lélia's contact with the dead. In the first, she talks about her desires and need for action. "Stretched out on the tombstones, I gave in to the fury of my imagination. I dreamed of the embraces of an unknown demon; I felt his hot breath burn my breast, and I dug my nails into my shoulders, thinking I felt the bite of his teeth" (*L*, 185). Her position on top of the tombstones, like a *gisante*, is a reminiscence of the more frenetic Gothic literature, but in the context of Sand's own psychology it implies much more, particularly when the second instance of Lélia's communication with the dead is examined.

In an underground chapel, whose entrance has been blocked by debris, Lélia finds a monk on his knees in an attitude of prayer. At first, she thinks he is alive, but then she realizes that he has been dead for thirty years and preserved in the airless cave. Or rather, his clothes have remained and become dust when Lélia touches them, revealing a skeleton underneath. "It was both frightening and sublime to see for the first time this monk's head whose tufts of grey hair were still stirred by the wind and whose beard was entwined in the emaciated fingers of his hands folded under his chin"

(*L*, 189). This scene is not ghoulish, as was the earlier one, but rather touching, particularly as Lélia goes on to make the dead monk her friend.

"J'enveloppai d'un nouveau vêtement la dépouille sacrée du prêtre. Je m'agenouillai chaque jour auprès d'elle. Souvent je lui parlai à haute voix dans les agitations de ma souffrance, comme à un compagnon d'exil et de douleur. Je me pris d'une sainte et folle affection pour ce cadavre. Je me confessai à lui: je lui racontai les angoisses de mon âme; je lui demandai de se placer entre le ciel et moi pour nous réconcilier; et souvent, dans mes rêves, je le vis passer devant mon grabat comme l'esprit des visions de Job et je l'entendis murmurer d'une voix faible comme la brise des paroles de terreur ou d'espoir." (*L*, 191)

"I covered the priest's remains with new clothing. Each day I knelt down beside him. He became the companion of my exile and sadness, to whom I spoke out loud of my suffering. I developed a saintly and crazy affection for this cadaver. I confessed to him. I told him of my spiritual anguish. I asked that he place himself as intermediary between heaven and me. And often in my dreams I saw him pass before my pallet like a spirit out of Job's visions, and I heard him murmur words of terror or hope in a voice as feeble as the breeze." (*l*, 123)

What is particularly interesting about this monk's return from the dead, so to speak, is that the scene recalls one told by George Sand in *Histoire de ma vie* about her and Deschartres's visit to her father's grave when it was opened to receive her grandmother's body. " 'You are going to see him who was your father . . . I've seen the skeleton. The head has already detached itself. I lifted it, I kissed it.' . . . We entered the crypt and I performed piously this act of devotion, as had Deschartres" (*Oa* I, 1106–1107). Lélia's friend from beyond the grave is identifiable with Sand's father, with whom she communicated in spirit, as she does here with the monk.

The special affinity between Lélia and Sand's private scenarios is made clear in *Histoire de ma vie*, where Sand ascribes the novel to what she calls the "school of Corambé."

Il portait trop le caractère du rêve, il était trop de l'école de *Corambé* pour être goûté par de nombreux lecteurs. Je ne me pressais donc pas, et j'éloignais de moi, à dessein, la préoccupation du public, éprouvant une sorte de soulagement triste à céder à l'imprévu de ma rêverie, et m'isolant même de la réalité du monde actuel, pour tracer la synthèse du doute et de la souffrance, à mesure qu'elle se présentait à moi sous une forme quelconque. (*Oa* II, 196)

It bore too strongly the character of a dream, it was too much of the school of Corambé to be appreciated by many readers. I was therefore not in a hurry, and I deliberately did not take the public into account, feeling a sort of sad satisfaction in giving in to the unforeseen train of my reverie, and isolating

myself from the reality of contemporary life to trace the synthesis of doubt
and suffering, as it presented itself to me in whatever form it liked.

The same vocabulary of reverie that characterizes Aurore Dudevant's childish creations, the evocation of Corambé and the intimation that *Lélia* is the
product of a kind of automatic writing inspired by her innermost feelings,
links the novel's content with that of Sand's other oedipal fantasies. Unlike
Corambé, the childhood stories, the convent romance, or the last two novels,
however, *Lélia* is not a positive, nurturing, and life-affirming creation.
Rather, it is the inverse of what came before, the surfacing of the underside
of Sand's usually benign vision.

Lélia links narrative, society, and personal psychology, as did *Indiana* and
Valentine, but in a negative way. Just as Sand describes two kinds of dreams,
two kinds of collective unconscious, one dark, the other healthy, so does
Lélia express what the previous works had not, at least not to the same
extent: the guilt, the despair, the fear occasioned both by her secret dreams
and by her condition as author, which was so dependent on these imag-
inings. Written in a period of depression, when nothing seemed to go right
and when the suicidal urges present in her mind for the past ten years
were strongest, *Lélia* decries the very impulses that made Sand's strength
and defined her character, precisely because that force and identity were
ill received by others, in the professional and personal spheres. Having
been repudiated by society, she turns that criticism upon herself but makes
it obvious that it was society that rejected her first.

Temptations, remorse, skeletons from the past, monsters within and
without, *Lélia* is clearly not the kind of novel that is usually associated with
Sand. Intensely personal and original, *Lélia* has no parallel in Sand's *oeuvre*,
partly because, as Sainte-Beuve noted, *Lélia* "is a work one only writes once"
(*L*, 594), which served as a kind of purgative, and partly because the book
was so badly received, even by its defenders. It is perhaps the final irony
that the novel was condemned for its negativity and scandalous frankness,
just as its heroine had been refused a place in the world. Ultimately, the
criticism leveled against *Lélia* concerned its unremitting pessimism and its
lack of constructive suggestions for change. "The general tone of the book
is one of anger in the mouth of Lélia, and one only has Trenmor's cold
stoicism to relieve it, to refresh oneself from this bitter and contrary wind"
(*L*, 592), wrote Sainte-Beuve. In *La France Littéraire*, Alfred Désessarts concluded: "Must I admit my whole opinion: this book strikes me as dangerous,
not because it destroys some modern prevailing ideas (what is the importance of today's system?), but because it prepares nothing" (*L*, 589). Past
literary renderings of the *mal du siècle* had contained some glimmer of hope

and consolation; at the end of René's story, Father Souël and Chactas reprove the young man's hypersensitivity. If, as D. G. Charlton points out, the *romans de l'individu* "are above all dialogues, not monologues from a single character or the author himself," preaching "moral affirmation," then *Lélia* clearly does not fit the paradigm on either score;[13] although dialogic in form, the combat is largely conducted between Lélia and Sténio, similar characters who become identified at the end. Furthermore, the two characters who are satisfied with their lives, the reformed criminal and the courtesan, have no secret formula to share with others, no hints to communicate to those who would emulate them, and are by definition social outcasts. Chateaubriand's faith in religion is not shared by Sand, who has no other palliative to offer. On the contrary, she demonstrates that for a woman, the Catholic church, at least as constituted in her time, is an impossible refuge. While she does not present Lélia as a model, any more than René was a model, Sand does intend her and the novel as a condemnation of the society that rejects her, and thereby goes beyond the individual to the general.

Sand's open expression of the despair of the woman artist was censured, leading to her own self-censorship. Sand took these criticisms of *Lélia* to heart and returned in her next works to the forms, style, and themes previously elaborated. She did not let the reactions to *Lélia* in the press go without protest, however. In her 1834 preface to a new edition of *Romans et nouvelles,* she states: "For the last several months, the attacks aimed at the author of *Lélia* have taken on such a coarse and personal nature, that a public response has become necessary."[14] What follows is less a justification of *Lélia* than a serious discussion of the inconsistences of critics, who take back their praise of an author when a new work does not suit their tastes or ideas. Still chafing from the calumnies, in her 1842 preface to the Perrotin edition of the *Oeuvres complètes* she again mentions the fury of the critics and serenely asserts her right as an author to raise in her novel the questions she deems essential. After *Lélia,* though, Sand's female voice went underground again and just a few years later she undertook to revise, indeed denature, the novel, which (re)appeared in 1839; as Jules Janin had recommended, she became a man once more in her fiction. She continued to express her own ideals and explore her particular themes, but more covertly, as in *Indiana* and *Valentine.* Significantly, her next openly "feminist" project, the one-sided fictional correspondence related in form to *Lélia,* the *Lettres à Marcie* (1837), aroused the antagonism of Lamennais, in whose journal *Le Monde* it appeared; because it advocated divorce, it was eventually censored by him.

Although *Lélia,* like *René, Obermann,* and similar novels that express the *mal du siècle*, is much less readable today than it was one hundred and fifty years ago, and the supposedly scandalous passages have lost most of their shock value, it is still a novel that was worth daring, to use Sainte-Beuve's phrase. It remains a searingly honest cry of a woman artist's soul, an indictment of, and a curse upon, a society in which she had no place.

6

LEONE LEONI
George Sand's Reading of Manon Lescaut

The tumultuous emotions that produced *Lélia* soon gave way to the very different if equally tempestuous passions of Sand's affair with Alfred de Musset, whom she had met while completing *Lélia*. In late December 1833, she and Musset left Paris for Italy, where they hoped to find inspiration for their work. Sand's seven months in Venice were to prove particularly fruitful, for she wrote three novels and two of her *Lettres d'un voyageur* in a short period punctuated by illness and romantic drama.

Before leaving Paris, George Sand had read *Manon Lescaut*. In March 1834, Sand sent the manuscript of *Leone Leoni* to François Buloz, her editor in Paris, who published it in the April 15 and May 1 editions of his *Revue des Deux Mondes*.[1] *Leone Leoni* is Sand's reading of *Manon Lescaut*.[2]

Unlike her earlier works, which followed literary models unconsciously, *Leone Leoni* represents Sand's deliberate decision to write her own version of an older novel. In *Leone Leoni*, Sand retains the narrative structure of *Manon Lescaut*, many of its key plot elements, and, most importantly, its depiction of masochistic love. Each of these components undergoes significant changes in Sand's hands, which reveal both her understanding of Prévost's work and her rebellion against it.

Like *Manon Lescaut*, *Leone Leoni* is a framed narrative. The extradiegetic narrator in both cases is a man who takes great interest in the person whose story constitutes the major portion of the text. Prévost's *Homme de qualité* is attracted first by the beauty and modesty of Manon, who seems superior to the other women who are being deported with her, and then by the suffering of Des Grieux. The narrator's initial motivation in approaching Des Grieux is curiosity: "Would you please satisfy my desire to know this beautiful woman, who does not seem at all destined for the sorry state in which I find her?"[3] This fascination with Manon becomes in Sand's novel a liaison between Bustamente, the extradiegetic narrator, and Juliette, the victim of a hopeless passion for Leone Leoni, a rake who had abandoned her two years before the opening of the story. Bustamente becomes her protector and her lover, first curing her of illness, then trying to imbue her with a desire to live. Bustamente's initial feeling is one of anger caused by jealousy, for, despite his efforts, Juliette cannot forget her perfidious lover Leoni. Sand has transformed Prévost's avuncular and rather detached narrator into a fatherly lover, so that Juliette's situation at the beginning of the novel resembles that of Indiana and her sisters.

L'homme de qualité helps Des Grieux after learning about his efforts to remain with Manon and go to the New World. When they meet again two years later, it is Des Grieux who spontaneously offers to tell his story as a sign of gratitude; he expects that his interlocutor will condemn him but also pity him. Conversely, it is Bustamente who encourages Juliette to reveal her adventures with Leoni to him. His project is a Freudian one *avant la lettre*: by talking about her misfortunes, Juliette will come to free herself from their spell, and Bustamente will be able to help her once he knows exactly what he must combat. The word "repressed" even appears in the text itself:

> "Je l'ai [ton mal] trop comprimé, tu l'as trop refoulé dans ton coeur. . . . Ainsi négligée et abandonnée, ta blessure s'est envenimée tous les jours, quand tous les jours j'aurais dû la soigner et l'adoucir. . . . Il faut montrer ta douleur, il faut la répandre dans mon sein; il faut me parler de tes maux passés. . . . Eh bien! prononçons-le ensemble ce nom maudit qui te brûle la langue et le coeur." (*LL*, 13–14)

> "I have repressed it [your unhappiness] too much, you have repressed it into your heart too much. . . . Your wound, thus neglected and abandoned, has become more inflamed every day, whereas I should have dressed it and poured balm upon it. . . . You must show me your sorrow, you must pour it out in my bosom, you must talk to me about your past sufferings. . . . Very well! let us pronounce it together, that accursed name that burns your tongue and your heart." (*ll*, 191–92)

Juliette agrees with this plan. "My sorrow is like a perfume that is always kept in a closed bottle; open the bottle and it quickly escapes. If I could speak constantly of Leoni, tell you the most trivial circumstances of our love, it would bring back to mind the good and the ill he did me . . ." (*LL*, 14). This "talking cure" will presumably free Juliette from her love and enable her to respond to Bustamente's marriage proposal; like many of Balzac's texts, *Leone Leoni*, too, is a contract narrative, where the telling of a tale is intended to produce a concrete change in the relations of the narrator and narratee.[4]

Juliette thus becomes the intradiegetic narrator, as does Des Grieux. Sand allows the woman character to tell her own story and to describe her own experience, as Lélia did, but again as a secondary narrator whose account is contained within a man's narrative. Sand's major change in her rewriting of *Manon Lescaut* is to reverse the genders of the protagonists, so that Juliette is the one who loves passionately a man whose life contains many other preoccupations that exclude her. This innovation was as deliberate as the decision to redo *Manon Lescaut*.

> [J]e m'étais dit que faire de Manon Lescaut un homme, de Desgrieux [*sic*] une femme, serait une combinaison à tenter et qui offrirait des situations assez tragiques, le vice étant souvent fort près du crime pour l'homme, et l'enthousiasme voisin du désespoir pour la femme.[5]

> [I] thought to myself that making Manon Lescaut a man and Desgrieux [*sic*] a woman would be a plot worth trying and which would offer fairly tragic situations, since vice is often very close to crime for a man, and strong emotion close to despair for a woman.

As in *Manon Lescaut*, Sand's title consists of the name of the beloved, rather than that of the narrator. The name Juliette reminds one instantly of Romeo and Juliette, who had made their appearance in Sand's early works through the intermediary of Zingarelli's opera, while Leone Leoni takes his name both from the symbol of the city of Venice and from the real-life sixteenth-century Italian sculptor.

Many aspects of the plot of *Leone Leoni* are copied from *Manon Lescaut*. Juliette and Manon are both sixteen at the outset of the stories and are both from bourgeois families, while their lovers are noble. Leoni and Juliette elope with the precious stones her father, a jeweler, had had sewn onto their costumes for a ball, and Leoni keeps them in a trunk until they get to Venice, where he sells them. Manon and Des Grieux plan to steal the pearls the young G . . . M . . . gives her, along with 10,000 francs. Lescaut, Manon's brother, is like an evil genius to Des Grieux and is killed at an opportune moment; similarly, Leoni has a friend, the marquis, who is a bad influence and whose death has a liberating effect on Leoni. Des Grieux also has a good friend in Tiberge, who tries to keep him from the path of debauchery. Henryet attempts to aid Juliette until he, too, is killed; his death in a duel foreshadows the final combat, as does Lescaut's duel, which probably inspired this narrative sequence. Des Grieux feels guilty that worry over his son hastened his father's death; similarly, Juliette's father succumbs to his grief at her elopement.

There are two crucial plot developments that Sand adapts from *Manon Lescaut* with important modifications. The first concerns the couple's idyllic love in a remote place. In *Manon Lescaut*, this episode comes at the end of the novel, when Manon and Des Grieux come to appreciate a simpler life in the New World, far from the temptations of Paris. The second is closely related, for it consists of the duel fought between Synnelet and Des Grieux to determine who will marry Manon. This episode precipitates the dénouement of the novel, as Manon and Des Grieux flee because they think Synnelet has been killed, and Manon subsequently dies in the desert. Sand has separated these two events in her novel, with interesting results.

Upon their elopement, Juliette and Leoni go to Switzerland, where they spend six happy months in relative isolation, living "on love and poetry in a perpetual tête-à-tête" (*LL*, 45). The advent of winter forces them to leave, and they go to Venice, where Juliette's trials begin. This rustic idyll is thus not the end of Juliette and Leoni's adventures, but rather their beginning. Juliette uses her memory of this utopian existence and the store of love and happiness she amassed then as a reference point for the rest of her experiences; her subsequent actions depend upon her conviction that Leoni did once love her and could love her again. It is appropriate that this period comes early in the novel, rather than at the end, for Sand's view of the kind of love Juliette and Leoni share does not admit of the moralistic ending of *Manon Lescaut*.

The events following this retreat take the nature of a fall from grace, whereas in *Manon Lescaut*, the edenic period comes after the sinful, Parisian episodes; thus, the narrative logic of *Leone Leoni* is entirely different. Much, but not all, of the ambiguity of *Manon Lescaut* is lost, as this period and its place in the story serve to confirm a first-person narrative that otherwise might strain credulity. Leoni himself admits in a conversation with friends that Juliette overhears that he loved her in Switzerland even if those feelings will never reawaken (*LL*, 72, 74), whereas Manon's feelings for Des Grieux remain enigmatic, at least until the end. Juliette quickly learns that Leoni has stolen her father's jewels, that he is a gambler, and that he has neither scruples nor principles. He leaves her in Venice to court a wealthy but dying woman in Milan, from whom he hopes to inherit a fortune; when Juliette shows up, he persuades her to pass as his sister and introduces her into the princess's household. Like Manon, Leoni displays convincing logic as he explains that this state of affairs is necessary for their fortunes and does not change their relationship. This ménage-à-trois, which recalls Manon's attempt to obtain the older G . . . M . . .'s money while making Des Grieux pass as her brother, with disastrous results, is followed by Leoni's use of the princess's money to support openly several mistresses. Like Des Grieux, Juliette must share her lover with many others.

Her final humiliation comes when she and Leoni are again without resources. Having been jailed, like Manon and Des Grieux, and forced to return the portion of the princess's inheritance already spent because a new will has been found, Leoni is freed only when Juliette uses what remains of her own inheritance to pay his debts. Never one to live frugally, Leoni cannot stand poverty. He finally agrees to allow Lord Edwards, an Englishman who had been soliciting Juliette's favors, to sleep with her, naturally without obtaining Juliette's consent to this bargain. In a scene that would be burlesque if it were not so deeply felt by the victim, Leoni speaks to Juliette from beside the bed so that she thinks it is really he who is seated next to her, and not Lord Edwards. She quickly realizes the truth and jumps out the window. Leoni stays around long enough to make sure she is not dead, then disappears for good.

This scene is reminiscent of Manon's procurement of a pretty prostitute for Des Grieux while she is entertaining the young G . . . M . . . . The lack of empathy and affection for the partner is truly extraordinary on the part of Manon and Leoni, although one infers a certain good-naturedness and sense of fairness in Manon's gesture, whereas Leoni is merely selfish and rapacious. Des Grieux and Juliette react very differently to this situation, as their genders prescribe; she is outraged and afraid, for her "protector" has essentially left her vulnerable to rape, and she envisages flight, even possible death, as the only way to maintain her personal and physical integrity. Des Grieux, on the other hand, is hurt and disappointed in Manon, yet so in love with her that looking at another woman is impossible. He is free to choose whether or not he spends the night with another person, in a way that Juliette is not.

With Leoni's betrayal, Juliette's tale of love and degradation ends. The telling of the story has cured her.

"Tout ce que je viens de te raconter m'a remis sous les yeux des infamies que j'avais presque oubliées. Maintenant je ne sens plus que de l'horreur pour le passé, et je ne veux plus y revenir. Tu as bien fait de me laisser dire tout cela; je suis calme, et je sens bien que je ne peux plus aimer son souvenir." (*LL,* 154)

"All this that I have told you has brought before my eyes anew a multitude of vile things that I had nearly forgotten. Now I feel nothing but horror for the past, and I do not mean for it to recur again. You have done well to let me tell it all to you. I am calm now, and I feel that I can never again love his memory." (*ll,* 329)

Furthermore, she agrees to Bustamente's marriage proposal, thus fulfilling the performative function of the narrative. Unlike *Manon Lescaut,* which ends when Des Grieux has finished his story, without the reappearance of the *Homme de qualité*, in *Leone Leoni* the extradiegetic narrator takes up the story again, thereby closing the frame and establishing a pleasing symmetry between the two opening chapters and the two closing ones.

These final pages contain decisive events that reverse the equilibrium achieved at the end of Juliette's narrative. Leoni and Juliette meet accidentally on the canal when she and Bustamente approach a gondola filled with merrymakers; she runs off with Leoni and sends Bustamente a letter of explanation. "[Y]ou know that I am not in control of myself, that an invisible hand governs me and throws me despite myself into the arms of that man" (*LL*, 158). As in the beginning, Bustamente's predominant emotion is anger, and he resolves to deliver himself once and for all from this rival. Having contrived a ruse to arrange a meeting with Leoni, Bustamente takes him to the Lido and challenges him to a duel. Bustamente kills Leoni and leaves him on the strand. As he returns to Venice with his gondolier, he sees Leoni and Juliette on the steamboat that is leaving for Trieste. He asks the gondolier whom he just killed and learns that his victim was not Leoni, but Leoni's evil friend the marquis.

Sand has collapsed the two final episodes of *Manon Lescaut*, the duel with Synnelet and the death of the protagonist, into one scene and then given that an ironic twist by adding a case of mistaken identity so that the protagonist does not die but is freed instead from a nefarious influence. The novel's final image is that of the two lovers, and not that of the two friends, Des Grieux and Tiberge, while the narrator, Bustamente, has a murder on his conscience and nothing else to show for his actions. His "talking cure" has not worked after all, for Juliette's love for Leoni is as strong as ever and beyond any rationalization on her part. The extradiegetic narrator's initial personal involvement with the intradiegetic narrator has led to far greater moral consequences; like the narrator of *Sarrasine*, Bustamente learns that narrative contracts are not always fulfilled, and that their effects often go far beyond those anticipated.[6]

Dramatically, as well as logically, Sand's ending works better than Prévost's. Instead of killing off the heroine at a time when she and the hero have found true happiness and contentment, as does Prévost, Sand avoids both the tragic ending of *Manon Lescaut* and the sentimental ending that the marriage of Bustamente and Juliette would have represented.

The death of Manon in the paradisiacal setting of the New World has often been viewed as problematic, for not only are she and Des Grieux prevented from living out the new, mutually loving existence they have created for themselves, but Manon, even more than Des Grieux, seems to be punished for past transgressions by dying suddenly and inexplicably during their flight from the colony. Whatever Prévost's motivations in resolving his story as he did, two messages seem implicit in his ending: reciprocal love is impossible, and a woman with a past like Manon's must be prevented from marrying and kept out of the social order.[7]

Sand does not destroy her heroine at the end, but rather allows her to continue to live and love. In addition, Sand remains faithful to the theme of irresistible passion common to both novels and makes it triumphant, whereas Prévost transmutes that passion into a more domesticated love, only to abort the relationship. This more moderate conjugality is seen in the marriage proposed by Bustamente, for, although he loves Juliette strongly enough to kill his rival, his love is not irrepressible and insurmountable, as is Juliette's for Leoni. Furthermore, Juliette feels grateful and respectful toward Bustamente but does not love him; indeed, Juliette remains cool toward Bustamente, even when she agrees to marry him. Sand rejects this plot possibility by having Leoni reappear and reawaken Juliette's passion, which, it should be noted, has a strong physical component.

Sand's plot, then, is more satisfying as well as more coherent than Prévost's. She has reversed his ending, as she switched the gender of his victim of love. It could be argued that Juliette, although alive at the end, remains a victim, and in fact resumes a relationship that has made her pay heavily in suffering and degradation for her love. Here, too, however, one must contrast Sand's vision of her theme with Prévost's. In *Manon Lescaut*, the victim of uncontrollable and unrequited passion is Des Grieux. He is freed from his enslavement to love only by Manon's death. In other words, it is not the lovesick partner who dies, but the object of that love. We have already seen how that resolution is less than convincing as well as artificial. Sand, on the other hand, has not only changed the gender of the sufferer, but has eliminated the fortuitous death of the lover so that the relationship continues. As Juliette herself predicts in her farewell letter to Bustamente, her own death will be the most likely end point of her torment: "But the storm envelops me and carries me away. In perishing on the reefs where I will be dashed, I will repeat your name . . ." (*LL*, 159). Suffering and death are associated within one protagonist, rather than being divided between two characters.

Sand had many models for the coupling of impossible love with death, beginning with the Tristan legend she had used to good effect in *Valentine*; in fact, the chronological distance between Prévost and Sand can be measured by her variation on his theme, for since Prévost's time novels depicting the death of doomed lovers had become popular. The most influential, of course, was Goethe's *Werther* (1774), which spawned many imitations, among them Juliana de Krüdener's *Valérie* (1804). In both cases, a young man loves a married woman who does not return his passion. Werther commits suicide, while Gustave succumbs to tuberculosis. Numerous other examples of hopeless and one-sided passion could be adduced, among them *René* and *Adolphe*; by the time *Leone Leoni* was written, the kind of suffering portrayed by Sand had become a romantic topos, as Sainte-Beuve mockingly pointed out in his preface to an 1840 edition of *Valérie*: "Indeed, the ending of these personal novels, inspired by memory, is hardly ever in conformity with the truth. . . . [B]ut one must continue the story, finish it according to the ideal, not the real. . . . One must kill off one's hero, whereas in real life he still lives somewhere, half-cured. . . . "[8]

Sand has inscribed her version of this doomed passion within a very specific tradition: that of women's literature of the early nineteenth century. This connection becomes evident when Juliette describes the readings recommended by Leoni as part of her sentimental education and reveals their influence on her.

> "C'étaient de beaux et chastes livres, presque tous écrits par des femmes sur des histoires de femmes: *Valérie, Eugène de Rothelin, Mademoiselle de Clermont, Delphine*. Ces récits touchants et passionnés, ces aperçus d'un monde idéal pour moi élevèrent mon âme, mais ils la dévorèrent. Je devins romanesque, caractère le plus infortuné qu'une femme puisse avoir." (*LL*, 31)

> "They were beautiful and pure books, almost all stories of women written by women: *Valérie, Eugène de Rothelin, Mademoiselle de Clermont, Delphine*. These touching and impassioned narratives, these glimpses of what was to me an ideal world, elevated my mind, but they devoured it. I became romantic, the most deplorable character that a woman can have." (*ll*, 208–209)

There are many examples in the novel of Juliette's *romanesque* perspective, one that allows her to be duped by Leoni and to remain under his domination.

Her description of him during their stay in Switzerland corresponds to the idealized portrait of the fictional hero. "How becoming the sunburn was to his manly face, and how it respected the large white forehead over the jet-black eyebrows! . . . He was generous, sensitive, refined, heroic" (*LL*, 50–51). Juliette herself admits to having a romantic imagination that is the stronger for her lack of experience and exposure to the ways of the world:

> "Leoni m'avait dit qu'il avait un secret terrible: j'imaginai mille infortunes romanesques. C'était la mode alors en littérature de faire agir et parler des personnages frappés des malédictions les plus étranges et les plus invraisemblables. . . . Je vous avouerai même que ma pauvre tête de jeune fille trouva un attrait de plus dans ce mystère impénétrable, et que mon âme de femme s'exalta devant l'occasion de risquer sa destinée entière pour soulager une belle et poétique infortune." (*LL*, 52)

> "Leoni had told me that he had a terrible secret. I imagined a thousand ro-

mantic catastrophes. It was the fashion then in books to introduce characters burdened by the most extraordinary and improbable maledictions. . . . I will even admit that my poor girlish brain found an additional attraction in that impenetrable mystery, and that my woman's heart took fire at the opportunity to risk its entire destiny to assuage a noble and poetic misfortune." (*ll*, 228–29)

Juliette and Indiana are sisters in their innocent conceptions of men and love.

That Leoni is aware of Juliette's propensity for the *romanesque* is clear to Bustamente and to Juliette, although each interprets Leoni's motivations differently." 'Leoni probably noticed that romantic tendency and took advantage of it?' I asked Juliette. 'Yes,' she responded, 'he did, but if he took so much trouble to deceive me, it was because he loved me, because he wanted my love at any price' " (*LL*, 52). Leoni's abuse of Juliette's naïveté and almost willing credulity is shown very clearly as Sand places him in the lineage of seducers such as *Indiana*'s Raymon.

Like Raymon, Leoni uses language to subjugate Juliette. She admits that "he spoke another language . . ." (*LL*, 30–31). After reporting at length one of Leoni's more specious dissertations on love, Juliette comments: "It was with such speeches that he assuaged my fears and dragged me, appeased and trusting, to the edge of the abyss" (*LL*, 67). Earlier, when he persuades her to flee with him, she cries, "[Y]our speeches are driving me mad" (*LL*, 40). Here, as elsewhere, he resorts to the sort of emotional blackmail common to lovers in women's fiction. This manipulation consists of his casting doubt on her love and obliging her to go against her own interests in order to prove her love to his satisfaction. Juliette does this again and again, first by leaving her parents and giving up her honor, later by posing as Leoni's sister to placate the princess Zagarolo. The sadistic nature of Leoni's love finds its clearest expression when he says: "I can make you die from grief, but I cannot let you go" (*LL*, 94). Juliette, like Indiana, responds in kind, calling herself a slave; she remains lucid enough in her misery to understand that she is being manipulated without, however, being able to end the situation.

> "Ces émotions continuelles m'affaiblissaient l'âme autant que le corps; je commençais à ne plus avoir la faculté de raisonner; le mal et le bien, l'estime et le mépris devenaient pour moi des sons vagues, des mots que je ne voulais plus comprendre, et qui m'effrayaient comme des chiffres innombrables qu'on m'aurait dit de supputer. . . . [J]e n'étais plus qu'une machine qu'il poussait à son gré dans tous les sens." (*LL*, 96)

> "These constant agitations weakened my mind as well as my body. I began to lose the faculty of reasoning; evil and good, esteem and contempt became

vague sounds, words which I no longer cared to understand, and which frightened me as much as if they were interminable columns of figures which I was
told to add. . . . [I] was simply a machine turned any way at his pleasure." (*ll*,
272)

Her very humanity has been taken away from her; she no longer understands language and becomes an automaton.

Leoni and Juliette's sadomasochistic liaison recalls more Léonce de Mondoville's relationship with Delphine, in Staël's novel of the same name, than
Des Grieux and Manon's affair, for Manon is never sadistic. *Delphine* is
mentioned in *Leone Leoni* in the passage where Juliette describes her readings. Léonce, like Leoni, whose name echoes his, can neither marry Delphine nor let her go. He constantly threatens suicide and uses this menace
to prevent Delphine from leaving him. Their love ends in death—twice in
fact, for Staël wrote two different endings; in the first, Delphine commits
suicide as Léonce, having been arrested during the Revolution by the Re-
publicans and condemned to death, is led to a firing squad, while in the
revised ending, Léonce goes off to war to be killed and Delphine dies of
shame.

Death seems to be a major feature of the other novels on Juliette's reading list as well: in *Valérie* and *Mademoiselle de Clermont* (1802), it is the male
protagonist who dies, while *Eugène de Rothelin* (1808) ends with the marriage
of Eugène and Athénaïs only after the tragic story of the marriage of
Eugène's parents and the untimely death of Eugène's mother has been told
and explained. Reading these works has done more than make Juliette
"romanesque"; they have taught her that love is painful, impossible to maintain in society, and usually leads to death. Juliette leads a novelistic life and
fully expects her end to be the same as that of her models.

Juliette's sense of an ending is not necessarily George Sand's, however.
Leone Leoni stops short of showing the heroine's death; it is Juliette who
anticipates a tragic end, and not her creator who grants her one. On the
contrary, the novel ends on a triumphant note, as Juliette and Leoni,
having both to some extent duped Bustamente, head off to a new city and
new adventures. There is a sense of freedom and liberation in the description of Juliette and Leoni as the boat pulls out: "They were scarcely on the
deck when the boat left with the speed of lightning. The couple leaned
over the rail to watch the wake" (*LL*, 168). They watch the wake the boat
leaves behind, as they are leaving Venice, with all its memories, behind
them; there is also a feeling of hope in this ending, particularly since the
man who had such psychological power over Leoni is dead. Sand leaves
Juliette's future open, rather than closing her novel on a definitively tragic
note.

Juliette's destiny is unusual and is experienced as such by the reader; the ending comes as a surprise, both within the context of the novel and with reference to *Manon Lescaut*. Neither married to Bustamente nor dead like Manon, nor even forelorn like Des Grieux, Juliette is suspended in time and space, looking back at Venice, and looking back, perhaps, at the destinies of women in past novels. It is particularly noteworthy that the marriage option is rejected by Sand not once but twice in this novel: first when Leoni returns and Juliette runs off with him, and then when Bustamente kills the wrong man, for presumably his intention in provoking Leoni was to kill him in order to remove him as a rival and thus marry Juliette, as was Des Grieux's purpose in fighting Synnelet. In fact, marriage to Bustamente is presented throughout the novel more in a negative than a positive way: he is overinsistent, overanxious to possess Juliette, and constrains her more than anything else. Curiously, when he tries to speak for her or to determine her destiny, Juliette vigorously rebuffs him. Clearly, for Sand as for previous women writers like Lafayette and Graffigny, marriage is not a satisfactory ending.[9]

Sand's feelings about marriage and fiction were ambivalent in her first novels as well. Although Indiana and Ralph live together, they are not legally married, while in *Valentine*, the final, happy marriage between Athénaïs and Valentin both displaces and replaces that of Valentine and Bénédict, who are joined only in death. Moreover, the death of a protagonist, always a convenient way of ending a novel, occupies a similarly ambiguous place in Sand's imagination. In the early novels especially, she seems to make an effort to avoid this ending, or at least to palliate it: Rose takes Blanche's place in the convent, Indiana and Ralph's suicide attempt is unsuccessful, Valentine and Bénédict live on in Athénaïs, Valentin, and their daughter. Only *Lélia*, written just before *Leone Leoni*, ends on an unreservedly mournful note. *Leone Leoni* thus diverges from its models but is consistent with Sand's own literary practice.

Sand has rewritten *Manon Lescaut* from a doubly female perspective, for both the protagonist and the author are women. In so doing, she has not only given Juliette a far different destiny from either Des Grieux or Manon, but she has also sharply distinguished her novel from its two sources, Prévost's work and women's novels of the previous generation. As has been seen, in her treatment of the theme of passion she remains closer to the women's tradition than to Prévost, diverging from both only in her ending, which nonetheless marks a return to earlier women's writing. This ending becomes the mark of her difference from male and immediate female predecessors, and contains her commentary on her literary models.

Manon Lescaut would seem to be an ideal spur to Sand's creative imagination, since it corresponds in theme and structure to her previous preoccupations with romantic triangles and unwavering love. *Leone Leoni* depicts a love triangle on which the very narrative depends for its existence; it is a stable one and does not evolve via complex substitution as do the triangles seen in earlier novels. The fleeting Henryet-Juliette-Leoni triangle later gives way to the Bustamente-Juliette-Leoni triangle, which comes chronologically at the end of the story but is present from the beginning of the narrative. Juliette, like Sand's previous heroines, is caught between two very different kinds of men and ultimately chooses to abandon the fatherly, overprotective Bustamente for the heroic Leoni. Juliette frees herself from the confines of Bustamente's paternalistic love, just as she breaks out of the plots imposed by previous literary models. Sand's rejection of marriage at the end is thus not only an avoidance of the expected dénouement, but also a repudiation of union with an overt father figure.

Despite her spare plot, Sand has nonetheless managed to incorporate into the novel another woman with whom Juliette shares Leoni; while the princess Zagarolo is not related to Juliette (on the contrary, Juliette passes as Leoni's sister, thereby making Juliette and Leoni putative siblings and introducing a note of incest into their relationship), a real sympathy and affection between the two women develops, despite Juliette's uncomfortable and humiliating position. Juliette comes not to mind her situation and accepts Leoni and the princess's public displays of affection. As in earlier novels, though, the other woman appears briefly, only to be eliminated in favor of her rival.

Leone Leoni shows Sand working against and among different literary traditions; its seamless originality demonstrates her own literary maturity in her ability to assimilate and adapt successfully prior texts. *Leone Leoni* has a rare equilibrium in Sand's *oeuvre* up to 1834—a balance of voice, where the female comes through strongly, an appealing plot, and Sand's usual exquisite style. It is a compelling work, worthy of being placed next to the novel that inspired it.

7

JACQUES
Incestuous Affinities

Written after *André* but published before, *Jacques* belongs to Sand's fertile Venice period. *Jacques* is one of a series of novels that bear a man's name as a title, rather than a woman's, as was the case with Sand's first three works. The title, like *Valentine* before it and *André* the following year, is one of convenience rather than a key to the novel, which could just as easily have been called *Fernande*, or *Jacques et Fernande*, or something totally different, for Jacques himself is by no means the main focus of the novel. Indeed, as a multivoice epistolary novel, *Jacques* allows several characters to be presented from different angles, forcing readers to draw their own conclusions as to how the characters and their actions should be judged.

George Sand was an indefatigable letter writer, as Georges Lubin's edition of her correspondence amply attests, and she had already used her epistolary talents in *Lélia*. In 1834, the year she wrote *Jacques*, Sand also began her *Lettres d'un voyageur*, a series of fictionalized travel and philosophical letters; 1837 saw the publication of her feminist *Lettres à Marcie* in Lamennais's *Le Monde*. Later in her career, she was still practicing the epistolary genre in *Mademoiselle La Quintinie* (1863). *Jacques* was Sand's first epistolary novel and, like *Leone Leoni*, marked a return to eighteenth-century models. Despite her use of a somewhat dated genre, even for her time, Sand created in *Jacques* a surprisingly modern novel.

Jacques is a streamlined version of the epistolary novel, without an editor's preface or cumbersome presentation.[1] Only a footnote from the "editor" reminds the reader that these letters are merely a selection culled from a larger correspondence in order to present the facts necessary for the understanding of the story; a final "editor's" note gives Jacques's fate (*J*, 353). There are five principal correspondents, plus two minor ones. The total number of correspondents Sand chose is ideal for this kind of novel—neither too many nor too few—so that Sand can sustain the exchanges without strain while providing multiple viewpoints on a very complex situation. Sand does not vary her tone much from writer to writer, unlike Laclos, although Fernande's letters are quite schoolgirlish, and Borel's, fittingly military. The epistolary form allows her again to present the women's stories in their own words, unmediated by a male narrator, and half the letters in the novel are written by the female characters.

Rather than being evenly distributed among the characters, the bulk of the letters instead fall into four distinct categories: the Jacques-Sylvia correspondence, which contains the greatest number of letters; the exchange between Fernande and Clémence, a convent friend and confidante; the letters between Fernande and Octave; and the Octave-Herbert correspondence. Although Herbert never directly appears in the novel, Octave's letters to him provide the reader valuable information on both Octave's character and Sylvia's background. He fulfills the traditional role of confidant, as do Clémence and Sylvia for Fernande and Jacques. Thus, although the novel details the formation and dissolution of their marriage, Fernande and Jacques exchange only five letters. Their story is revealed through their writings to others. On the level of narrative, then, the non-communication between Jacques and Fernande is mirrored in their limited correspondence, while the heavy exchange of letters between Jacques and Sylvia is an indication of the true extent of their relationship. Furthermore, the epistolary form, with its exchange of letters, reflects the plot, which concerns an exchange of partners.

Jacques therefore has four main correspondences that reveal three story lines: Jacques and Fernande's marriage, Sylvia and Octave's relationship, and Octave and Fernande's affair. The second fizzles out fairly quickly as Octave turns his attention to Fernande. Similarly, as Octave becomes Fernande's confidant and Clémence betrays increasing alarm at Fernande's relationship with Octave, the Fernande-Clémence correspondence ceases. By Part III, the longest of the novel's three parts, Octave and Fernande's affair, as well as the unexplained story of Sylvia's origins and her relationship to Jacques, becomes the focus of the novel, as the characters recombine to form new attachments. A fourth story line then becomes apparent in the hidden but ultimately essential story of Sylvia and Jacques.

Gérard de Nerval was the first to notice a resemblance between *Jacques* and Goethe's *Elective Affinities*, published in France in 1810.[2] In both novels, a married couple come together with two friends only to find their marriage dissolving as they experience attraction to the newcomers. These new affinities, as Goethe's title suggests, are almost chemical in nature, as though the four protagonists are participating less in a human interaction than in a laboratory experiment. The inexorability of the formation of new couples proceeds from this immutable attraction, as does the amorality of the situation, which is shown to be unavoidable and thus not subject to the usual social sanctions. The scientific nature of these permutations is underscored by recurring images from nature, particularly that of magnets and iron. Both novels deal almost exclusively with desire and love within and outside of marriage and avoid extraneous subplots or description. *Jacques* is especially spare, due to the epistolary form that enables the author to avoid unnecessary narrative. In *Jacques*, as in *Elective Affinities*, the raw struggles of human beings trying to come to terms with their passions are presented as starkly as possible.

The similarities between the two novels go deeper than the mere quadruple situation. In both novels, a child is born to the married couple, only to die. The children are clearly symbols of the parents' transgressions. Goethe's Otto resembles not his mother and father but the lovers his parents were thinking of when he was conceived, while Sand's twins are constitutionally weak, a manifestation of the instability of Jacques and Fernande's marriage; furthermore, the boy prefers Sylvia, the girl, Octave, or the parents' love objects.

Elective Affinities, like *Jacques*, is a novel about similarity and difference. Charlotte and the Captain are more nearly alike than Charlotte and Eduard, while Ottilie soon takes on many of Eduard's characteristics. Octave and Fernande find that they have more in common with each other than with their respective lovers, just as Jacques and Sylvia have the same world-weary, stoical perspective. These affinities, however, are more than mere attraction between like personalities. They explore the boundaries between like and unlike, interrogating the collapse of difference that is present in consanguineous relationships. Goethe's title, *Wahlverwandtschaften*, contains the word "kinship," so that the affinities chosen are more than friendships; they are relations as well.

It is surely no coincidence that the name Otto appears four times in *Elective Affinities*. Eduard's name is Eduard-Otto, and he was originally called Otto, until his friendship with the Captain, also named Otto, required that one of them go by another name. The child of Eduard and Charlotte, who resembles the Captain, is called Otto to honor his two fathers, as it were. Charlotte contains the sounds of Otto. Finally, Ottilie's name is a feminine form of Otto. Eduard prizes a glass that had been his as a child and bears his initials, E-O, which he now takes to represent his and Ottilie's initials. The fact that this glass survives intact when it is meant to be broken at the christening of a new summer house strikes Eduard as a sign of the rightness of his love for Ottilie. In fact, though, Eduard and Ottilie seem to be the same person, as Ottilie's ability to play music as badly as Eduard and her adoption of his handwriting indicate. Perhaps that is why their relationship is doomed to lead only to suffering and death, rather than happiness, for their similarities preclude the difference necessary for a healthy marriage; in any case, their situation is another illustration of Peter Brooks's thesis that in incestuous scenarios, possession is mortal.[3] Instead of demonstrating the happy recombination of elements described in chapter 4 of the novel, where limestone and sulfuric acid form gypsum and a gaseous acid, *Elective Affinities* shows the destructive products that the reaction of two substances can produce. The four characters do not form other, better partnerships during the course of the novel; on the contrary, by the end two are dead, with the resurrection the only hope of being united, while those who are left do not seem on the verge of marrying.

Sand has taken this experiment several steps further with entirely different results. She complicates Goethe's already close relationships by making Jacques, Sylvia, and Fernande blood relations. As Henry James correctly put it:

> In "Jacques" there is the oddest table of relations between the characters. Jacques is possibly the brother of Silvia, who is probably, on the other side, the sister of his wife, who is the mistress of Octave, Silvia's dismissed *amant!* Add to this that if Jacques be *not* the brother of Silvia, who is an illegitimate child, he is convertible into her lover. *On s'y perd.*[4]

Although the revelation to the reader of this consanguinity does not come until the latter part of the novel, Jacques is aware all along of the fact that Sylvia is Fernande's half sister, and that Sylvia's mysterious mother is none other than Mme de Theursan, a bigoted aristocrat who has successfully hidden the birth of this illegitimate daughter. It is difficult to know if Jacques's hatred of Mme de Theursan is motivated by his aversion to hypocrisy or by the fact that her simultaneous affairs with two different men, including his own father, have prevented all the parties involved from knowing who is Sylvia's father and thus preclude any marriage between Jacques and Sylvia. In this tangle of real and presumed kinship, James is right to say that one does indeed get lost; instead of Goethe's relatively simple exchange of partners, Sand sets up her usual system of evolving triangles.

Jacques's motives for marrying Fernande are noble: he wishes to save her from her mother's bad influence and share his wealth with her, for they are poor nobility while he is a rich bourgeois. For the first time, Sand shows a man of lower rank marrying an aristocratic woman, so that intermarriage and the sharing of wealth between classes is accomplished in a different way than in previous novels. Jacques is also very attracted to Fernande, and he acknowledges that he cannot possess her without marrying her. However, since he is aware of his feelings for Sylvia, and he knows Sylvia is Fernande's sister, his choice of Fernande as a wife has curious resonances for the reader beyond the ones he alleges in his letter to Sylvia (*J*, 35).

Jacques and Fernande's marriage is unusual in Sand's fiction up to this point in that it is a love match and not a forced union. Fernande is very inexperienced, as were young girls fresh from the convent, but is sure that her feelings for Jacques are those of love. Jacques has quite a past, if his fellow soldiers are to be believed, and has always been indulgently treated by women. He is old enough to recognize his feelings for Fernande. Nonetheless, however certain Jacques and Fernande are of their emotions, and however different the circumstances of this courtship and marriage might be from those of previous novels, the results are the same: it is apparent in a frighteningly short time that Jacques and Fernande are not happy together. "Only six months of love, how short a time!" (*J*, 128). The rest of the novel (two-thirds of the book) is devoted to an examination of the formation of new ties and the study of love, marriage, and society. It is permissible to surmise that Sand used her own experience of marriage to paint this portrait of a couple who, despite the best of intentions on both their parts, are not made for each other.

No one is to blame for this failed relationship. "I do not know whose foot slipped, but the grain of sand has fallen," writes Jacques to Sylvia (*J*, 111). Jacques is quite harsh in his judgment of Fernande, who in her inexperience and youth seems to do everything wrong. She throws herself at Jacques's feet to beg his forgiveness, a gesture she probably learned in novels and that he abhors. He, on the other hand, does not handle Fernande properly. Instead of assuaging her jealousy of his numerous past loves by reassuring her, he creates mystery and unhappiness for his oversensitive wife.

The portrait of both characters is a balanced one, thanks to the epistolary form, where there is no single narrator or point of view; letters 30 and 31, from Fernande and Jacques to their confidants, recount the same events, but from differing perspectives. The characters are presented through their own letters and those of their correspondents. Jacques and Fernande both have faults, as can be seen by the reader as well as their friends, who advise them on behavior. Letters 25 and 26, for example, the first from Clémence to Fernande, the second from Sylvia to Jacques, try to prevent the couple's marriage from deteriorating further, although the advisors' opinions are not infallible. Clémence is a particularly good counselor for Fernande, one who very much understands the workings of marriage and who foresees before anyone what will transpire. Clémence is a young widow who is reluctant to remarry, perhaps because situations such as Fernande's lead her to prefer her freedom. Fernande resists her advice, however, and as she and Octave become more drawn to each other, she drops Clémence as a correspondent, for Clémence's prescience is felt to be inconvenient. Despite Clémence's seeming good sense and clear-eyed perspective, though, she is called a "prude" by Jacques's friend Capt. Borel (*J*, 268), and Octave, for less disinterested reasons, calls Clémence a "false and bad friend" (*J*, 233), which rounds out the portrait of Fernande's confidante and leaves an ambiguous image of the character and her advice.

Although the novel focuses on both Jacques and Fernande and their changing emotions with marriage, Jacques, as the older and more legally responsible of the two, is also the more concerned about the course of action to take and becomes the central figure. He agonizes over the death of his marriage, which was contracted to assure his happiness in his mature years. Divorce is an impossibility, while the kind of brute force suggested by Borel, clearly a figure related to *Indiana*'s Delmare, is repugnant to Jacques: "Borel, in my shoes, would have calmly beaten his wife, and then he would probably not have blushed to invite her into his bed, sullied with his blows and his kisses" (*J*, 300). When first his daughter and then his son dies, Jacques feels he has no future to live for, while the discovery that Fernande is pregnant by Octave removes the option devised by Jacques of remaining as a "father" to Fernande and Octave as his "children." Jacques decides to commit suicide in such a way that only Sylvia knows for sure that his death is not accidental: he walks off into the Alpine snows, and an editor's note tells us that he was never seen again and is presumed to have fallen into a crevice and died. The naïve wish, expressed by Octave in a letter to Fernande that Jacques reads, that Jacques would die, of old age or some other cause, freeing his widow to remarry, is fulfilled by Jacques himself, and one imagines that Fernande and Octave, absorbed in their love and the plans for their future child, did not mourn his loss excessively.

Jacques, then, depicts the man's side in the tragedy of unhappy marriage, whereas Sand's earlier novels had shown the case from the woman's perspective only. Sand demonstrates that men and women both pay dearly when an unsuccessful marriage is indissoluble. Jacques's sufferings are shown compassionately, and it is easy to empathize with the death of his dreams of love and domesticity, although his character is odd enough and his romantic history sufficiently varied to make one feel that he is not entirely blameless for the failure of his marriage, particularly in his refusal to reveal more of his past to Fernande. On the other hand, the effects of a bad marriage on a woman are not neglected, as Borel's portrait of Fernande indicates: "I believe she has a good heart; before her marriage, at least, she was charming. I didn't recognize her when you brought her back to us with caprices, convulsions and excesses of which in the past I would never have thought her capable" (*J*, 273–74).

Despite the shift in emphasis to the man's suffering, though, the opinions of marriage expressed in the text remain the same as in Sand's previous works. Sylvia calls laws, beliefs, and social custom "chains of iron" (*J*, 47), a by now familiar phrase to Sand's readers, while Jacques calls marriage a barbaric institution whose abolition will unfortunately not take place in his century because men and women are too crude and cowardly to allow a freer union, preferring instead the "heavy chains" of the "law of iron" (*J*, 36). Furthermore, Jacques says of the vows of fidelity and obedience required in the marriage ceremony: "One of them is an absurdity, the other is contemptible" (*J*, 67). He goes on to establish his own moral code: "Lying is what degrades women. What constitutes adultery is not the hour she accords her lover, but the night that she then spends in the arms of her husband" (*J*, 301). This was Sand's precept in her other novels as well, and one of the innovations she brought to literature: not only was extra-marital love not condemned, but fidelity to the lover, not the husband, was prescribed. The laws of love took precedence over those of marriage.

Jacques was not particularly well received because of its daring ending, which contains both the satisfaction of the wife's adulterous passion and the husband's suicide. Jules Janin, in a long critical article on Sand in *L'Artiste*, provides an interesting perspective on the way the novel was read at the time of its publication:

Après quoi, il faut ajouter que George Sand nous a un peu réhabilités, nous autres hommes, dans un dernier roman, intitulé *Jacques*; ce roman est écrit en lettres, et, à l'embarras de la narration, à la confusion des personnages, à un certain malaise général qui se fait sentir dans tout ce livre, on voit que cette justification de l'homme contre la femme, réparation tardive et incorruptible des excès de *Lélia* a dû coûter beaucoup à George Sand; d'ailleurs, même dans ce plaidoyer en faveur des hommes, faites-y attention, vous allez trouver une trahison de l'auteur. *Jacques* [*sic*] . . . est un héros manqué qui joue à la fois le plus grand et le plus niais des rôles. Jacques, voyant sa femme aussi malheureuse en ménage qu'*Indiana* et *Valentine* [*sic*] avec leurs ignobles maris, Jacques, digne homme, ne trouve rien de mieux que de donner un amant à sa femme, et, quand il est bien déshonoré, d'aller se jeter dans un abîme, la tête la première.[5]

After which, it must be added, George Sand rehabilitated us a little, we men, in a last novel called *Jacques*; this is an epistolary novel and, in the confused narration, the tangle of characters, a certain general unease that makes itself felt throughout the book, we can see that this defense of man against woman, belated reparation for the excesses of *Lélia*, must have cost George Sand a great deal; besides, even in this defense of men, watch out, you will find a betrayal on the part of the author. *Jacques* [*sic*] is a failed hero who plays both the greatest and silliest of roles. Jacques, seeing his wife as unhappy in marriage as *Indiana* and *Valentine* [*sic*] with their ignoble husbands, Jacques, the worthy

man, cannot find a better solution than to give his wife a lover and, when he
is thoroughly dishonored, to go throw himself into the abyss, head first.

Balzac, in a letter to Mme Hanska, strikes a similar note, although in his
opinion, the novel is at least as much about Fernande as about Jacques:
"This one is empty and false from beginning to end. A young *naïve* girl,
after six months of marriage, leaves a *superior* man for a young whipper-
snapper, an important man, passionate, in love, for a dandy, without any
physiological or moral reason."[6] This view of *Jacques*, especially the characterization of the men, says at least as much about Balzac as about Sand's
novel.

Sand herself, in the preface written in 1855, felt compelled to state that
the novel was the fruit of a sad and bitter period in her life.

> C'est un livre douloureux et un dénoûment désespéré.
>   *Jacques* n'est cependant pas l'apologie du suicide; c'est l'histoire d'une passion,
> de la dernière et intolérable passion, d'une âme passionnée: je ne prétends pas
> nier cette conséquence du roman, que certains coeurs dévoués se voient réduits
> à céder la place aux autres et que la société ne leur laisse guère d'autre choix,
> puisqu'elle raille et s'indigne devant la résignation ou la miséricorde d'un époux
> trahi. (*J*, 4)

> It is a painful book and a despairing ending.
>   *Jacques* is not an apologia for suicide, however; it is the story of a passion,
> the last and unbearable passion, of a passionate soul. I do not pretend to deny
> this consequence of the novel, that certain devoted hearts will see themselves
> reduced to giving up their place to others, and that society doesn't offer them
> much other choice, since it jests and turns indignant at the resignation or the
> forgiveness of a betrayed spouse.

She goes on to urge the reform of marriage, as Jacques does in the novel
itself. As we have already seen, Henry James was not any more favorably
disposed toward the novel at the end of the century than the critics at the
time of the novel's publication. Examination of the criticisms of *Jacques*
shows that not only was the novel perceived as morally shocking for its
defense of adultery and seeming approval of suicide, but it was also seen
to be somehow unbalanced, for there is some disagreement even as to the
novel's subject. Jules Janin takes *Jacques* as a plea for men, while Balzac
sees it as an exaltation of an adulterous woman. James, for his part, is the
most lucid in his perception of the novel. Read in the context of Sand's
other novels of the period, though, *Jacques* appears surprisingly simple, for
it displays precisely the same obsessive pattern of relationships seen previously.

Beyond *Jacques*'s obvious theme of unhappy marriage and the difficulties of forming new ties when divorce is prohibited lies a search for a better partner, a more suitable relationship, similar to that found in *Indiana*. Jacques, like Delmare, is old enough to be his wife's father. This discovery surprises and dismays Fernande, who had thought the thirty-five-year-old Jacques no older than twenty-five. As she is seventeen, there is an eighteen-year difference between them. Her friend Clémence is certain that this age gap is too great and that Jacques is not the right match for Fernande. Jacques considers Fernande as his daughter but promises to do so only in his heart. In one of his two premarital letters to Fernande, Jacques foresees his old age and the day when she will no longer see him as a husband: "Remember, Fernande, that when you find me too old to be your lover, you can take your cue from my white hair and seek from me a father's tenderness" (*J*, 67–68). These paternal instincts become stronger as Fernande's love for Jacques wanes, and he deliberately masters his own love; his dream of being as a father to Fernande and Octave has already been mentioned. Fernande's relationship with Octave, then, is a turning away from the father to a man who is more nearly her contemporary. It is also, again as in *Indiana* and the other works, a union with the same.

The similarity between Fernande and Octave, on the one hand, and Jacques and Sylvia, on the other, is underlined many times in the novel by Fernande and Octave. "Jacques and Sylvia are one, you and I are another; they understand each other in everything, just as we do." (*J*, 222–23). When Fernande has read Octave's life story, she feels that she has read her own; she regrets that Jacques and Sylvia are not married, for each alone seems capable of appreciating the other. Octave draws the same conclusion and wonders how he could ever have loved Sylvia, for in *Jacques*, as in the previous novels, Octave comes to Fernande only after having been Sylvia's lover (and the carnal nature of Sylvia and Octave's affair is discreetly but firmly made clear). Sylvia is Mme de Theursan's daughter and thus Fernande's half sister. Again, as in *Indiana* and *Lélia*, a sister becomes the sexual intermediary through whom the ultimate lovers are joined. Thus, the triangle Octave-Sylvia-Fernande, where Fernande tries to reconcile the lovers Sylvia and Octave, gives way to the Fernande-Octave dyad.

Let us now look at the mirror image of this triangle, that of Jacques-Sylvia-Fernande, where Sylvia is the mediator between the estranged couple Fernande and Jacques. Sylvia and Jacques are truly ideally suited to each other, and the only obstacle to their union is the fact that they are possibly half brother and sister. Jacques's need to marry Fernande can be seen as a subconscious desire for her sister Sylvia, as his late admission that he always used another woman as a distraction from possible sexual thoughts of Sylvia reveals: "[M]y desires and my ecstasies always placed between us, as a safeguard, a lover who received my caresses, but who did not prevent my veneration from rising evermore to you" (*J*, 351–52). His marriage also allows Sylvia to come and live in his house, which sets the novel's plot in motion.[7] Since Fernande and Sylvia are sisters, this triangle resembles all the others in its sexual component. Furthermore, if the two half sisters can be read as mother-daughter figures, the brother can be considered to represent the father, not only in psychoanalytic terms but from indications in the text itself. Jacques is seen as a father not only to Fernande but to Sylvia as well, having learned at his father's deathbed about the circumstances of her birth. He sought out Sylvia and became her tutor and guardian; when Sylvia first sees him she thinks he is her father come to claim her, and cries: "There is my father, my father has been found!" (*J*, 85). This brother-and-two-sisters triangle simply stands in for the traditional mother-father-daughter arrangement.

Sylvia's story is not completely unveiled for the reader—and for Sylvia herself—until near the end of the novel, when Mme de Theursan is revealed to be Sylvia's mother; no one, not even Mme de Theursan, knows whether Sylvia's father is also Jacques's father. This unresolvable uncertainty means that Jacques and Sylvia can never be more than brother and sister. Jacques and Sylvia's tragic love story is clearly the hidden plot of *Jacques*, and it is one that Sand has very poorly explored, for it could have made a fascinating novel, particularly since this situation was not completely impossible in real life. The French family often comprised step- and half siblings because of frequent remarriage after the death of a spouse; in addition, inadequate (or nonexistent) contraception led to the birth of children out of wedlock or to mothers whose husbands were not the children's biological fathers. All three circumstances can be found in Sand's own family, where Sophie and Maurice Dupin each had an illegitimate child before meeting, making Hippolyte Chatiron and Caroline Delaborde her half siblings. Sand also thought, incorrectly in Georges Lubin's view, that her friend Félicie Molliet was Maurice Dupin's daughter and thus another half sister (*C* IV, 425). Finally, her own daughter, Solange, was in all likelihood not fathered by Casimir Dudevant, although she bore his name as the *Code Civil* required. This web of relationships was not unique to Sand's family, so that a study of possible kinship between two lovers would doubtless have touched a responsive chord in her readers. Yet rather than focusing on the emotions and anxieties of a couple whose relationship must forever remain ambiguous, unless they are willing to take a decisive step and marry despite their possible consanguinity, Sand has instead raised the issue of incest only to have it short-circuited by Jacques's death. Sylvia is not even allowed to join Jacques in death, for he expressly forbids her to take her own life, on the ground that her suicide would give credence to the gossip that their relationship was more than fraternal. *Jacques* thus both creates a literal incest scenario and denies it fulfillment, while nonetheless also establishing a parallel, nonconsanguineous relationship that asserts what has been repressed.

It is evident that Jacques does not even realize that Sylvia returns his passion, and their mutual confidences come too late in the novel for them to be the basis of any action. In the third letter from the end, Sylvia proposes to Jacques that they start over in the New World.

> Nous adopterons, si tu veux, quelque orphelin; nous nous imaginerons que c'est notre enfant, et nous l'élèverons dans nos principes. Nous en élèverons deux de sexe différent et nous les marierons un jour ensemble à la face de Dieu, sans autre temple que le désert, sans autre prêtre que l'amour. . . . (*J*, 345–46)

> We will adopt an orphan, if you like; we will imagine that he is our child and we will bring him up according to our principles. We will raise two of different sexes, and one day, we will marry them together in the sight of God, with no other temple than the desert, no other priest than love. . . .

This is truly a dream of perfect endogamy: a brother and sister raise two children as brother and sister, who, because they are not related, can marry as their parents could not.

The relationship between Jacques and Sylvia, as possible siblings, is literally incestuous, whereas in *Indiana*, *Valentine*, and later *Mauprat*, the relationships are incestuous only in the figurative sense that the couples seem like brother and sister or, in the case of Indiana and Ralph, father and daughter as well as brother and sister. The latter couple, as well as Bernard and Edmée Mauprat, are cousins, a degree of consanguinity deemed incestuous by the Catholic church, which nonetheless offered dispensation for marriage with some frequency. Jacques explicitly rejects incest, once when he refers to Fernande as having become like a daughter to him, "and any other thought would seem to me like incest" (*J*, 341), and then again when he tells Sylvia in his penultimate letter that he dies pure and unsullied by impious thoughts of her. Jacques's death is therefore motivated not only by his willingness to free Fernande from her marriage vows but by his fear that he will succumb to his desire for his sister. This sacrifice resembles Julie's in *La Nouvelle Héloise*.

Sand depicts in other texts of the period relationships where the characters show an awareness of the incestuous nature of the affairs in which they are involved and absolutely reject that relationship, even if socially and legally the liaison would be accepted. What is important is not the literal status of the relationship but that the character experiences it as incestuous. In "Metella" (1833), a short story reminiscent of *Corinne*, which itself depicts a man involved with two sisters, Olivier falls in love with Sarah, Metella Mowbray's niece and more his contemporary. He has been Metella's lover for many years, and she is now older and declining in beauty. In order not to hurt Metella, for whom Olivier still has great respect and affection, he leaves, vowing not to return until Sarah has married someone else. Having loved the "mother," Olivier cannot then become the adoptive daughter's husband.

This same scenario is repeated, with many embellishments, in *La Dernière Aldini* (1837), a heavily framed narrative whose title character, a young noblewoman, falls in love with a singer who had formerly been a gondolier, as well as her mother's lover. Unlike Sarah, Alezia Aldini learns who Lélio really is and understands his refusal to marry her. Lélio's knowledge that the woman he has come to love is in fact Bianca's daughter comes when Alezia recounts what can only be described as a primal scene, in which Lélio recognizes himself as one of the participants:

> "Une nuit, je fus réveillée dans la chambre de ma mère, où mon petit lit se trouvait placé, par la voix d'un homme. . . . On ne se méfiait pas de moi. On parlait librement. . . . [J]'entendais le bruit de leurs baisers. Il me semblait connaître cette voix d'homme; mais je ne pouvais en croire le témoignage de mes oreilles." (*DA*, 144–45)

> "One night, I was roused from sleep in my mother's bedroom, where my little bed was placed, by the voice of a man. . . . They did not suspect I was listening, and continued speaking. . . . [I] heard the sound of their kisses. The voice of the man seemed familiar to me, but I could not credit the evidence of my ears." (*LA*, 74)

Lélio is thunderstruck by this confession, and his reaction is worth quoting in detail:

> Mille pensées contraires et toutes sinistres s'emparèrent de ma tête. Je vis s'agiter devant moi, pareilles à des fantômes, les images du crime et du désespoir. Emu du souvenir de ce qui avait été, effrayée de l'idée de ce qui eût pu être, je me voyais à la fois l'amant de la mère et le mari de la fille. Alezia, cette enfant que j'avais vue au berceau, était là, devant moi, me parlant en même temps de son amour et de celui de la mère. (*DA*, 151)

> A thousand conflicting and unworthy thoughts took possession of me. I saw before me like phantoms, images of crime and despair. Moved by the remembrance of what had been, terrified at the idea of what might have been, I saw myself at once the lover of the mother and the husband of the daughter. Alezia, this child whom I had seen in her cradle, was then before me, speaking at the same time of her own love and that of her mother! (*LA*, 76)

For Lélio, an affair with his former mistress's daughter is akin to an "inceste intellectuel" (*DA*, 152), for he considered himself like a father to Alezia. Alezia underscores the unhealthy aspect of the situation by insisting on the fact that she has never discussed her experience with anyone else; her confession to Lélio represents the first time she has brought her story to light. Thus, Alezia's narrative is a *mise-en-abyme* of Sand's novels. In all of these works, the man recognizes the incestuous nature of his relationship and withdraws, leaving the woman free to mourn him and regret his departure. Similarly, Sand's father died, and she remained behind.

Jacques contains the clearest and most streamlined version of the configurations we have been following throughout Sand's work. There is no structural necessity for Jacques and Sylvia's fraternity, or at least there is no reason for the ambiguity of their relationship; nor is Jacques and Sylvia's dilemma explored, so that one is impelled to ask why Sand has set up her novel in such a confusing way. Only Sand's subconscious could have dictated such an arrangement, for *Jacques* denies twice, in Jacques and Sylvia's unconsummated relationship and in Fernande's rejection of her paternal husband, what it finally proclaims: happy union with the same.

Early in the novel, Fernande tries to argue that she and Octave cannot be more than friends because they are too much alike:

Jacques et Sylvia se ressemblent et ne nous ressemblent pas, et c'est pour cela que nous les aimons tant; voilà pourquoi nous avons pu avoir de l'amour pour eux, mais nous ne pouvons pas en avoir l'un pour l'autre. Pour alimenter l'amour, il faut, je crois, des différences de goûts et d'opinions. . . . (*J*, 233)

Jacques and Sylvia are alike, and are not like us, and that is why we love them so; that is why we could love them, but not each other. To nourish love, one needs, I think, differences of taste and opinions. . . .

This is the conclusion of Goethe's *Elective Affinities*, where Eduard and Ottilie become locked in a narcissistic relationship that, like Narcissus's own experience, ends in death. As Fernande and Octave fall more in love, though, they realize that they are made for each other, "his being is of the same nature as my own" (*J*, 255). At the end, they are expecting a child who symbolizes the goodness of their relationship and its future. Unlike its model, but true to Sand's previous works, *Jacques* presents productive, joyous incest.

Like *Valentine*, which also asserts the incest it denies, *Jacques* is greater than the sum of its parts. Yet although it is not Sand's most successful work, it is an important one on many levels. Thematically, *Jacques* broadens Sand's social criticism to embrace the man's viewpoint; economically, the marriage of bourgeois fortune and aristocratic blood differs from those of her past novels in that the rich bourgeois is a man, not a woman. *Jacques* raises the question of incest, even if the novel refuses to explore the issue fully, and prepares *La Dernière Aldini* and *François le champi*. Finally, Sand's use of the letter form shows again her ability to write well in different registers. Her handling of the polyphony of the epistolary genre is controlled and convincing, while the very open-ended nature of the novel, with its ambiguous conclusion and multiplicity of viewpoints, places the responsibility for synthesis on the reader. In that sense, *Jacques* forms a bridge between the eighteenth-century form and twentieth-century literary concerns.

8

EDUCATING WOMEN
André *and* Mauprat

Published in 1835, but composed in Venice before *Jacques* the previous year, *André* is perhaps the most self-assured of the works Sand had written until then, narrated in a certain, unwavering voice. Curiously, the gender of the narrator cannot be determined, for there are no authorial interventions. Instead, the *récit* is smooth and flowing, the plot simple and direct. The point of view, though, is clearly female. Sand's style, too, already well developed in previous novels, is here at its most pure, most lyrical. Georges Lubin, in his introduction to a recent reedition of *André*, is close to the mark when he says: "except for its sad conclusion, this study of country mores and of the little city of L . . . (La Châtre, of course) would be one of G. Sand's prettiest novels . . . " (*A*, ii). However, Lubin is not quite accurate in his assessment of *André*, for it is not merely the conclusion but the whole last third of the novel that is not only sad, but tragic. *André* is a cautionary tale that depicts once again society's lack of place for unusual women.

André is a retelling of the Pygmalion story, but with an emphasis on what happens after Galatea awakens and achieves full cognizance of her situation. Sand makes the parallel explicit when she has André say: "She is my Galatea . . . ; but she has only come alive to look at the heavens. Will she come down from her pedestal, and will she put her feet on the ground next to mine?" (*A*, 123). Although André does not physically create Geneviève as Pygmalion does Galatea, he becomes her teacher and spiritual creator. Like Galatea, however, Geneviève is different from all the other women, showing her individuality in dress, conduct, and lifestyle. Geneviève's passage from a calm, semieducated maker of artificial flowers who does not have an inkling of the meaning of passion to a loving, knowledgeable artist parallels, and then surpasses, Galatea's transformation from inert marble to warm flesh. When Venus grants Pygmalion's wish and brings his "ivory girl" to life, they produce a daughter nine months later and live happily ever after.[1] Geneviève's awakening does not have the same joyous future; although she, too, becomes pregnant, her child dies while still in the womb and Geneviève herself dies giving birth. This is the sad ending to which Georges Lubin referred in his introduction.

George Sand explores the myth of Pygmalion and Galatea in a way that no one else has by showing Galatea's side of the story instead of Pygmalion's and by asking herself what Galatea's reactions to the world might be after her awakening. Furthermore, by making Geneviève's emotional and moral transformation so profound as compared with Galatea's mere physical change in Ovid or even G. B. Shaw's later cultural improvement of Eliza Doolittle, Sand turns her story into an epistemological inquiry, one that seeks to define the use and meaning of knowledge to a woman.

Although she was living in Venice, Sand chose again her beloved Berry as the setting for *André*. In *André*, Sand also turns her attention to a milieu that had not yet attracted her notice and that was little represented in literature at the time. Neither nobles nor peasants, nor even solid bourgeois, the women who are the focus of the novel are members of the urban working class. These women Sand calls *artisanes* (*A*, 18), a local word that the narrator asks permission to use. Littré states that the feminine *artisane* designates the wife of an *artisan*, and notes that the word was unapproved by the Académie Française. Dictionaries of the *berrichon* dialect do not list either the masculine or the feminine of this word. The only exception is H. F. Jaubert's *Glossaire du centre de la France*, where *artisanne* [sic] is defined as: "Femme de la classe des artisans (Voy. *André* de G. Sand, et *apprentisse*)." In the absence of further proof, it is hard to say if Jaubert's reference is a case of a literary usage becoming the dictionary definition, or if Sand's use of the word was indeed the norm for her region, as she implies.[2] It is clear, though, that *artisane* was not standard French to designate a female worker, known as an *ouvrière*. Sand's adoption of this regionalism therefore represents the imposition on the French reading public not only of a dialectical word but, more important, of a feminine dialectical word for a particular kind of woman. Sand's description of her province is dependent on her use of the regional language, and in the later pastoral novels, of which *André* is a prototype, the *berrichon* language is extensively present in the texts as Sand's own special voice. Aurore Dudevant's very first fictional work, *La Marraine*, contains some local dialect, which the "editor" excuses because of the difficulty of rendering these expressions in what she terms more "refined" style (*LM*, 31–32). From the beginning, she was aware of the distinctiveness this language brought to her writing and of the originality and difference it lent to her work. *André* thus amplifies and refines the trend begun in *La Marraine* and continued in *Valentine*.

The *artisanes* who figure in *André* are also *grisettes*, that is, seamstresses and needleworkers. Sand does not use this word in quite the same way as her male contemporaries, for whom the *grisette* was synonymous with the working girl who made ends meet by prostituting herself or rather by becoming the mistress of a young bourgeois or noble, often a student. The portrayal of the *grisette* by Hugo, Musset, and Murger, as well as in Béranger's popular songs, made her a familiar romantic figure. Here, Sand designates women who earn their living at manual trades and who, although far from being prostitutes, are not immune to the attentions of young men, mostly in the hope of marrying one of them.

> Ainsi une jeune fille y peut, sans se compromettre, agréer les soins d'un homme libre et ne pas désespérer de l'amener au mariage; si elle manque son but, ce qui arrive souvent, elle peut espérer de mieux réussir avec un second adorateur . . . . (*A*, 19)

> Thus a young woman can, without compromising herself, accept the attentions of an available man and not despair of leading him to the altar; if she misses her goal, which often happens, she can hope to succeed better with a second admirer . . . .

The definition of the *grisette* has not changed so much as the emphasis; the accent is on their work and not on their amorous experiences, which seem in addition to be without financial entanglements. As in *Lélia*, Sand paints a positive, sympathetic portrait of the sexual woman and shows that women are not defined entirely by their sexuality. Neither are these *grisettes* fallen women, doomed to death or repentance like their romantic sisters; the above quotation makes it clear that the *grisette*'s behavior did not marginalize her socially but often was successful in achieving matrimony and thus status and position. As presented by Sand, the *grisette* becomes a living character, not a woman who has been "killed into art," in Gilbert and Gubar's phrase, like the *grisette* of male fantasy, the man's helpmeet who is denied any but the place men assign her.[3]

In describing these young women, Sand tells us that:

> L'indépendance et la sincérité dominent comme une loi générale dans les divers caractères de ces jeunes filles . . . . [C]ette espèce de ligue contre l'influence féminine des autres classes établit entre elles un esprit de corps assez estimable et fertile en bons procédés. (*A*, 18–19)

> Independence and sincerity dominate as a general rule in the diverse characters of these young women. [T]his sort of league against the female influence of the other classes establishes among them an esprit de corps that is very estimable and the source of good deeds.

Thus, these young women know the meaning of sisterhood well before the term has been invented. Henriette is typical of this kind of woman. She describes herself as a "woman of legal age, established, mistress of her own actions" (*A*, 45). At age twenty-five, she is independent and supports herself as a seamstress while training and supervising three younger girls. Although uneducated and quick to act before reasoning thoroughly, Henriette is basically a good person. She serves as a foil for Geneviève, whose situation is similar but whose experience is quite different because of her greater intellectual capacities.

Geneviève is a particular kind of *grisette*, for she does not suffer men's attentions. Rather, she lives alone, as she is an orphan and without family, and devotes herself entirely to her art. Geneviève's reserve makes her somewhat of an outsider among her companions: "She had gotten used to living outside of the society that surrounded her" (*A*, 52). However, her singularity is not cause for sadness, as Geneviève finds happiness in her freedom and her work. Geneviève is the prototype of the independent working woman who earns her living and needs no one to make her life complete. One thinks of Colette's Renée Néré as an example of this kind of woman, whose lifestyle will not become a social reality, or even a fictional one, until well after Sand's time.

Geneviève is not only an *artisane*, but an *artiste* (*A*, 171), even a *poète* (*A*, 51), a creator whose medium is artificial flowers. She imitates flowers but not in a crude, careless way. Except when forced by clients to falsify reality by making flowers in colors not found in nature, for example, Geneviève is faithful to her observations and makes of her flowers works of art. Geneviève is a poet whose humble art led her to an appreciation of the outside world and a desire to learn, which in turn improved her creations. She inspires several lyrical pages on poetry that reveal George Sand's concept of her own art.

> On dit que la poésie se meurt; la poésie ne peut pas mourir. N'eût-elle pour asile que le cerveau d'un seul homme, elle aurait encore des siècles de vie, car elle en sortirait comme la lave du Vésuve, et se fraierait un chemin parmi les plus prosaïques réalités. En dépit de ses temples renversés et ses faux dieux adorés sur leurs ruines, elle est immortelle comme le parfum des fleurs et la splendeur des cieux. (*A*, 49)

> It is said that poetry is dying; poetry cannot die. Even if it only had for asylum the mind of a single person, it would still have centuries of life, for it would flow from his mind like lava from Vesuvius and find a path among the most prosaic realities. Despite overturned temples and false gods worshiped on their ruins, poetry is immortal like the perfume of flowers and the splendor of the heavens.

Sand makes the telling point that poetry can be found everywhere, even, or perhaps especially, "at women's spinning wheels" (*A*, 49). Poetry is born of two elements: "beauty found in nature and the feelings given to all ordinary intellects" (*A*, 51). This is a democratic view of art, which is within reach of all, and contrasts with the prevailing notions of the period of the artist as magus, one of the elect chosen to lead the many.

Since she does not frequent dances or spend time with young men, Geneviève is truly free, as Henriette is not. Once she begins seeing André, however, Geneviève is open to the scorn of the whole town, not because she has a suitor, but because of the secrecy of their meetings. The gossips do not understand the nature of André and Geneviève's relationship, and that she meets him only to improve her knowledge of botany, not for romantic trysts. Henriette's meddling and the necessity of not alienating her clientele force Geneviève into an engagement with André that she would otherwise never have undertaken, simply to conform to social custom. From the moment she becomes involved with André, Geneviève loses her free and independent status and becomes instead subject to the rules set up by men.

Despite the differences in their standards and goals, Henriette and Geneviève are ultimately both victims of the men they love. The same view of the disparity between men and women's concepts of love appears in *André* as in Sand's previous novels. Henriette, by being true to the nature of the *grisette*, is not socially ruined by her affair with Joseph Marteau, but she is nonetheless very much used by him. As has been pointed out, the ultimate goal of the *grisette* is marriage with her lover. Joseph's ends are quite different. He sees his relationship with Henriette as a mere dalliance: "[I] allow her to cherish as much as she likes the illusion of one day becoming madame Marteau. I want to be her lover, that's all," he confides to André (*A*, 131). To Henriette, he shows his displeasure at André and Geneviève's impending marriage, for his purpose in bringing them together was to provide André with a mistress, not a bride. Henriette's reaction shows her horror at Joseph's intentions. "Good God! It strikes you as natural and just to seduce a girl and abandon her; but to marry her when you've ruined her reputation, you call that a wild idea, a crazy idea!" (*A*, 129). Henriette realizes just how faithless men can be and is appalled by this discovery, although she remains with Joseph for some months longer. In any case, she has more inner resources than Geneviève and is better able to take love's misfortunes in her stride in the hope of succeeding at another time.

Geneviève therefore finds herself engaged to a man whom she esteems but does not love. This engagement is not immediately followed by marriage, however, for two reasons: André hopes that Geneviève will come to love him as he loves her, and he is afraid that his father will not give his consent to the marriage. André, as has been established from the beginning, is a weak man.

> André tenait peut-être de sa mère, qui était morte jeune et chétive, une in- surmontable langueur de caractère, une inertie triste et molle, un grand effroi de ces récriminations et de ces leçons dures dont les hommes peu cultivés sont prodigues envers leurs enfants. (A, 6)

> André had perhaps inherited from his mother, who had died young and feeble, an insurmountable languor of character, a sad and indolent inertia, a great fear of those recriminations and hard lessons that uneducated men give gen- erously to their children.

This inability to stand up to his father and exercise his own will causes André to put off his marriage until Geneviève's pregnancy makes it im- perative, and then to resist either reconciling with his father or demanding his mother's inheritance by legal means, a step to which Geneviève is op- posed.

In his constant hesitation and inaction, André puts Geneviève in the worst possible position for a woman: pregnant, unable to earn her living, because her clientele has been stolen by another *fleuriste*, she is totally dependent on an unreliable man who himself, as Joseph had warned him, is inapt for any profession, despite his education, and who cannot maintain the posi- tion as tutor he finally obtains. Geneviève's biggest fear is for her child and his or her welfare, for she realizes that were she to die, this child would be at the mercy of a brutal grandfather and an ineffectual father who is more like a child himself. "She felt that she was chained down, that she had to live or die under the yoke of her father-in-law" (A, 218). Given these cir- cumstances, it seems more of a blessing than a tragedy that Geneviève's child is never born. What is tragic is Geneviève's own death, which for her represents a deliverance from suffering and ignominy. Enslaved by her physical condition and financial dependence, Geneviève has come a long way from the solitary freedom she enjoyed before she met André. Both education and love have led her not to greater heights but to despair and death.

The educational program André devises for Geneviève has a dual pur- pose. He not only teaches her facts about botany and science but tries also to inspire her with the beauties of poetry so that she might understand and share his love. André succeeds in his task: "He saw passion being born in this virginal soul, and recieved into his bosom the first effusions of the love he had taught her" (A, 128). In fact, it can be argued that he succeeds only too well: "Geneviève reached her lover's level, but this equality was not of long duration. More open and more intelligent, she soon surpassed him"

(*A*, 128). Geneviève does not remain a passive Galatea, the mirror of Pygmalion's desire. Instead, she grows beyond her lover's level and is able to take his measure.

In making her Galatea neither Pygmalion's inferior nor even his equal, but his superior, and then depicting such a disastrous outcome, Sand raises the question of the usefulness of learning. André compares Geneviève to Eve, and himself both to God and to Adam: "He was proud to raise her up to him and to be both the creator and the lover of his Eve" (*A*, 90). Like Eve, to whom the serpent promised equality with God, Geneviève expects that knowledge will improve both her art and her life. To a certain extent, her learning does provide inner joy: "Every day she found an enthusiastic pleasure in the development of her mind that entirely transformed her character and before which her timid prudence disappeared . . . " (*A*, 91). But rather than allowing her access to a higher social class or other social rewards, her education, impossible to acquire except under irregular circumstances, leads to a fall from grace, as those young *bourgeoises* who had originally admitted her to their group despite her simple origins reject her once she has imitated, or so they think, the loose behavior of the other *grisettes*. For a time, she uses her increased wisdom to discount the calumnies of the town: "But since her rapid education had strengthened her intellect, she felt her forces and her pride grow day by day" (*A*, 101). Soon, however, Geneviève herself realizes that her education has led only to unhappiness.

> "C'est vous [les livres] qui m'avez perdue. . . . J'étais avide de savoir vous lire, mais vous m'avez fait bien du mal! Vous m'avez appris à désirer un bonheur que la société réprouve et que mon coeur ne peut supporter. Vous m'avez forcée à dédaigner tout ce qui me suffisait auparavant. Vous avez changé mon âme, il fallait donc aussi changer mon sort!" (*A*, 171)

> "It is you [books] who ruined me. . . . I was avid to be able to read you, but you did me much harm! You taught me to desire a happiness that society reproves and that my heart cannot bear. You forced me to disdain all that sufficed for me before. You changed my soul, you should have changed my fate, too!"

This exclamation is very revealing, for it shows how far Geneviève has come since her calm, undisturbed life of the beginning. She now desires more and cannot be fulfilled. Geneviève dies regretting her costly education, which has made her unfit for any social stratum. "She missed her ignorance and the calm of her imagination, as well as the tender reveries during which she happily fell asleep, when she knew nothing about anything in the universe" (*A*, 224).

Are we to conclude from this tragic ending that Sand does not support

education for women? On the contrary, education is not criticized in this
novel at all; rather, it is the insufficiencies of society—first in not educating
women and then in not finding a place for those who somehow manage
to attain some learning—that are denounced. Even the limited social mobility available to men of the period through the professions, as seen in
Sand's novel *Simon* (1836), based in part on the true story of Michel de
Bourges's social ascension, simply did not exist for women. If anything,
education was a liability for women as things stood, making them unfit for
any station in life and endowing them with intellectual appetites that could
not be satisfied. Even woman's traditional form of social mobility, marriage,
is denied Geneviève in that her marriage ends with her death. Society, in
the form of André's father, disapproves of the disproportion in condition
between André and Geneviève, for despite her education and qualities, the
grisette is not the right match for the son of a marquis. George Sand is not
reneging on her social theories, however, for a successful marriage between
Geneviève and André would still be possible were André able to press his
lawsuit against his father. André's insufficiencies are at least as much to
blame for Geneviève's death as his father's prejudices. *André* is thus merely
a particular case and not an indictment of marriage across class lines. A
society that could not fully integrate women into its ranks, as well as men
who were not up to dealing with the new independent woman, surely a
situation Sand had experienced herself, are castigated.

In light of its negative resolution, it might seem paradoxical, even per-
verse, to call *André* the most feminist of Sand's early novels. Yet despite
its melancholy dénouement, *André* offers a great deal that is encouraging
for women. It depicts independent women who earn their living and answer
only to themselves. The women have a collective name and band together
for protection. More important, they are not privileged members of the
upper classes but are representative of the large number of French working women. Geneviève is herself called both a "poète" and an "artiste," and
the rose she creates under a sudden wave of inspiration is no mere imitation
of nature but a work of art in itself, born of the combination of intelligence
and nature, which was the definition of poetry given in the novel (*A*, 51).
"It is as beautiful a thing in its class . . . as the work of an old master; it is
nature rendered in all its truth and all its poetry" (*A*, 126). Sand makes it
clear that women can truly be artists, that they are capable of understanding
the most complex and abstract concepts if only they are exposed to them.
André furnishes a view of women that must have been cheering to the female
reading public. *André* thus joins *Lélia*, the novel that preceded it, in thought
but with an entirely different tone. The anger is gone and has been replaced
by a mixture of hope and sadness. The woman artist still fails to be accepted

by the world, still is unable to find her spiritual match, but the other *artisanes* remain, as does *André*, to encourage and inspire women for the future.

If *André* chronicles Geneviève's education, *Mauprat* puts a woman in the role of educator. Edmée de Mauprat becomes not only a teacher but also the designer and overseer of a difficult pedagogical program aimed at civilizing her cousin Bernard, "the wild child of La Roche-Mauprat" (*M*, 188, 425). *Mauprat* is, as Yvette Bozon-Scalzitti points out, a retelling of "La Belle et la Bête," but with Beauty in charge, rather than the Beast.[4] In the original story, the Beast is conscious of his situation vis-à-vis Beauty, namely that he is a prince who can be transformed only by her love, whereas in *Mauprat*, it is Edmée who not only knows her own heart, but plans everything so that Bernard can become her husband.

Edmée's purpose in educating Bernard is not to turn him into another M. de La Marche, her fiancé at the novel's opening, a very correct though boring gentleman. Rather, she hopes to bring him up to her level, to make him her equal, not her inferior. As Edmée tells him at the end, marriage between them would have been impossible, were it not for her persistence in teaching him: "One thing is certain, and that is you would have made a detestable husband; you would have made me ashamed of your ignorance, you would have wanted to dominate me, and we would have destroyed one another . . ." (*M*, 428). Bernard had to make great progress before Edmée could finally become his wife.

Geneviève's education was both practical and spiritual and led her far beyond her teacher, as we have seen. Bernard's experience is quite different. Some traditional subjects are excluded from the curriculum; in particular, Latin is considered unnecessary, given the belated nature of his schooling. The emphasis in Bernard's program is on the spiritual and the social; the ferocious bandit must be taught to live within polite society and to control the natural impulses that have ruled him heretofore.

The epistemological questions so acutely posed in *André* are not an issue in *Mauprat* at all, because education for men was the norm, whereas it was not for women; the Loi Guizot of 1833, for example, established primary education in France, but education for girls had to wait until the 1850s or later to become a serious reality. Education is assumed to be good and efficacious because it succeeds for Bernard, as it did for men in general. It would be wrong, however, to assume that Bernard's education transforms him completely, the way the Beast gives way to a handsome prince in Leprince de Beaumont's tale. "Here is a great question: 'Are there invincible tendencies in us, and can education merely modify them or wholly destroy them?' As for me, I would not dare to answer . . ." (*M*, 53). *Mauprat* is thus not (or not only) a paean to progress, the story of the triumph of culture over nature, the confirmation of man's innate goodness (*pace* Rousseau); despite Edmée's use of Rousseau's *Emile* as a basic text, Sand and Jean-Jacques part company on many key issues.[5] Bernard remains somewhat feral, the animal in him lurking just below the surface.

This quality is evident in the description of the eighty-year-old Bernard at the novel's beginning, where he is shown to retain certain wild features and behavior: "His face would have appeared extremely handsome to me had not a certain harshness of expression brought before my eyes, despite myself, the shades of his forefathers" (*M*, 37). He is very polite to his guests but raises his voice at the servants and swears terribly when a door is left open. Bernard himself admits to being "a bit rough" (*M*, 38), and it is evident that his education has only changed him to a certain extent. He is gracious and well informed, but also temperamental.

In fact, Bernard has become just like Edmée. Except for the reference to Edmée's "delicate beauty," Bernard's description of Edmée could be a self-portrait: "She was a proud and intrepid young woman as well as a sweet and affable chatelaine. I often found her haughty and disdainful; Patience and the poor of the district always found her humble and debonair" (*M*, 155). Both he and she use similar images of wood to describe themselves; Bernard calls himself "an old branch happily detached from a rotten trunk and transplanted into good soil, but still knotty and rough . . ." (*M*, 38), while Edmée characterizes her Mauprat ancestors to the abbé: "Even those whom education has smoothed the most have many knots . . ." (*M*, 187). Instead of a linear depiction of Bernard's socialization, *Mauprat* describes a circular movement, in which the change in Bernard is one of degree rather than kind.

Bernard and Edmée are alike right from the beginning. They are cousins and share the same last name. Thus the novel's title is significant, as it designates either Bernard or Edmée, or both, and posits the novel as a family saga; it is the first of only a handful of Sand's works to bear just a last name. Bernard is immediately, if crudely, attracted to Edmée, while Edmée tells him that she has wished to meet him for a long time, for she knows of her father's earlier hope of adopting Bernard and having him eventually marry her, a dream reminiscent of Sylvia's proposal to Jacques. The greatest difference between Edmée and Bernard is Bernard's wildness, which far outweighs his good qualities. Edmée, on the other hand, tempers her proud and untamed side with learning and charity. Under her tutelage, Bernard learns to do the same. By the time of their marriage, Bernard and Edmée have become as similar as two people can be, and in marriage they continue to share the same name.

They are also equals, with his legal control over her offset by her greater moral authority over him, as in Raymon and Laure's marriage. Edmée herself reveals to her confessor long before marriage with Bernard is anything but a remote possibility that she will allow no man to dominate her: "[I] will never suffer the tyranny of a man, not the violence of a lover any more than a husband's slap across the face . . ." (*M*, 189), which shows her awareness of the masculine power to which marriage would subject her. She manages to checkmate this potential situation by choosing Bernard over M. de La Marche.

In making this choice, Edmée demonstrates that she, too, has changed, along with Bernard, and that her sentimental education began at La Roche-Mauprat, when Bernard's general education did, although her realization of her progress comes well before his. During the same conversation with her confessor, she admits that her "love" for M. de La Marche consists of confidence and friendship, not passion. In the sequel to this conversation, which is delayed until the very end of the novel for reasons of suspense, since Bernard must not yet learn that she loves him, she describes the evolution of her feelings for her fiancé: "M. de La Marche appears insipid and stiff to me ever since I got to know Bernard" (*M*, 427). Her meeting with Bernard has been decisive for her as well as for him, for she has learned what she really wants in a husband by comparing the two men who vie for her hand. She has dared more in choosing Bernard, but she has also received far more from him emotionally than she ever would have from M. de La Marche, as Bernard himself immodestly points out: "There came a time when I understood Edmée; such a time would never have come for M. de La Marche" (*M*, 154). The peasant philosopher Patience also, with his characteristic perspicacity, knows from the beginning that "that La Marche fellow isn't her type" (*M*, 175). Thus, Edmée and Bernard's marriage represents the completion of the circle as the two who were already similar become even more so.

If their relationship does not represent a vast transformation on the personal level, it does so on a social level, for it is hardly accidental that *Mauprat* takes place at the end of the *ancien régime* and runs approximately up until the novel's publication date, 1837, a period encompassing massive social changes in France. The American and French revolutions play prominent roles in the book, while the Napoleonic era is glossed over. Edmée and Bernard marry after the American Revolution, in which Bernard fought with Lafayette, and just before the French Revolution, which changed their status and fortune without affecting their relationship.[6] It is significant that their marriage comes at a historical time when liberty was the watchword and when an old way of life was forever destroyed, for this egalitarian union is precisely the kind of marriage that should have existed in postrevolutionary France. The First Republic did much to ease laws relating to marriage; divorce was permitted for the first time, and many took advantage of this option, while marriages were concluded and dissolved with a great deal of freedom. Indeed, Sand's own mother was supposed to have been married and divorced at this time, despite the fact that no certificates have been found. Although women's status was far from optimal during the Revolution (it will be remembered that Olympe de Gouges, author of the "Déclaration des droits de la femme et de la citoyenne," was guillotined, as were Manon Roland and others), women definitely had a civil freedom unknown previously.

This lack of constraint (some called it license) was cruelly repressed by Napoleon and the *Code Civil*, under which women's status in France reached a nadir from which it has not fully recovered today. George Sand had felt the effect of these laws in her own marriage, where her husband had jurisdiction over her property, and in her recent separation procedure, for divorce had been banned in 1816, to be reinstated in 1884, after Sand's death. Separation was possible, however, and it is that for which Sand sued, eventually winning back control of her money and property as well as custody of her children. This was a long and painful process and is detailed in her correspondence. Just one example from a letter to her brother about her husband shows clearly Sand's, and every other woman's, situation before the law:

> Quand même tu lui attacherais une corde au pied pour le retenir aux environs de Paris, n'ai-je pas à Paris, un domicile qu'il a le droit de violer, un mobilier, fruit de mon travail, qu'il a le droit de vendre, une propriété littéraire dont il a le droit de toucher la rente chez mon éditeur? Comment veux-tu que je reste à la disposition d'un homme qui est fou et furieux, au point de prendre un fusil quand il est de mauvaise humeur? (*C* III, 127)

> Even if you attached a rope to his feet to keep him in the Paris area, do I not have a home in Paris that he has the right to enter, furniture, the fruit of my labor, that he has the right to sell, literary property whose income he has the right to collect from my publisher? How can you want me to be at the beck and call of a man who is absolutely crazy, to the point to threatening me with a shotgun when he is in a bad mood?

This was what the Revolution had led to, and subsequent regimes had only ratified the provisions of the *Code Civil*. Even the 1830 revolution, which Sand had followed with concern from Nohant, had effected nothing but a change of monarch. By 1837, the promises of freedom made by the Revolution were clearly unfulfilled, not only for all the French but for women especially.

By setting her novel against the prerevolutionary background, Sand has proven *a contrario* what the Revolution should have wrought but did not.

Bernard, with his feudal upbringing, Enlightenment education, and egalitarian marriage, symbolizes the France of the past as well as the future. In this context, his trial becomes not merely a plot device but emblematic of the events of 1789 and suggestive of a new aftermath of the Revolution: the verdict in Bernard's trial is not the one expected when he is indicted. This is the second time Sand used historical events to show the insufficiencies of contemporary society. In *Indiana*, the revolution of 1830 is depicted in the novel and followed by the marriage of Laure and Raymon, an unconventional kind that would only later become socially acceptable. On the île Bourbon, Ralph and Indiana purchase freedom for slaves well before the Second Republic, which in 1848 finally and belatedly put an end to slavery in French territory. Both novels rewrite history by showing the circumstances that led to a particular revolution and proposing an outcome different from the one that actually took place.

Mauprat is thus a social novel, but not only the kind of social novel that it has been recognized to be. It is true that Sand became familiar with, and influenced by, Pierre Leroux's socialist doctrines around the time of composition of *Mauprat*. Yet the kind of equality and economics shown in *Mauprat* differs very little from that seen in Sand's previous novels. Patience and Marcasse eat at the Mauprats' table and are treated as equals, but so do Bénédict, Athénaïs, and Valentine eat, play, and practically live together. Bernard and Edmée ungrudgingly give up part of their money and property when required to by the Revolution, but they obviously retain enough wealth to provide advantageously for their four surviving children. Valentine, too, was happy to live on 1200 francs a year and would have gladly exchanged her château for a cottage. Patience and Marcasse are also exceptional characters, and neither represents *le peuple* in all its ordinariness, as would be the case later in the *romans champêtres*. While *Mauprat* does contain an unmistakable social message and foreshadows Sand's great programmatic social novels, *Le Compagnon du tour de France* and *La Comtesse de Rudolstadt*, I would suggest that this social agenda is not the only thesis Sand illustrates, or even the most powerful one. Equality among citizens, fairer distribution of wealth, impartiality of justice, all are Sand's goals and are present in *Mauprat*. But preeminent among her aims are equality in marriage and justice for women.

These themes are not new in Sand's work, either, for she had sounded the same note since *Indiana*, striving in her novels for better-assorted relationships than those arranged by social custom (Ralph-Indiana instead of Delmare-Indiana, Valentine-Bénédict instead of Valentine-Lansac). Unlike the novels that preceded it, though, *Mauprat* depicts the constitution of a happy marriage according to Sand's ideals and not the dissoluton of unhappy unions based on male authority and woman's subjugation. *Mauprat* even recalls these earlier novels in its *berrichon* setting, particularly Edmée's flight through the woods; in the socially correct if emotionally unsatisfying engagement of Edmée and M. de La Marche, *Mauprat* reinscribes *Valentine*. Edmée herself is a French Indiana without the latter's Creole ignorance but with the same self-mastery and devotion to her cause. In fact, the short story that Sand expanded over several years into a novel seems to have been originally conceived as a remake of *Indiana*: a young woman, married to a much older man, is saved by another young man with whom she falls in love. This situation is clichéd in the extreme, as she must have felt, for she radically modified it into the plot we find in *Mauprat*.

Mauprat, then, is a continuation and culmination of Sand's feminist and social thought as developed over the previous seven years. It is also one of the most successful depictions of her thesis, for not only does *Mauprat* end happily and unambiguously for both protaganists, but the novel is also artistically satisfying. Masterfully narrated, well, if somewhat overly, plotted, *Mauprat* keeps the reader in suspense right up until the end. Sand has ably integrated many subgenres into the novel: Gothic novel, historical novel, mystery story, adventure novel, and social treatise, without making *Mauprat* seem like a *fourre-tout*. *Mauprat* is a framed narrative that relies again on the romance tradition.

Novel of education, *Mauprat* conducts its *Bildung* on three levels. Like *Jacques*, where the form reflects the contents, *Mauprat* educates while portraying an education, as did Rousseau's *Emile*, whose educational theories Edmée put into practice. Bernard tells his story to the narrator, a young man who, as an author, is characterized as "inquisitive and chatty" (*M*, 39). Furthermore, he is a "faithful historiographer" (*M*, 39), who will transmit Bernard's story to others and both purge the reputation of Bernard's Mauprat ancestors and pass on to his readers the moral of Bernard's story. This shrewd framing comprises one more, extratextual level, for the author of this *mise en scène* is of course George Sand, who is educating her audience. This tripartite narrative situation conceals some very clever sex-change operations, as seen in other Sand novels: Edmée educates Bernard, Bernard educates the male narrator, who in turn takes responsibility for the novel's frame. This narrator even resembles a woman, in his characterization by Bernard as a "*little* young man" (emphasis Sand's) and as belonging to an "effeminate generation" (*M*, 39). Ultimately, it is a woman who writes the novel and who is known as such by her public despite her male name.

Like Edmée, Sand takes on the task of pedagogue, orchestrating, again like her character, a subtle program of sex education aimed at both male and female readers. It will be remembered that Edmée's education of Bernard was designed to teach him not so much facts and figures but moral principles and the ability to reason; basically, though, it is a program that teaches him to understand her, to live with her without oppressing her or dominating her but allowing her to be spiritually free. This is Sand's agenda for her readers, too. As in *André*, Sand shows explicitly what had been implicit in her previous critiques of society: the importance of modifying men's behavior if woman's condition is ever to improve. The earlier novel had depicted the tragic consequences of André's inability to fulfill Geneviève's needs, while *Mauprat* presents both a more optimistic prognosis and specific guidelines for change.

At the highest scriptural level, as at the deepest representational level, the director of operations in *Mauprat* is a woman. Although using a masculine name and a male narrator, Sand is very much in control of her creation and her message. She has found safety in this disguise, just as her revisionist view of marriage is hidden by the more anodynic political and moral lessons of *Mauprat*. Sand's masculine stance really has become very subversive. By employing male narrators, whether overtly as in *Mauprat*, or subtly as in *Simon*, where a brief comment indicates the narrator's gender, Sand both shows her solidarity with men and uses it to her own advantage.[7] She says, in effect, I am one of you, and states what she is not—a silly woman writer to be patronized by male critics and readers. One has only to read Sand's friend Sainte-Beuve's articles on women writers, or Juliette Decreus-van Lietland's study of Sainte-Beuve, to realize just how limited, and limiting, this criticism was.[8] The use of a male narrator is thus reassuring to the male literary elite, for it distinguishes Sand from other women writers while effecting a rapprochement with male writers and critics. This mode of narration defuses, and seemingly diffuses, the feminist message of her novels, for as a "male" writer, Sand can be thought to take up a role familiar to men and dear to their heart, that of chivalrous defender of women, but whose defense does not include liberating them from legal and social constraints. Having lulled men into a false security with a conspiratorial wink, Sand is then free to tell them exactly what she thinks of their laws and their society. It is a brilliant stratagem and one that seems to have worked very well, if the critical reception given to Sand's early novels is any indication. Except for *Lélia*, Sand's novels were read and applauded despite their acknowledged criticism of contemporary mores and their call for vast social change. This success led to their wide distribution and strong influence for many decades throughout the world.

With *Mauprat*, Sand has come a long way from the struggle so painfully apparent in *La Marraine*, whose narrative situation bears some similarity to *Mauprat*'s in that a man tells his life story to a narrator who has run short of ideas (*LM*, 23; *M*, 37). It will be remembered that in *La Marraine*, the female narrator had difficulty giving narrative authority to a man but was unwilling to assume control herself. In *Mauprat*, Sand and Edmée are firmly

in charge, Edmée within the novel and Sand without, while Bernard and
the unnamed narrator are merely agents of Sand's power.

If *Mauprat* repeats the theme of previous novels and offers a solution to
women's oppression, the novel also repeats the triangular structure apparent in Sand's other works as well. Here, too, a suitable resolution can
be seen, one that is at one and the same time more stable and more disturbing than other such relationships described in earlier novels. The abbé
tells Edmée during a decisive conversation: "It is impossible for this adventure at la Roche-Mauprat to be anything but a sinister dream" (*M*, 190),
and, in a sense, all of *Mauprat* is some sort of bad dream, of the kind that
half a century later Freud would be only too happy to analyze. The narrator,
too, speaks of hair-raising stories that he will not communicate to the reader,
"grieved that I am that they ever darkened (*noirci*) and pained my memory"
(*M*, 36). The word *noire* comes up in the following paragraph, where he
excuses himself for telling such a disagreeable tale:

> Je vous demande pardon, au contraire, de vous envoyer aujourd'hui une nar-
> ration si noire; mais dans l'impression qu'elle m'a faite, il se mêle quelque chose
> de si consolant, et, si j'ose m'exprimer ainsi, de si sain à l'âme, que vous m'ex-
> cuserez, j'espère, en faveur des conclusions. (*M*, 37)

> On the contrary, I must ask your pardon for unfolding so sombre a tale. Yet,
> in the impression which it has made on me there is something so consoling
> and, if I may venture the phrase, so healthful to the soul, that you will excuse
> me, I hope, for the sake of the result. (*m*, 3)

We are entitled to ask ourselves what there is in *Mauprat* that is both dark
and healthy for the soul; an examination of the complex relationships in
the novel will help provide an answer.

Mauprat describes in accurate detail the working out of what Freud would
later call the Oedipus complex. It does so for both Bernard and Edmée,
so that in the end he has achieved union with the mother and she with the
father. This is obviously a rather unhealthy situation, but it is presented in
a very positive way, as we have seen before, heralding both new sexual
equality and the reign of social justice. Like *Jacques*, then, *Mauprat* portrays
the same situation for two different characters, but with positive outcomes
for both. Let us begin by looking at Bernard's experience.

Bernard loses his mother at the age of seven, around the same time as
Edmée loses hers; it is later revealed that both deaths were caused by Bernard's uncle Jean. He is adopted by his grandfather and uncles, the brigands of La Roche-Mauprat. At age thirteen, he has his first run-in with

Patience, one of the many father figures in which the novel abounds. Patience describes himself as Edmée's "foster father" (*M*, 398) and admits to Bernard that he came to love him as his own child, thus claiming paternity to both of them (*M*, 358). However, these statements come well after his initial turbulent meeting with Bernard, who has killed Patience's tame owl. As a punishment, Patience hangs Bernard up in a tree, with the dead owl above the boy's head; the owl's blood drips down on Bernard, who is powerless to move. It is a chilling scene, a warning of future corrections should Bernard not reform. It is not difficult to read into Patience's act a threat of castration, particularly since it follows upon Bernard's threat to harm Patience, who had supposedly spoken ill of the Mauprats. The son's desire to kill the father is met with a rude reminder of the father's superior strength. Much later, Patience also threatens to avenge Edmée's death by killing Bernard; fortunately, Bernard is not guilty and Patience then helps to exonerate him. The relationship between Bernard and Patience is typical of the uneven struggle between father and son, and moves from combat to affection after Bernard has won his wife. Too, the theme of castration is apparent in the sobriquets given to the two branches of the Mauprat family—"Coupe-Jarret" (Hamstringcutter) and "Casse-tête" (Head-breaker), especially the former.

After his escape from La Roche Mauprat, Bernard is adopted by his uncle Hubert, whom he sees as a father, a good one after all the ill-treatment he had received from his uncles. He admits that his love for Hubert "took hold of me at the same time as a violent love for the daughter . . ." (*M*, 134). This triangular relationship, seen so many times in Sand's other novels, becomes not the uncle-daughter-cousin relationship it is in reality, but the father-mother-son triad described by Freud, where Edmée becomes the mother to Bernard.

Sand uses various family terms to describe Bernard and Edmée's relationship, ranging from cousin, which is their real blood tie, to brother and sister, one of her favorite terms for lovers, to mother-son. This latter comes up frequently, and is used from the beginning of their acquaintance. Edmée calls Bernard "mon enfant," not once but twice right after their meeting, even though she knows they are the same age (*M*, 96, 103); her kiss reminds Bernard of his mother's last kiss. Later, as Bernard's education progresses, he tells his listeners: "If there never was a stronger or more reserved fiancée, never was there a more tender mother than she" (*M*, 213). Upon his return from America, changed and matured, Bernard again uses the same word: "Edmée was a true mother to me" (*M*, 278). Edmée herself reveals her pride in Bernard's progress: "[I] took pleasure in it with true maternal pride" (*M*, 280). After all their trials and after many years of marriage, Bernard insists that "during the whole course of my life I gave myself up entirely to her reason and integrity" (*M*, 431), the way a child is led by his mother. The link between Edmée and his mother, who died before she could complete his education, is made explicit by Bernard himself: "With this sole influence, which I remember, and that of another woman that I subsequently endured, there was enough to make something of me" (*M*, 53).

In order to win the mother, the child must eliminate the father. This has already been pointed out in Bernard's relationship with Patience. The combat between Hubert and Bernard appears in the noisy philosophical arguments Bernard picks with his uncle once he has acquired a bit of education. Bernard enjoys demonstrating the superiority of his learning over Hubert, and the two spend many evenings quarreling. Eventually, Bernard does succeed in killing the father, but in an indirect way.

It is significant that when Edmée first enters La Roche-Mauprat and hears shots, she assumes that they are directed at her father, who she supposes has come to rescue her. Her infernal agreement with Bernard to give herself first to him is made so that he will save her father, who in fact is in no danger. This linking of Bernard and sexuality with the death of the father is hardly accidental. Following an argument between Bernard and Edmée, a scene that we will examine later in more detail, Edmée is shot by Antoine de Mauprat, one of Bernard's brothers and, for the moment, a stand-in for Bernard. Edmée thinks it is Bernard who has shot her, and repeats: "*You are killing my father!*" (*M*, 398). The witnesses to this outburst do not understand the portent of Edmée's words and think that she mistakenly believes that her father has been shot also. It is clear from the context, however, that Edmée is telling Bernard that by killing her, he has killed her father, who lives only for his daughter. And, in fact, she is right, for Hubert enters a second childhood as a result of her accident and recovers only long enough to join Bernard and Edmée's hands before dying. At Bernard's trial, Edmée insists that her words right after the shooting had no meaning and were due to delirium. However, she betrays the truth of her feelings afterwards, as well as the extent of her denial, when she asks: "And if I loved you enough to absolve you in my heart and to defend you before the world, at the cost of a lie, what have you to say against that?" (*M*, 425), which indicates that in her heart she accused him of killing her father.

Bernard thus attains what every boy dreams of, union with the mother. His marriage is happy and successful and lasts over forty years without a cloud, surviving revolution and personal hardship. We must now go back and examine this relationship from Edmée's perspective. If anything, the Oedipal configuration is even more clear in her case, although the roles are different: Edmée remains the daughter, and her conflict is the resolution of her feelings for her father in the ability to transfer that love to another man, Bernard, who nonetheless, as in all Sand's novels, is still a father figure.

Edmée's father is clearly the most important person in her life. Motherless, without siblings or close relatives, she has been brought up by a doting father, who, along with Patience and the abbé Aubert, father figures all, forms her only society. She tells the abbé, "I feel that I only love one person with passion, my father . . ." (*M*, 195). At the end of the novel, after everything has been concluded but her marriage, she admits to Bernard that had they married earlier, before Bernard's education had been completed, they would have been miserable; "it would have driven my father to despair, and, as you know, my father had to be considered before everything else!" She goes on to make a clear statement of her motives for waiting so long to agree to marry him: "I sacrificed you to my father, my poor Bernard, and heaven, which would have cursed us if I had sacrificed my father, rewards us today by giving us to each other, tried and invincible" (*M*, 428). She preferred her father to Bernard, and in fact later accepted Bernard by transforming him into her father. Since Bernard has also become a mirror image of Edmée, one could easily give the novel a new title: *My Father, Myself*.

In his old age, when he recounts his story, Bernard greatly resembles the old Hubert. He is quick to anger and has a temper. Edmée's portrait of her father could apply to Bernard as well: "You see that, despite his adorable goodness, my father is sometimes so mettlesome that he breaks his snuffbox by slamming it down on the table when your political arguments get the better of his . . ." (*M*, 187). Bernard notes that during the course of an argument, his uncle "stamped his foot on the burning logs in his fireplace" (*M*, 212). This image is reminiscent of Bernard's ironic comment to the narrator upon inviting him to approach the hearth: "Mauprat though I am, I won't put you in there instead of a log" (*M*, 39).

Edmée's acceptance of this transference of desire from the father to Bernard takes place during the long illness caused by her accident. Her refusal to marry Bernard even after their six-year separation while he was in America and his evident social and intellectual development is explicable only by her stronger attachment to her father. When she thinks her father dead, she experiences a rebirth, even assuming a fetal position, and does not recognize him when doctors bring him into her room, so convinced is she that her father is dead. Her grave illness is not attributable to her wounds, which heal easily, but to her distress over her father's death. When in fact she recovers enough to understand that her father is not dead, only very ill, she cares for him like a child. "But she didn't understand anything that wasn't him" (*M*, 392). When she hears Bernard's name, she faints, unable to bear her father's imminent death and replacement by Bernard. Only as she grows stronger can she accept her father's death and Bernard as her husband. Through this crisis, she has been able to come to terms with her feelings both for her father and for her cousin. As I have pointed out, though, since Bernard so much resembles his uncle, Edmée is losing nothing by marrying him, but combining father and outside love object into one man. Furthermore, she is fulfilling her father's plan by marrying Bernard.

The scene of Edmée's shooting is a crucial one in the novel, for it marks the end of Edmée's resistance both to Bernard and to the love she feels for him. It is the third scene to take place at the Tour Gazeau, Patience's old habitat and the site of Bernard's early punishment. Two of Bernard's brothers had died there on the night Edmée was brought to La Roche-Mauprat. Bernard and Edmée have come full circle from that awful night when Bernard made Edmée swear she would belong to him before any other man, and their argument before the Tour Gazeau is the culmination of the rape Bernard tried to accomplish when he first met Edmée. *Mauprat* can be said to be the transformation, over some 400-odd pages, of the impulse to rape into conjugal sexuality; it is not insignificant that Bernard and Edmée later have six children, symbols of their successful marital relations.

Bernard and Edmée meet just after Bernard has vowed to possess the next woman to appear at the brigands' lair. He tries to force himself on Edmée, whom he takes for a prostitute, until she manages to make her identity known and to persuade him to help her escape. She is less afraid of Bernard than of his brothers, for she knows that unless she can incite Bernard's pity, she will be "violated and assassinated two hours from now . . ." (*M*, 103). Later, she puts it another way: "[B]ut it's a strange sort of jealousy that would allow a man to possess his mistress at ten o'clock and then turn her over at midnight to eight drunken men who will return her to him tomorrow as filthy as the mud of the roads" (*M*, 105). The word *viol* (rape) is never used, only such well-known euphemisms as "outragée" (insulted, violated), "victime des autres brigands" (victim of the other brigands) (*M*, 236), "déshonorée" (dishonored) (*M*, 378). It is evident, though, that rape is what Edmée fears at La Roche-Mauprat and what Bernard contemplates at the Tour Gazeau: "Edmée never knew what peril her honor was in during that minute of anxiety" (*M*, 344).

Indeed, frustrated by seven years of waiting and by the very confusing signals given by Edmée, Bernard nearly allows his wild side to take over. He manages to control himself, however, and runs away only to hear a shot fired, the shot that wounds Edmée. Clearly, Antoine de Mauprat's shooting of Edmée is a displaced figuration of Bernard's desire to dominate the proud Edmée, and it is important to note that Antoine succeeds where Bernard must not, for it would be impossible for Edmée to continue to love a man who had treated her so brutally. The crime is committed, albeit symbolically, and causes the crisis at the end of which Bernard and Edmée's marriage is decided.

Among other things, then, *Mauprat* describes a marriage that is the culmination of a process not only of cultural education but of libidinal education as well: male brutality against women is countered and transformed into healthy sexuality, where man does not abuse his superior strength. Edmée had already expounded this theory to Bernard when contradicting his brothers' assertion that women are liars: "Bernard, do you want to know why they think women are liars? . . . It's because they use violence and tyranny with those who are weaker than they are. Every time one makes oneself feared one risks being deceived" (*M*, 165).

In keeping with her dual focus on Bernard and Edmée, Sand manages to have things both ways in *Mauprat*, for she illustrates both sexual violence in men and its result for women. Despite the displacement, Edmée is nonetheless a victim of aggression, and the fact that Antoine's attack leads to her marriage indicates that sexuality, particularly initially, can be a traumatic, searing experience, even if it is ultimately successfully assumed by the woman.[9] Edmée is frightened of Bernard throughout the novel, frightened by his potential for violence, sexual or not. This potential, like every other aspect of Bernard's character, is not eliminated by the novel's end but merely suppressed, more or less dominated by more positive energies. This is evident on the first page of the novel, where Bernard's destruction of La Roche-Mauprat is described. ". . . [A]s if to give a slap to the memory of his ancestors, he ordered the entrance gate to be torn down, had the North tower gutted (*éventrer*) and a breach made from top to bottom in the enclosure wall (*mur d'enceinte*) . . ." (*M*, 35). Bernard "guts the tower" (but the verb *éventrer* contains the noun *ventre*, associated with the womb, as well as the belly), "slits from top to bottom the enclosure wall" (again, the word *enceinte* also means *pregnant*), images all of rape and violence against women. Overtly, Bernard's action is aimed at his bad "fathers," the Mauprats, but covertly, the destruction of La Roche-Mauprat shows his repressed acts against Edmée that have been sublimated. *Mauprat* thus rewrites in a positive manner the situation of *Rose et Blanche*, where Horace rapes Denise, attempts to possess Rose and later falls in love with her, only to return to Blanche and literally frighten her to death as she assumes her wedding night will repeat the earlier rape. Rose cannot marry such a man, whereas Edmée is free to marry Bernard, while Antoine bears the opprobrium of the aggression and is eliminated. The ambivalence of sexuality, and of incestuous desire, is illustrated in *Mauprat*, as in Sand's other works.

While *Mauprat* is dark, it is also consoling. Sand has written a streamlined variation on her usual structure, where the accent is on fathers, good and bad. *André* and *Mauprat* form a diptych not only in theme but in structure, as did *Indiana* and *Valentine*, where one novel is a positive illustration of a given situation and the other a negative one. *André* and *Mauprat* both exhibit the same couple-plus-father trio first introduced in *Leone Leoni*. In these two novels, the older men are literally fathers—the marquis is Geneviève's father-in-law and André's father, Hubert is Edmée's father—whereas in past novels the men whom the women rejected had been merely father figures (Horace, Delmare, Jacques, Bustamente). For this reason, the familiar sister dyad and shared lover are superfluous, since union with the real father would be impossible. Nonetheless, in *André*, Sand makes a half-hearted and unsuccessful attempt to involve Joseph Marteau in a triangle with Geneviève and André while Joseph is still courting Henriette, testifying to the influence this structure had on her imagination.

In *Mauprat*, Edmée must turn away from Hubert to Bernard, who is identified with the father by his blood relation to Hubert as well as by Hubert's plan to adopt Bernard as his son. There is no need for the intervention of another woman to establish Bernard's equivalence with the father. *André* shows the tragic outcome of the same triangular situation, but where the husband and wife are unequal and the brutality of the father, symbol of society and its laws, overcomes the efforts of Geneviève to placate him. She cannot form a lasting relationship with André, who has inherited his mother's weak character, because he is incapable of fulfilling the role defined by the heroes of previous Sand novels and of challenging the rule of the father by replacing it with an egalitarian, noncoercive arrangement. Geneviève therefore becomes a victim of the marquis's violence, in a scene reminiscent of Delmare's aggression against Indiana, which leaves a mark on her forehead; as a result, her child dies *in utero* and Geneviève's own death follows. This attack clearly has sexual overtones, in addition to its social and familial resonances. The bad father wins in *André*, making it one of two novels of this early series (the other being *Lélia*) to have an unequivocally tragic ending. *André* and *Mauprat* both show, albeit in opposite ways, that men must change if women are to find a meaningful place in a new society.

CONCLUSION

In the ten years following the "Voyage au Mont d'Or," George Sand produced an admirable and extensive body of work. She treated her major subject, woman in male society, in a variety of ways and a multiplicity of forms. Women of all classes and diverse professions make their appearance in these early novels, which place particular emphasis on the woman artist. Women are portrayed in an unaccustomed light: prostitutes are sympathetically drawn, female friendship and solidarity are repeatedly promoted, androgyny in thought and action, rather than traditional femininity, is valorized. Sand's novels as a group manifest not only a fresh, new talent but a decidedly female point of view in the handling of theme, plot, form, and, especially, narration. The woman's voice remains audible despite Sand's consistent adoption of a male narrator.

Sand's economic theories, featuring intermarriage between classes and the more equitable distribution of wealth, were also original and were developed well before she came under the influence of Pierre Leroux or any other social reformer. They were born of her own education, experience, and observation. In later novels, she would take on industrialization (*La Ville Noire*, 1861) or turn even more to peasant society (among others, *Le Meunier d'Angibault*, 1845, where Sand describes the formation of a profit-sharing operation). Concomitant with economic change is social improvement, where marriage is no longer a financial transaction but the union of loving equals; slavery, literal and figurative, is ended; and education is available to all. Sand's rewriting of both the French Revolution and the revolution of 1830 served as a prelude to her active *engagement* in the short-lived revolution of 1848.

Sand's celebration of the Berry and its inhabitants, which reached its apogee with the *romans champêtres*, began with her first fictional work, *La Marraine*. There, too, we see the first use of the *berrichon* language that Sand would eventually transform into a distinctive and personal literary voice, most notably in *Jeanne* (1844). Her realization of the differences between men's and women's language, in "La Fille d'Albano," *Indiana*, and *Leone Leoni*, was not limited to a mere identification of the problem but led ultimately to a solution that consisted, on the one hand, of rewriting her local dialect, as she does with the word "artisane" in *André*, and, on the other, of the early development of an exquisite prose style that is completely hers and absolutely unmistakable.[1] Her own voice is thus always present and palpable in the form of an original literary language, the "woman's sentence" Virginia Woolf described.[2]

These thematic and narrative accomplishments can all be attributed to Sand's own family romance, both to her personal identification as a writer with a kind, heroic, and artistic father figure, and to her working out through her plots of an oedipal scenario whose resolution occasions political reforms. In elaborating her own family plot, Sand turned to genres and narrative forms that reproduced her own obsessions. Thus, the romance, with its oedipal origins, was her dominant mode. Also attractive to her as models were more or less explicitly oedipal plots, such as that of *Manon Lescaut* or *Elective Affinities*, while she established further triangular situations in her novels even when they were ancillary to the main story line. Her female oedipal plot, with its variance from the male version, motivated her rewriting and reimagining of traditional narratives.

As early as her initial texts, we see Sand limning her scenario, as she turns away from her mother as textual receiver in the "Voyage au Mont d'Or," creates the androgynous singer in "Histoire du rêveur," imagines a family triangle in *La Marraine*, and has the eponymous Fille d'Albano reject her constraining, bourgeois fiancé for a life of artistic freedom with her brother. Sand's first novel, *Rose et Blanche*, sets up situations and relationships among characters that will reappear regularly in future works, although this inaugural plot lacks the completion and resonance of its later developments. *Indiana* achieves final equilibrium in a way *Rose et Blanche* does not, but it does so through a more complicated series of exchanges among partners. Similar configurations govern *Valentine*, whose ambiguous focus and ending indicate the unconscious force of this scenario and its conflictual nature when the mother figure remains present. The novel's Berry setting, like that of *La Marraine* and *Mauprat*—indeed, Sand's preference in all these works for the country, her father's territory, over Paris, her mother's sphere—strengthens the connection between Sand's personal considerations and her fiction.

With its lack of traditional plot and mixture of narrative modes, *Lélia* almost demands an incomplete presentation of the scenario. Nonetheless, we do find the crucial central figure, which consists of two sisters involved with the same man, while Trenmor appears as a surrogate father, although his link with Lélia and the dynamics of the triangle are not the same as in the other novels. *Jacques* returns to the four-character plot of *Rose et Blanche*, without mediating characters, and explicitly introduces the possibility of incest into the plot. As in *Valentine*, the ending both affirms and denies endogamy, but with the negation as the psychoanalytic equivalent of an avowal. In *Leone Leoni*, both the plot and the narration depend upon the triangle, which again consists of an avuncular protector, a young woman, and her dashing lover. Similar in structure to *Leone Leoni*, *André* and *Mauprat* feature real fathers in the place of fatherly husbands who are rejected in favor of younger men; however, the difference in character between André and Bernard de Mauprat means the victory of the father's order in *André*, with all its negative social ramifications, as opposed to the successful marriage of the Mauprat cousins.

The novels published after *Mauprat* are too numerous to catalogue easily. Some merely repeat old works, while others represent exciting new achievements: *Consuelo* and *La Comtesse de Rudolstadt* (1842–44) are masterpieces of description and female plot; *Jeanne* is a graceful adaptation of the Joan of Arc story to Sand's era and province; *La Petite Fadette* (1849) tells of growing up female at a time when adolescence was hardly recognized as a separate part of the life cycle; *Laura* (1865) is an adventurous novel of the *merveilleux*.

Even during the decade that separated the "Voyage au Mont d'Or" from *Mauprat*, Sand had begun exploring other literary genres. The *Lettres d'un voyageur*, published from 1834 to 1836, represent another foray into travel literature and are a felicitous combination of philosophy and fiction. These letters prepared both the *Lettres à Marcie* (1837) and *Un Hiver à Majorque* (1842), the description of her stay on the island with Chopin and her children. In 1833 Sand wrote her first play; however, *Aldo le rimeur*, a "poem in dialogue," was not meant to be performed. *François le Champi* was the first of many novels to be adapted for the theater. Sand also wrote directly for the stage with some success, often trying out her plays beforehand in the puppet theater at Nohant. The brilliant *Histoire de ma vie*, sketched in the "Voyage," was on Sand's mind in the 1830s, when she signed a contract to write her autobiography, but was not begun until 1847. Her last texts, collected in the *Contes d'une grand-mère*, return to her earliest inspiration, the fantastic.

In many of Sand's later novels, the scenario I have described in this book as engendering social and economic as well as personal transformation reappears, either intact or with variants. The situation in *Jeanne* has strong affinities with that of *Rose et Blanche*. *La Mare au diable* (1846) presents the attempted seduction of Marie by the man who would be her employer, and her marriage with Germain, a man twelve years her senior, who is a paternal figure to the sixteen-year-old. Marie takes the place of Germain's first wife, Catherine, even wearing the dead woman's wedding ring, while Germain's son Petit-Pierre completes the family triad. *Le Dernier Amour* (1867) depicts an affair between Félicie, who is married to the older Sylvestre, and her younger cousin, Tonino. The novel explicitly refers to the situation in *Jacques*. Several of Sand's subsequent novels show her usual configuration with a reversal of genders. Thus, *François le Champi* (1850) ends with the quasi-incestuous marriage of the foundling and his foster mother. *Le Piccinino* (1847) describes a young man in love with a woman he later learns is his own mother.

Germaine Brée cites *La Confession d'une jeune fille* (1865) to illustrate her thesis regarding Sand's triangular situation between her mother and her grandmother.[3] Yet, although this extremely complexly plotted novel does feature several maternal figures, notably Jennie Guillaume, clearly the kind of mother Aurore Dupin would have desired, father figures play a preeminent role. Lucienne loves her tutor, later her foster mother Jennie's fiancé. Much of this two-volume novel is taken up with Lucienne's ambivalent feelings about Frumence Castel, which eventually are transmuted into filial affection. Jennie is aware of Lucienne's emotions and is willing to step aside to allow Lucienne and Frumence to marry, a selfless gesture (and a bit of wish fulfillment) that recalls Rose and Blanche's situation. Jennie and Frumence finally marry, although theirs is a curiously chaste, passionless union, and Lucienne resumes her role as daughter. Lucienne must then decide whether or not to marry the Scotsman Mac-Allan, who had once been her stepmother's lover. Thus, Lucienne again finds herself in the same situation as before, the rival of her "mother." Fortunately for Lucienne, it turns out that her real mother had committed adultery, so that M. de Valangis was not her father after all, and her stepmother was therefore of no blood or legal relation, leaving Lucienne free to marry Mac-Allan. This convenient outcome allows the union of Lucienne with the exotic and dashing father figure. In fact, the novel, like Balzac's *Le Lys dans la vallée*, is a long letter sent to Mac-Allan by Lucienne, her confession about her past, with a request for his approval. Their marriage is therefore sanctioned by the father figure himself. A very psychologically revealing document, *La Confession d'une jeune fille* deals with naming, identity, and family relationships, and descends in a direct line from Sand's earlier novels.

George Sand's *oeuvre*, extending over nearly fifty years, is rich and varied, as was her own existence. The product of a unique set of circumstances, Aurore Dupin Dudevant dared to create her own lifestyle and, as George Sand, to impose it on society. In her fiction, most especially in her first works, she elaborated a particularly female literary vision that remains vibrant and influential a century and a half later.

Abbreviations

A	George Sand,	*André*, prés. par Georges Lubin (Paris: Editions d'Aujourd'hui, 1976).
C		*Correspondance*, ed. Georges Lubin (Paris: Garnier), Vol. I, 2d ed., 1964; Vol. II, 1966; Vol. III, 1967; Vol. IV, 1968; Vol. VI, 1969.
DA		*La Dernière Aldini* (Paris: Michel Lévy Frères, 1866).
FA	J.S.	"La Fille d'Albano," *La Mode*, 15 May 1831, pp. 157–68.
Hr	George Sand,	"Histoire du rêveur," ed. Thierry Bodin, *Présence de George Sand* 17 (June 1983): 2–39.
I		*Indiana*, ed. Pierre Salomon (Paris: Garnier, 1962).
i		*Indiana*, trans. George Burnham Ives (1900; rpt. Chicago: Cassandra Editions, 1978).
J		*Jacques* (Paris: Michel Lévy Frères, 1866).
L		*Lélia*, ed. Pierre Reboul (Paris: Garnier, 1960).
l		*Lélia*, trans. Maria Espinosa (Bloomington: Indiana University Press, 1978).
LA		*The Last Aldini: A Love Story* (Philadelphia: B. Peterson and Brothers, n.d.).
LL		*Leone Leoni* (Paris: Perrotin, 1840)
ll		*Leone Leoni*, trans. George Burnham Ives (1900; rpt. Chicago: Cassandra Editions, 1978).
PD	Jules Sand,	"La Prima Donna," *Revue de Paris* (April 1831): 234–48.
M	George Sand,	*Mauprat*, préf. de Jean-Pierre Lacassagne (Paris: Gallimard [Folio], 1981).
m		*Mauprat*, trans. Stanley Young (Chicago: Cassandra Editions, 1977).
ML		*My Life*, trans. and adapted Dan Hofstadter (New York: Harper and Row, 1979).
Oa		*Oeuvres autobiographiques*, ed. Georges Lubin, 2 vols. (Paris: Gallimard [Pléiade], 1970, 1971).
RB	J. Sand,	*Rose et Blanche, ou la comédienne et la religieuse*, 5 vols. (Paris: B. Renault, 1831).
V	George Sand,	*Valentine* (Paris: Michel Lévy Frères, 1869).

Translations are my own unless otherwise indicated, and conform as much as possible to Sand's own style and phrasing. I have occasionally been aided by the translations of Sand's works cited, which I have also sometimes modified.

Notes

INTRODUCTION

1. Freud addressed several times the question of the girl's oedipal development and its asymmetry with the boy's, notably in "The Psychogenesis of a Case of Homosexuality in a Woman," in *The Standard Edition of the Complete Psychological Works of Sigmund Freud*, ed. James Strachey (London: Hogarth Press, 1955) (known as *SE*), vol. 18, pp. 147–72; "The Dissolution of the Oedipus Complex," *SE*, vol. 19 (1961), pp. 173–79; "Some Psychical Consequences of the Anatomical Distinction between the Sexes," *SE*, vol. 19, pp. 248–58; "Female Sexuality," *SE*, vol. 21 (1961), pp. 223–43; "Femininity" (in *New Introductory Lectures on Psychoanalysis*), *SE*, vol. 22 (1964), pp. 112–35. Psychoanalysts since have revised and refined Freud's formulations, retaining the basic oedipal triangle but debating mostly the concepts of "penis envy" and "castration," which do not enter into my argument. Recent feminist analyses have been especially fruitful in exploring the descriptive rather than prescriptive aspects of Freud's theories and their sociohistorical dimension. See Nancy Chodorow, *The Reproduction of Mothering*: *Psychoanalysis and the Sociology of Gender* (Berkeley: University of California Press, 1978), and Juliet Mitchell, *Psychoanalysis and Feminism*: *Freud, Reich, Laing and Women* (1974; rpt. New York: Vintage Books, 1975), both of whom recapitulate the various studies of the female Oedipus complex from Freud on, as well as Luce Irigaray's trenchant rereading of "Femininity" in *Speculum de l'autre femme* (Paris: Minuit, 1974).

2. Leslie Rabine, "George Sand and the Myth of Femininity," *Women and Literature* 4, ii (1976): 10.

3. Otto Rank, *Das Inzestmotiv in Dichtung und Sage*: *Grundzüge einer Psychologie des dichterischen Schaffens*, 2d ed. (1926; rpt. Darmstadt: Wissenschaftliche Buchgesellschaft, 1974).

4. Marthe Robert, *Origins of the Novel* (Bloomington: Indiana University Press, 1980), p. 170.

5. Peter Brooks, *Reading for the Plot*: *Design and Intention in Narrative* (New York: Alfred A. Knopf, 1984), p. 109.

6. Jean-Jacques Rousseau, *Julie, ou la Nouvelle Héloïse* (Paris: Garnier, 1960), p. 729 (VI, xii).

7. Germaine Brée, "George Sand: The Fictions of Autobiography," *Nineteenth-Century French Studies* IV, 4 (Summer 1976): 442.

8. I have made a distinction throughout the book between the child Aurore Dupin; Aurore Dudevant, the young woman who wrote a series of works leading to *Rose et Blanche*; and George Sand, the author she became.

9. Gislinde Seybert, *Die unmögliche Emanzipation der Gefühle*: *Literatursoziologische und psychologische Untersuchungen zu George Sand und Balzac* (Frankfurt am Main: Materialis Verlag E2, 1982), p. 17.

10. Bruno Bettelheim, *The Uses of Enchantment* (New York: Alfred A. Knopf, 1976), p. 112.

11. Brooks, *Reading for the Plot*, p. 64.

12. Jacques Lacan, "Fonction et champ de la parole et du langage," in *Ecrits* (Paris: Seuil [Points], 1966), vol. I, pp. 157–58.

13. After this book was written, I noted that Wendy Deutelbaum and Cynthia Huff had also investigated Aurore Dupin's identity with her father, but found their conclusions as to Sand's conservatism to be unwarranted and somewhat unfair. See "Class, Gender and Family System: The Case of George Sand," in Shirley Nelson Garner, Claire Kahane and Madelon Sprengnether, eds., *The (M)other Tongue: Essays in Feminist Psychoanalytic Interpretation* (Ithaca and London: Cornell University Press, 1985), pp. 260–79.

14. Béatrice Didier, "Femme en voyage," in *L'Ecriture femme* (Paris: PUF écriture, 1981), p. 176.

15. This "novel" concerns a couple who meet when they come to pray in front of the madonna, clearly a mother figure. Aurore was unable to make them fall in love, despite the conventions of the genre; "I didn't have it in me," Sand declares (*Oa* I, 940). Both characters eventually take holy orders instead of marrying. Her refusal to unite the characters is perhaps a denial of the underlying content of the story. This sketchy plot summary makes this story seem like so many of the others Sand describes in *Histoire de ma vie*, as well as like her novels.

16. Philippe Berthier, "Corambé: Interprétation d'un mythe," in Simone Vierne, ed., *George Sand: Colloque de Cerisy* (Paris: CDU-SEDES, 1983), p. 19.

17. Helene Deutsch, *The Psychology of Women* (New York: Grune and Stratton, 1944), vol. I, p. 312. Although I concur with her reading of Corambé, I otherwise disagree totally with Deutsch's unnecessarily censorious, and to my mind erroneous, interpretation of Sand's life and character.

18. The exact length of time Sand took to write *Indiana* is unknown, but the novel was composed quickly, probably between January and May 1832.

19. Henry James called Sand "the great *improvisatrice* of literature—the writer who best answers to Shelley's description of the skylark singing 'in profuse strains of unpremeditated art.'" "George Sand," in *French Poets and Novelists* (London: Macmillan and Co., 1878), p. 197. Nietzsche was far less complimentary in expressing the same view of Sand's supposedly effortless writing, which he described as flowing like the milk of a cow. See "Streifzüge eines Unzeitgenössen," *Götzen-Dämmerung*, no. 1, *Werke* (Leipzig: Naumann, 1895), vol. VIII, p. 117.

20. Sigmund Freud, "Family Romances," *SE*, vol. 9 (1959), pp. 237–41. Brée also uses the term "family romances" for her version of Sand's triangular relationships.

21. Chodorow, *Reproduction of Mothering*, p. 110.

22. Seybert, *Die unmögliche Emanzipation*, p. 34.

23. Yvette Bozon-Scalzitti, "Vérité de la fiction et fiction de la vérité dans *Histoire de ma vie*: le projet autobiographique de George Sand," *Nineteenth-Century French Studies* 12, iv & 13, i (Summer–Fall 1984): 101.

24. Dianne Sadoff, *Monsters of Affection* (Baltimore and London: The Johns Hopkins University Press, 1982).

25. Elaine Showalter, *A Literature of Their Own: British Women Novelists from Brontë to Lessing* (Princeton: Princeton University Press, 1977), p. 61.

26. Margaret Hennig and Anne Jardim, *The Managerial Woman* (Garden City, N.Y.: Anchor Press/Doubleday, 1977).

27. Showalter, *A Literature of Their Own*, p. 64.

28. Madelyn Gutwirth, *Madame de Staël, Novelist: The Emergence of the Artist as Woman* (Urbana: University of Illinois Press, 1978), pp. 39–42.

29. Recent studies have detailed Sand's reception and influence outside of France. See, for example: Carole Karp, "George Sand and the Russians," in *George Sand Papers, Conference Proceedings, 1976* (New York: AMS Press, 1980), pp. 151–61; Annarosa Poli, *George Sand vue par les Italiens: Essai de bibliograhie critique* (Paris: Marcel Dider, 1965); Patricia Thomson, *George Sand and the Victorians: Her Influence and Reputation in Nineteenth-Century England* (New York: Columbia University Press, 1977).

30. Georges Lubin's edition of Sand's correspondence includes copies of her book

contracts. Curtis Cate's excellent study, *George Sand: A Biography* (Boston: Houghton Mifflin Co., 1975), also documents the financial aspect of Sand's literary career. Her book contracts with her editors were usually wisely drawn to maximize her share of the sales, while her correspondence shows that she was not shy about demanding her royalties.

1. WRITING A SELF:
FROM AURORE DUDEVANT TO J. SAND

1. As noted in the Introduction, Aurore Dupin wrote throughout her adolescence. In the convent, she composed skits for her fellow students; however, none of these texts are extant, and they can only be known from Sand's descriptions of them in her autobiography. A notebook in the Bibliothèque Nationale (N.a.fr. 13641) bearing the date 1822 contains entries from approximately 1818 (Aurore's convent days) to 1823, the year of the birth of her son, Maurice. The entries include financial notations, useful addresses, historical facts and dates (probably schoolwork), and a few creative passages, mostly brief poems or prose compositions.

2. Georges Lubin states in his introduction to the "Voyage" that the work was written in 1829, based on his dating of the letter that accompanied the manuscript. Aurore Dudevant's trip took place in 1827, and the opening date of Sunday 12 August could only refer to August 12, 1827. This fact, plus the spontaneous tone of the work, leads me to believe that the "Voyage" was written at least in part in 1827, although Aurore Dudevant may have recopied it and even made corrections in 1829; a letter from Jane Bazouin on October 12, 1827, indicates that Aurore had recently sent her three pages describing her trip. See *Oa* II, 499–501. I have chosen to use the title Aurore Dudevant gave the manuscript, with its nineteenth-century spelling of Mont-Dore.

3. Lubin treats this dedicatory missive as a letter. It can be found in *C* I, 561–64. The original manuscript of *La Marraine* is in the Collection Lovenjoul, number E821, along with two copies. Reference to the manuscript will be to the copy by Lina Sand numbered E823 and will bear the initials *LM*.

4. Tzvetan Todorov, *Introduction à la littérature fantastique* (Paris: Seuil [Points], 1970), pp. 49–50.

5. Tricket, who also appears in "Le Grillon," might owe his name to the English translation of *grillon*, "cricket," or else to the English word *trick*.

6. The terms *extradiegetic* and *intradiegetic* can be found in Gérard Genette, "Discours du récit," in *Figures III* (Paris: Seuil, 1972), p. 238.

7. The same angel-demon opposition appears in *Lélia*, where it is thought to have influenced Baudelaire's *double postulation*. Here, the language itself anticipates Baudelaire's. Aurore Dudevant may have gotten her inspiration for this dichotomy from Byron.

8. Thierry Bodin's new edition of "Histoire du rêveur" contains two previously unpublished fragments of the story, neither of which is found in the most complete manuscript of the tale. Fragment A contains approximately two paragraphs detailing Amédée's reaction upon awakening and his conversation with the innkeeper who had originally warned him of the presence of spirits on the mountain. It does not add anything to the story. Why Aurore Dudevant did not include this ending in her other copy of the manuscript cannot be said for certain, for she obviously anticipated continuing her narrative by writing "Chap. 4me de l'histoire du rêveur" (*Hr*, 28). Perhaps she felt that the story was complete as written, and so eliminated as inadequate the sequel she had devised, while nonetheless leaving space for a better continuation, should she come up with one.

Fragment B describes a musical soirée held by an Italian prince, where Amédée makes an episodic appearance. It is not in any way a continuation of "Histoire du rêveur" as we now know it, and lacks a beginning. It does, however, anticipate "La Prima Donna" (1831), an Aurore Dudevant–Jules Sandeau product.

9. See Thierry Bodin's edition of "Histoire du rêveur" for details on the different manuscripts, as well as the *variantes* listed in his notes. It should be noted that he does not include references to the manuscript 0114 in the Bibliothèque Historique de la Ville de Paris, which provides yet another version of "Le Chanteur" and "L'Eruption." The existence of these manuscripts and diverse fragments indicates that Aurore Dudevant may have composed other texts that are now lost.

10. George Sand, *L'Histoire du rêveur, suivie de Jehan Cauvin* (Paris: Montaigne, 1931), p. 121. Aurore Lauth-Sand, George Sand's granddaughter, published both "Histoire du rêveur" and "Jehan Cauvin" together, although they were written in different notebooks. While "Histoire du rêveur" is very inaccurate, her edition of "Jehan Cauvin" is quite correct.

11. Pierre Fauchéry points out that women authors of the eighteenth century often wrote about small pet animals such as birds. See *La Destinée féminine dans le roman européen du 18ᵉ siècle* (Paris: Armand Colin, 1972), p. 218.

2. J. SAND: BECOMING A WOMAN ARTIST

1. Curtis Cate, *George Sand: A Biography* (Boston: Houghton Mifflin Co., 1975), p. 178.

2. The opera Gina sings is Zingarelli's *Romeo et Giuletta* [*sic*], a work Aurore Dudevant knew. See *C* I, 486, where the same misspellings appear, as well as *Valentine*, p. 229. Thérèse Marix-Spire also attributes the inspiration for "La Prima Donna" to Aurore Dudevant and the style to Sandeau. She sees Gina as the first in the long line of artists that George Sand will create for her novels, but overstates her case when she describes the subject of the story as "the artist, superior by definition, who languishes and pines away because of her contacts with the dryness and coldness of prosaic life . . . ." See *Les Romantiques et la musique: le cas George Sand 1804–1838* (Paris: Nouvelles Editions Latines, 1954), p. 232.

3. Alphonse Signol, *Le Commissionnaire*, 4 vols. (Paris: B. Renault, 1831). This "posthumous" work by a recently deceased author is a series of sketches, rather than a novel. Aurore Dudevant's contributions are difficult to identify, and it is possible that she and Sandeau enlisted the help of others of their *berrichon* friends to fill the four volumes.

4. See *C* I, 940–942.

5. This is not far from the explanation she gives in *Histoire de ma vie*, although her memory is not always trustworthy. See *Oa* II, 138. Comparison of the two editions of *Rose et Blanche* shows that most of the original was retained in the second edition, published two years later. Except for the Denise episode, which became the prologue, and "La Dévote," which was moved forward five chapters, the order of the chapters remained the same, although the numbers did not, as the original five volumes became two. The vulgarisms, as well as several pointless digressions, were cut, while punctuation and paragraph divisions were changed. Otherwise, the two editions are identical. It is not likely that Sand would have reworked and republished this novel if she had not contributed in large part to its existence. Sandeau's biographer agrees that many scenes are unmistakably Aurore Dudevant's. See Mabel Silver, *Jules Sandeau: L'Homme et la vie* (Paris: L'Entente Linotypiste, 1936), pp. 33–36. Tatiana Greene also finds that Aurore wrote most of the novel. See "De J. Sand à George Sand: *Rose et Blanche* de Sand et Sandeau et leur descendance," *Nineteenth-Century French Studies* IV, 3 (Spring 1976): p. 171.

6. See *C* I, 792–97, 801. Her tone is quite different in *Histoire de ma vie*, as regards both the man and his novel, which she describes as being based on a "revolting plot device" (*Oa* II, 149), forgetting that the same could be said of *Rose et Blanche*.

7. J. Sand, *Rose et Blanche*, 2 vols. (Paris: H. Dupuy, 1833).

8. Denise also recalls the doll Olympia, whose name appears in the text as that of Soeur Olympie, from E. T. A. Hoffmann's "The Sandman."

9. Honoré de Balzac, "Adieu," in *La Comédie humaine* (Paris: Gallimard [Pléiade], 1979), vol. X, p. 1006.

10. Balzac has a much better understanding of the psychological mechanisms at work here. Stéphanie protected herself from the horror of war and separation from her lover by retreating into madness, while Denise emerged from her rape, after a long illness, an intelligent, sensitive young woman, with no trace of her supposedly congenital idiocy. The transformation only makes sense if seen in a broader, metaphorical way as Aurore Dudevant's hope for her own independence.

11. Mabel Silver attributes the rape scene to Sandeau, because a modified form appears in two of his later works. Comparison of these versions with that of *Rose et Blanche* reveals that the scenes have absolutely nothing in common except the names Horace and Denise. See Silver, *Jules Sandeau*, p. 36.

12. Feelings of depression began in 1824 and afflicted Aurore Dudevant until well into the 1830s, leading her to contemplate suicide on several occasions. See *C* I, II, III, as well as *Histoire de ma vie*, passim.

13. The particularly Rousseauistic concept of liberty expressed in *Histoire de ma vie* is worth noting; the phrase "by depending on all, one really depends on no one," echoes Rousseau's "each in giving himself to all gives himself to no one" (J.-J. Rousseau, *Du contrat social* [Paris: Garnier, 1962], p. 244).

14. Aurore Dudevant uses the expression "la Muse de mon département" well before Balzac, in the dedicatory letter to *La Marraine*, p. 2, also published in *C* I, 563.

15. In the second edition of the novel, this letter is written in standard French, as though the newly successful George Sand no longer wanted or needed to let this example of Rose's ignorance remain.

16. Sandra M. Gilbert and Susan Gubar call this fear the "anxiety of authorship" and analyze its appearance in the work of British and American women writers. See *The Madwoman in the Attic: The Woman Writer and the Nineteenth-Century Literary Imagination* (New Haven and London: Yale University Press, 1979), pp. 48–53. Sand's fears derive less from lack of tradition than from her particular historical circumstances, as will be seen.

17. Germaine Brée, *Women Writers in France* (New Brunswick, N.J.: Rutgers University Press, 1973), p. 40.

18. References to Staël are minimal in Sand's works, a telling omission. At least twice she compared herself to her predecessor, and "Metella" (1833) was clearly inspired by *Corinne*, but she also criticized Staël, for which she incurred Sainte-Beuve's wrath. This dispute is quite instructive, for it shows Sand's uneasiness vis-à-vis Staël, as well as Sainte-Beuve's insistence on a solidarity among women writers that he would not have demanded of men. See *Oa* II, 752, 1453, as well as *C* III, 434, 458; IV, 353–54.

3. *INDIANA*: HEROIC ROMANCE AND BOURGEOIS REALISM

1. After this chapter was written, I was pleased to see that Yvonne Bozon-Scalzitti makes the same link between George and Georgeon in her article "Vérité de la fiction et fiction de la vérité dans *Histoire de ma vie*: le projet autobiographique de George Sand," *Nineteenth-Century French Studies* 12, iv & 13, i (Summer–Fall 1984): 115.

2. Isabelle Naginski sees the name George Sand as being "mid-way between masculine and feminine," rather than as the fusion of the two sexes, in her inter-

esting article "George Sand. Gynographie et Androgynie," *Bulletin de la Société des Professeurs Français en Amérique* (1983–84): 21.

3. See the very incomplete but still useful *Catalogue de la bibliothèque de Mme George Sand et de M. Maurice Sand* (Paris: A. Ferroud, 1890).

4. Félix Decori, ed., *Correspondance de George Sand et d'Alfred de Musset*, Nouvelle édition (Bruxelles: E. Deman, 1904), p. 11.

5. Northrop Frye, *Anatomy of Criticism: Four Essays* (1957; rpt. Princeton: Princeton University Press, 1973), pp. 186–206. Further references are in the text as Frye.

6. Fredric Jameson, "Magical Narratives: Romance as Genre," *New Literary History* VII, i (Autumn 1975): 158. Further references are in the text as Jameson.

7. The notion of Raymon as catalyst is derived from Jameson's view of Heathcliff as mediator rather than villain. See Jameson, p. 149.

8. The site of Ralph and Indiana's suicide attempt is doubly significant, for it combines a mountaintop and a waterfall. James M. Vest has thoroughly analyzed water imagery, so important to the romance, in *Indiana*. See "Fluid Nomenclature, Imagery, and Themes in George Sand's *Indiana*," *South Atlantic Review* 46, 2 (May 1981): 43–54. For a discussion of mountaintops and ceremonial ladders that link earth to sky in traditional symbolic systems, see Mircea Eliade, *Images et symboles: Essais sur le symbolisme magico-religieux*, 2d ed. (Paris: Gallimard, 1952).

9. Angels as the symbols of providence or luck appear twice in the text before this scene. Raymon describes Indiana as his "bon ange" (*I*, 77), for caring for him when he is brought wounded into the salon at Lagny; an angel is said to save Indiana herself from succumbing to Raymon's rhetoric when she seeks refuge in his room (*I*, 214). As Jameson has pointed out (p. 144), the magical elements of the romance have been secularized in the art romance; in *Indiana*, angelic intervention has become a metaphor for protection or, better, self-preservation.

10. "The initiatic work is the drama of a rebirth; the initiatic work illustrates the principle 'dying to be reborn.' The higher level which the hero reaches is in fact that which he had left before his fall; the rebirth is thus a reintegration into society." Léon Cellier, "Le Roman initiatique en France au temps du Romantisme," in *Parcours initiatiques* (Grenoble: Presses Universitaires de Grenoble, 1977), p. 123.

11. Gérard Genette, "Discours du récit," in *Figures III* (Paris: Seuil, 1972), p. 203.

12. Stirling Haig, "La Chambre circulaire d'*Indiana*," *Neophilologus* LXII, 4 (Oct. 1978): 507.

13. See Ellen Moers, *Literary Women* (Garden City, N.Y.: Anchor Books, 1977), pp. 369–401, for a discussion of female sexual imagery.

14. Frye remarks that "the hero travels perilously through a dark labyrinthine underworld . . ." (p. 190). Here, that underworld has become the heroine's own home.

15. See Hans Mayer, *Outsiders*, trans. Denis M. Sweet (Cambridge, Mass.: MIT Press, 1982), for an enlightening study of the outsider in literature.

16. Carol Gilligan, *In a Different Voice: Psychological Theory and Women's Development* (Cambridge, Mass., and London: Harvard University Press, 1982).

17. Leslie Rabine, "George Sand and the Myth of Femininity," *Women and Literature* 4, ii (1976): 14.

18. The comparison between the two novels is not arbitrary but is occasioned by Sand's own parallel in a letter of July 1832 where she recounts a scene in which Jules Janin, after having praised *Indiana* as the best novel of manners of the period, is visited by an angry Hugo, hurt that his novel was passed over. This exuberant letter, one of Sand's funniest, is, I think, not to be taken literally, particularly since no such review by Janin has been found. An anonymous article in the *Journal des Débats*, for which Janin was theater critic, appeared two weeks later (July 21) and used somewhat similar language, but there is no indication that Janin wrote it; he did write a major article on Sand much later, in 1836.

Even if the anecdote is false, as I suspect, it is nonetheless important to note that Sand again chooses to compare herself favorably to Hugo, as she had in "Jehan Cauvin." See *C* II, 119–20.

19. Quoted in Annarose Poli, "George Sand devant la critique," in Simone Vierne, ed., *George Sand: Colloque de Cerisy* (Paris: CDU-Sedes, 1983), p. 96.

20. Carol V. Richards's article "Structural Motifs and the Limits of Feminism in *Indiana*," in *The George Sand Papers: Conference Proceedings 1978*, Hofstra University Center for Cultural and Intercultural Studies 2 (New York: AMS Press, 1982), pp. 12–20 came to my attention after this chapter was written. She covers some of the same ground, but from a different viewpoint and with different conclusions.

21. See René Girard, *Mensonge romantique et vérité romanesque* (Paris: Grasset, 1961). Sand was aware of the importance of this triangular mechanism, for she assigns it a role in the structure of woman's desire as well: "Women's hearts are so made that they begin to see a man in a young boy as soon as they see him esteemed and caressed by other women." *La Petite Fadette* (Paris: Garnier, 1958), p. 164.

22. Mme de Fonbreuse is "seated under the mantelpiece of a huge gothic fireplace" in *La Marraine*, p. 327.

23. Quoted by Salomon in *Indiana*, p. 293.

24. Mireille Bossis, in her article "Les Relations de parenté chez George Sand," *Cahiers de L'Association Internationale des Etudes Françaises* 28 (mai 1976): 297–314, underscores Ralph's paternal role throughout the novel and his father-daughter relationship with Indiana, which is fully assumed by both at the end. She describes him as a "unique and all-powerful character who removes the incest taboo . . ." (p. 309). I think she underestimates the sexual nature of the bond, apparent in the passage she quotes from the novel, and I find her final mother/child image applicable, in part, only to the dynamics of Ralph's earlier relationship to his mother, as she shows.

25. Ellen Moers points out that Austen is always very specific about the sums of money involved in her novels. See *Literary Women*, p. 102.

26. Sand's private notebooks contain much information, dating from her teens, on her financial affairs: money spent, profits received or anticipated from Nohant, and so forth.

27. According to Jean-Hervé Donnard, "Balzac carefully documented a social phenomenon that was to occur more and more frequently . . ." (p. 148). "On the other hand, during Napoleon's reign, society was so mixed that there weren't too many social obstacles to the marriage of a young nobleman and the daughter of a shopkeeper. Under Louis XVIII, such a marriage would have been scandalous; in any event, it would not have taken place so easily" (p. 251). See *Balzac: Les Réalités économiques et sociales dans La Comédie humaine* (Paris: Armand Colin, 1961).

28. Leslie Rabine is partly correct in her assessment that "George Sand did not settle accounts with the existing ideology . . ." ("Myth of Femininity," p. 13), in the sense that traditional class distinctions are maintained and the social order is not radically changed, as it would be if a noblewoman were to marry a peasant. However, her linking of Sand's class values to Noun seems to me to be wrong on several counts. Not only is there a long literary tradition of the nobleman marrying the poor woman, but this option is explicitly raised and thoroughly examined by the narrator (*I*, 52–53) and discarded not on account of class differences but rather because Raymon no longer loves Noun. Furthermore, this kind of union does appear in *Valentine*. As I have shown, Noun is eliminated from the novel for other reasons.

29. Victor Hugo, "Sur Walter Scott: A propos de *Quentin Durward*," in *Oeuvres complètes* (Paris: Le Club Français du Livre, 1967), vol. 5, p. 131.

30. *Journal des Débats*, July 21, 1832, p. 3.

4. *VALENTINE*: TRISTAN AND ISEUT IN THE BERRY

1. Little attention has been paid to later adaptations of the story of Tristan and Iseut. Denis de Rougement, in *L'Amour et l'occident* (Paris: Plon, 1939), treats rather superficially the texts in which the theme of love as death can be found. Most important among these for Sand's *oeuvre* is Rousseau's *La Nouvelle Héloïse*. For a study of literal renderings of the story, see Wolfgang Golther, *Tristan und Isolde in den Dichtungen des Mittelalters und der neuen Zeit* (Leipzig: S. Hirzel Verlag, 1907).
2. There is no one "Tristan story." Instead, there are several versions of a legend that seems to date back to the Celts. A lost text of the story, composed around 1150, gave rise to versions by Eilhart von Oberge, Béroul, and Thomas. The latter's poem was a model for Gottfried von Strassburg's *Tristan*. There is also a lengthy French prose version, composed ca. 1215–35 and printed in 1489, as well as a German one of the fifteenth century. Joseph Bédier's reconstitution of the original legend, *Le Roman de Tristan et Iseut*, is perhaps the best-known version today, although as a source it is unreliable. The form in which Sand learned of the story can only be surmised. As Francisque Michel remarks in his edition of the Thomas fragments: "Everyone knows, at least by name, Tristan of Lyoness and his lover Yseult of the blond hair, wife of Marc king of the land of Cornwall." See *Tristan, recueil de ce qui reste des poëmes relatifs à ses aventures* (Londres: Guillaume Pickering; Paris: Techner, 1835), vol. I, p. i. It should be noted that Sand's library contained the *Bibliothèque universelle des romans*, in which a much-reduced account of the prose version appears in the April 1776 issue, vol. I, pp. 53–238. The publication in 1804 of Walter Scott's *Sir Tristram* had generated much discussion and attests to the contemporary interest in the story. In *Le Compagnon du tour de France* (1840), Sand would name her heroine Yseult. When I refer to the Tristan story, it is not to any specific text but to those elements which have over the centuries become associated with the legend, particularly the magic philter, Tristan and Iseut's love in the forest, the two Iseuts, and the rose and the vine.
3. "El beivre fud la nostre mort / Nus n'en avrum ja mais confort; / A tel ure duné nus fu / A nostre mort l'avum beü" (The drink was our death / We will never more have rest / It was given us at such a time / That we drank it to our death). Bartina H. Wind, *Les Fragments du roman de Tristan, poème du XIIe siècle par Thomas* (Leiden: E. J. Brill, 1950), p. 157.
4. Joan M. Ferrante, *The Conflict of Love and Honor: The Medieval Tristan Legend in France, Germany and Italy* (The Hague, Paris: Mouton, 1973), p. 55.
5. In his article "Un modèle d'*Indiana*?" *French Review* 50, ii (Dec. 1976): 317–20, Mario Maurin successfully demonstrates similarities between *La Princesse de Clèves* and *Indiana*, which would make the rapprochement between the avowal scene here and Lafayette's even more plausible.
6. "Sine wurden aber niemer mê / in allen ir jâren / sô heinlîch sôs ê wâren, / nochn gewunnen nie zir fröuden sît / sô guote stat sô vor der zît" (But never again in all their days were they so close and familiar as they had been, nor did opportunity ever again so favor their amours). Gottfried von Strassburg, *Tristan*, ed. Karl Marold (1912; rpt. Berlin: Walter de Gruyter and Co., 1969), p. 246; *Tristan*, trans. A. T. Hatto (Baltimore: Penguin Books, 1960), p. 274.
7. Although the rose and vine do not appear in Thomas's version, and Gottfried's breaks off before the end, it is nonetheless an undisputed part of the Tristan legend, found in Eilhart and both prose versions. Marie de France, in her lai "Chèvrefeuille," uses the image of the honeysuckle and the hazel. Bénédict plants honeysuckle and clematis over his doorway (*V*, 243).
8. I cannot agree with Nancy K. Miller that *Valentine* contains "Sand's nostalgia

for essentially feudal values . . . ." Miller herself makes the case that the novel "is grounded precisely in the history of a domain sold 'as national property during the Revolution, and redeemed under the Empire' . . . ." The subsequent sale and repurchase of the estate by the Lhérys shows Sand's particular economic vision, which, far from being feudal, was ahead of her time. See "Writing (from) the Feminine: George Sand and the Novel of Female Pastoral," in Carolyn Heilbrun and M. Higonnet, eds., *The Representation of Women in Fiction*: *Selected Papers from the English Institute. 1981*, n.s., no. 7 (Baltimore and London: The Johns Hopkins University Press, 1983), pp. 151, 124.

9. Mireille Bossis, "Eléments pour une lecture de Valentine," to appear in *Friends of George Sand Newsletter*.

5. *LÉLIA*

1. *Le Journal des Dames et des Modes* 46 (20 août 1833), p. 362.

2. Annarosa Poli, "George Sand devant la critique," in Simone Vierne, ed., *George Sand*: *Colloque de Cerisy* (Paris: CDU-Sedes, 1983), p. 98, describes Musset's unpublished article.

3. Félix Decori, ed., *Correspondance de George Sand et d'Alfred de Musset*, nouvelle éd. (Bruxelles: E. Deman, 1904), p. 11.

4. Poli, "George Sand," p. 98.

5. Jules Janin, "George Sand," in *L'Artiste* 12, 13e livraison (1836): 153–54.

6. Shelley I. Temchin, "Straining the Structures of Romanticism: George Sand's *Lélia* Reconsidered" (Ph. D. diss., Tufts 1981), p. 140.

7. Peter L. Thorslev, Jr., *The Byronic Hero*: *Types and Prototypes* (Minneapolis: University of Minnesota Press, 1962), p. 189.

8. D. G. Charlton's essay "Prose Fiction" includes *Delphine* and *Corinne* in his list of novels that describe the *mal du siècle*. See D. G. Charlton, ed., *The French Romantics* (Cambridge, Eng.: Cambridge University Press, 1984), vol. I, pp. 167–80.

9. I cannot agree with Eileen Boyd Sivert, who asserts that "Lélia does not know how to question masculine society or its discourse." Lélia knows how to question and criticize; what she does not know is how to change masculine society. See "*Lélia* and Feminism," *Yale French Studies* 62 (1981): 54.

10. See Sidney D. Braun, *The "Courtisane" in the French Theater from Hugo to Becque (1831–1885)*, The Johns Hopkins Studies in Romance Literatures and Languages, Extra Volume XXII (Baltimore: Johns Hopkins University Press, 1947), for a consideration of the courtesan in French literature.

11. Sandra M. Gilbert and Susan Gubar, *The Madwoman in the Attic*: *The Woman Writer and the Nineteenth-Century Imagination* (New Haven and London: Yale University Press, 1979).

12. See Joseph Barry, *Infamous Woman*: *The Life of George Sand* (Garden City, N.Y.: Anchor Press, 1978), p. 157.

13. Charlton, "Prose Fiction," pp. 174, 178.

14. George Sand, "A propos de *Lélia* et de *Valentine* (Préface de *Romans et nouvelles*)," in *Questions d'art et de littérature* (Paris: Calmann-Lévy, 1878), p. 44.

6. *LEONE LEONI*: GEORGE SAND'S READING OF *MANON LESCAUT*

1. Pages 79–84 of the Perrotin edition I have used are not in the original *Revue des Deux Mondes* text but were added when the novel was published in book form. Pages 81–84, describing the gambler, are taken from *Lélia* (L, 29–31).

2. See George Sand's 1853 *Notice* to *Leone Leoni* in *Oeuvres illustrées* (Paris: Hetzel, 1853), vol. IV, p. 78.

3. Antoine-François Prévost d'Exiles, *Histoire du chevalier Des Grieux et de Manon Lescaut* (Paris: Garnier-Flammarion, 1967), p. 35.

4. Roland Barthes describes this kind of narrative in *S/Z* (Paris: Seuil [Points], 1970), p. 95.

5. Sand, *Notice*, p. 78.

6. Barthes, *S/Z*, pp. 218–19.

7. For a longer development of this perspective, see Leslie W. Rabine's stimulating article "History, Ideology, and Femininity in *Manon Lescaut*," *Stanford French Review* V, i (Spring 1981): 65–83.

8. Juliana de Krüdener, *Valérie*, Nouvelle édition, préface de Sainte-Beuve (Paris: Charpentier, 1840), p. xxi.

9. Nancy K. Miller, in her excellent article "Emphasis Added: Plots and Plausibilities in Women's Fiction," *PMLA* 96, i (Jan. 1981): 36–48, studies women novelists' attempts to create a destiny for their heroines outside of male fictional conventions. Her discussion of *La Princesse de Clèves* is particularly germane to George Sand, and doubly so, for Sand, like Lafayette, chooses not to end her novel with a marriage. Sand's debt to Lafayette can be seen in *Indiana*, as Mario Maurin has shown, as well as in *Valentine*. See M. Maurin, "Un modèle d'*Indiana*?" *French Review* 50, ii (Dec. 1976): 317–20.

7. *JACQUES*: INCESTUOUS AFFINITIES

1. My analysis of *Jacques* as an epistolary novel has been aided by Janet Gurkin Altman's excellent study of the genre, *Epistolarity: Approaches to a Form* (Columbus, Ohio: Ohio State University Press, 1982).

2. Gérard de Nerval, *Oeuvres* (Paris: Gallimard [Pléiade], 1966), vol. I, p. 798. Goethe's novel had been translated as *Les Affinités électives* in 1810. It is interesting to note that in *Le Dernier Amour* (1865), another incestuous story, Sand refers both to her own novel *Jacques* and to Goethe's *Affinités électives*. See *Le Dernier Amour*, prés. Simone Vierne (Paris, Genève: Ressources [Slatkine], 1980), pp. 257, 301.

3. Peter Brooks, *Reading for the Plot: Design and Intention in Narrative* (New York: Alfred A. Knopf, 1984), p. 109.

4. Henry James, "George Sand," in *French Poets and Novelists* (London: Macmillan and Co., 1878), p. 226.

5. Jules Janin, "George Sand," *L'Artiste* 12, 13e livraison (1836): 154.

6. Honoré de Balzac, *Lettres à l'étrangère* (Paris: Calmann-Lévy, 1899), vol. I, p. 196.

7. In "Les Relations de parenté chez George Sand," *Cahiers de L'Association Internationale des Etudes Françises* 28 (mai 1976) 297–314, Mireille Bossis asks if "this marriage with Fernande is a protection that he imposes on himself" (p. 311), while nonetheless admitting that by marrying Fernande, Jacques is setting the stage for the rest of the novel. She makes some of the same points I do about *Jacques*, but her negative conclusions about the role of family relationships in Sand's work stand in direct opposition to mine.

8. EDUCATING WOMEN: *ANDRÉ* AND *MAUPRAT*

1. Ovid, *Metamorphoses*, trans. Rolfe Humphries (Bloomington and London: Indiana University Press, 1972), pp. 241–43.

2. H. F. Jaubert, *Glossaire du centre de la France* (Paris: Chaix, 1856), vol. I, p. 93. Jaubert's earlier work, *Vocabulaire du Berry et de quelques cantons voisins par un amateur du vieux langage* (Paris: Roret, 1842) does not list *artisan(e)*, which lends strength to the theory both that Sand created this particular usage and that Jaubert's subsequent reference shows literature influencing lexicography.

3. Sandra M. Gilbert and Susan Gubar, *The Madwoman in the Attic: The Woman Writer and the Nineteenth-Century Literary Imagination* (New Haven and London: Yale University Press, 1979), p. 41.

4. Yvette Bozon-Scalzitti, "*Mauprat*, ou la Belle et la Bête," *Nineteenth-Century French Studies* X, 1 & 2 (Fall–Winter 1981–82): 1–16.

5. See Suzanne Mühlemann, "*Mauprat* ou la création de l'homme," and Yves Chastagneret, "*Mauprat* ou du bon usage de l'*Emile*," *Présence de George Sand* 8 (Mai 1980): 7–15, for two considerations of Sand's adaptation of Rousseau.

6. See Claude Sicard's edition of *Mauprat* (Paris: Garnier-Flammarion, 1969), pp. 16–17, for a discussion of the novel's chronology.

7. "It is commonly believed that women alone know the secret of these little vain rivalries. I call all men of good faith to witness: is there one of us who has not had the urge to throw out of the window a rival lucky enough to touch the woman we love with his songs?" George Sand, *Simon*, in *La Dernière Aldini*, p. 292. This quotation is doubly significant, for Sand adopts a male persona while nonetheless using a female perspective to debunk a myth about women.

8. Juliette Decreus-van Liefland, *Sainte-Beuve et la critique des auteurs féminins* (Paris: Boivin, 1949).

9. In a letter to her half brother Hippolyte just before his daughter's marriage in 1843, Sand makes abundantly (and unabashedly) clear the possible traumas sex can inflict on an inexperienced young woman and prescribes a reasonable solution: "Stop your son-in-law from brutalizing your daughter on her wedding night, for many weak organs and painful births have no other cause in delicate women. . . . Nothing is more awful than the fear, the suffering and the disgust of a poor child who knows nothing and finds herself raped by a brute. We raise our daughters as best we can to be saints, and then we turn them over like fillies" (*C* VI, 43).

CONCLUSION

1. Sand did not simply transcribe dialectal words and phrases but adapted the local idiom and even invented words of her own to express herself better, as well as to figure the peasants' speech, since they could not be made to speak in the French of the Académie Française. Clearly, though, realism was not her only goal in adopting the language of her province. See Alexander Herman Schutz, "The Peasant Vocabulary in the Works of George Sand," *The University of Missouri Studies* II, i (January 1, 1927): v–114.

2. Sand could thus take her place among the women writers described by Sandra M. Gilbert and Susan Gubar in their interesting study of women and language, "Sexual Linguistics: Gender, Language, and Sexuality," *New Literary History* XVI, 3 (Spring 1985): 515–43.

3. Germaine Brée, "George Sand: The Fictions of Autobiography," *Nineteenth-Century French Studies* IV, 4 (Summer 1976): 447–48.

Index